Commercial and Economic Law in Hungary

Commercial and Economic Law in Hungary

János Bóka
Katalin Gombos
Tekla Papp
András József Pomeisl

This book was originally published as a monograph in the International Encyclopaedia of Laws/Commercial and Economic Law.

Founding Editor: Roger Blanpain
General Editor: Frank Hendrickx
Volume Editors: Jules Stuyck & Evelyne Terryn

Wolters Kluwer

Published by:
Kluwer Law International B.V.
PO Box 316
2400 AH Alphen aan den Rijn
The Netherlands
E-mail: international-sales@wolterskluwer.com
Website: lrus.wolterskluwer.com

Sold and distributed in North, Central and South America by:
Wolters Kluwer Legal & Regulatory U.S.
7201 McKinney Circle
Frederick, MD 21704
United States of America
Email: customer.service@wolterskluwer.com

Sold and distributed in all other countries by:
Air Business Subscriptions
Rockwood House
Haywards Heath
West Sussex
RH16 3DH
United Kingdom
Email: international-customerservice@wolterskluwer.com

Printed on acid-free paper

ISBN 978-94-035-1322-5

e-Book: ISBN 978-94-035-1353-9
web-PDF: ISBN 978-94-035-1384-3

This title is available on www.kluwerlawonline.com

Printed in the United Kingdom.

The Authors

János Bóka is an associate professor at the Károli Gáspár University of the Reformed Church, Hungary. Since 2018 he serves as Secretary of State for European Union and international judicial cooperation at the Ministry of Justice, Hungary.

He obtained his Law degree from the University of Szeged, Hungary in 2001. Until July 2009, he worked as a legal and policy advisor at the European Parliament. He obtained an MA degree in European Integration and Development at the VUB, Belgium. He defended his PhD thesis in 2012 at the University of Szeged. In 2014–2015 he worked as a senior legal advisor at the Curia (Supreme Court) of Hungary specialising in economic and commercial law. In 2017–2018 he was Director of the Hungarian Academy of Justice.

As visiting professor, he has lectured on Commercial Law, Contract Law and Comparative Law at universities in France, mainland China and Taiwan.

He has good command in English, French and Russian.

He has published in Hungarian, English and French in the area of International and EU Law, Contract Law and Private International Law as well as Comparative Law.

Katalin Gombos is a dr. habil. associate professor and head of Department at the National University of Public Service, Budapest, Hungary, Faculty of International and European Studies, Department of European Public and Private Law. Since 2013, she is a judge of Curia of Hungary (Hungarian Supreme Court).

She obtained her Law degree and postgraduate degree in European Law from the University of Szeged, Hungary, where she taught in the Department of International and European Law until 2016. She defended her PhD in 2008 and obtained the habil. title in 2015 at the University of Szeged.

She is a member of the Public Body of the Hungarian Academy of Sciences, the Scientific Board of the Competition Research Centre. She is a member of the European Law Institute (ELI) and institutional participant of the events of the Association of European Competition Law Judges.

She was a member of the Codification Committee of the new Code of Private International Law of Hungary (2017) and a member of expert board of the new Code of Procedural Law of Hungary (2016).

She is a member of the editorial board of journal *Európai Tükör* (*European Mirror*).

Tekla Papp graduated from the Faculty of Law at the University of Szeged, Hungary in 1991 and passed the Bar examination in 1995. In 2004 she obtained her PhD for her thesis on the *Concession Contract in Hungary and Europe*. In 2010, she habilitated at the University of Szeged, finishing a project on the atypical contracts in Europe as well as the legal aspects of the Hungarian companies without legal personality. She is a full professor of law since 2014. Currently she is working as the head of Institute of Civil Law, Faculty of Science of Public Governance and Administration at the National University of Public Service, Hungary.

In 2011, she was elected as an arbiter of the Chamber of Commerce and Industry of Hungary.

She represents Hungary in the European Model Company Act Study Group. She is the vice-president of the Societas Central-East Europe – Company Law Research Network, member of European Law Institute, Society of European Contract Law and Society of Juridical and Administrative Sciences.

She has over 250 publications in Hungarian, English, German and Serbian (including 5 monographs).

András József Pomeisl is working at the Curia (Supreme Court) of Hungary as a senior advisor in the Civil Department since 2013. He obtained his Law degree from the Péter Pázmány Catholic University, Hungary in 2002. He worked at the Supreme Court of Republic of Hungary as a section notary between October 2002 and July 2006, then as a court secretary between August 2006 and December 2012. He has been also the Head of the Department of International Relations and European Law between May 2010 and January 2012. He also teaches Private Law at Ferenc Deák Postgraduate Training Institute at Péter Pázmány Catholic University, Hungary as a mandated lecturer since 2015.

He was a member of different Working and Theme Groups of the Codification Expert Committee of the new Code of Civil Procedure of Hungary.

He speaks and writes in English, German and Latin.

He has published in Hungarian on civil procedure and judicial enforcement, on NGOs and on private law issues as well as constitutional law matters and ECHR case law.

The Authors

Table of Contents

List of Abbreviations

AA	Accounting Act – Act C of 2000 (*Számviteli törvény* [Sztv.])
ARA	Arbitration Act – Act LX of 2017 (*Választottbírósági törvény* [Vbtv.])
ASP	Act on Setting Prices – Act LXXXVII of 1990
B2C	Business-to-Consumer
BA	Bankruptcy Act – XLIX of 1991 (*Csődtörvény* [Cstv.])
BCE	Budapest Commodity Exchange
BCSE	Budapest Commodity and Stock Exchange
BDT	Casebook of the Courts (*Bírósági Döntések Tára*)
BH	Court Order (*Bírósági Határozat*)
BSE	Budapest Stock Exchange
CC	Civil Code – Act V of 2013 (*Polgári Törvénykönyv* [Ptk.])
CCP	Central Counterparty
CM	Capital Market Act – Act CXX of 2001 (*Tőkepiaci törvény* [Tpt.])
CP	Code of Civil Procedure – Act III of 1952 (*Polgári perrendtartás* [Pp.])
Crim. P.	Code of Criminal Procedure – Act XIX of 1998 (*Büntetőeljárási törvény* [Be.])
CSD	Central Securities Depository
DSNP	Debt Settlement Procedure for Natural Persons – Act CV of 2015 (*Magáncsőd törvény*)
EBH	Decision of the Supreme Court (*Legfelsőbb Bíróság döntése*)
ECA	Economic Chambers Act – Act CXXI of 1999
ECC	European Consumer Centre
ECN	European Competition Network
EEA	European Economic Area
EU	European Union
GVH	Hungarian Competition Authority (*Gazdasági Versenyhivatal*)
FA	Firm Act – Act V of 2006 (*Cégtörvény* [Ctv.])
HCA	Act LVII of 1996 on the Prohibition of Unfair and Restrictive Market Practices (Hungarian Competition Act)
HNAM	Hungarian National Asset Management

List of Abbreviations

HUF	Hungarian Forint (national currency) (*magyar forint*)
ÍH	Decision of the High Court of Appeal (*Ítélőtáblai Határozat*)
IPCs	Insolvency Practitioner Companies
KGD	Administrative and Economic Law Report (*Közigazgatási és Gazdasági Döntvénytár*)
LB	Supreme Court (*Legfelsőbb Bíróság*)
NAA	Act on National Assets – Act CXCVI of 2011
NBH	National Bank of Hungary – Magyar Nemzeti Bank
NGOs	Non-governmental Organisations
NJC	National Judicial Council
NOJ	National Office for the Judiciary
OECD	Organisation for Economic Co-operation and Development
PIL	Act on Private International Law – Act XXVIII of 2017 (*Nemzetközi magánjogi törvény* [Nmjtv.])
SA	Act on the issue of securities, investment services and the stock exchange – Act CXI of 1996 (*Értékpapírtörvény* [Épt.])
SAA	Act on State Assets – Act CVI of 2007
SAMO	State Aid Monitoring Office
TFEU	Treaty on the Functioning of the European Union
VAT	Value Added Tax

General Introduction

§1. General Background of the Country

I. Geography

1. Hungary is a small-to-medium size landlocked country located in the Carpathian Basin in Central Europe. It covers an area of 93,030 sq kms and has 2,106 kms of land boundaries. Hungary borders with Slovakia to the north, Ukraine to the northeast, Romania to the east, Serbia to the south, Croatia to the southwest, Slovenia to the west and Austria to the northwest (Figure 1).

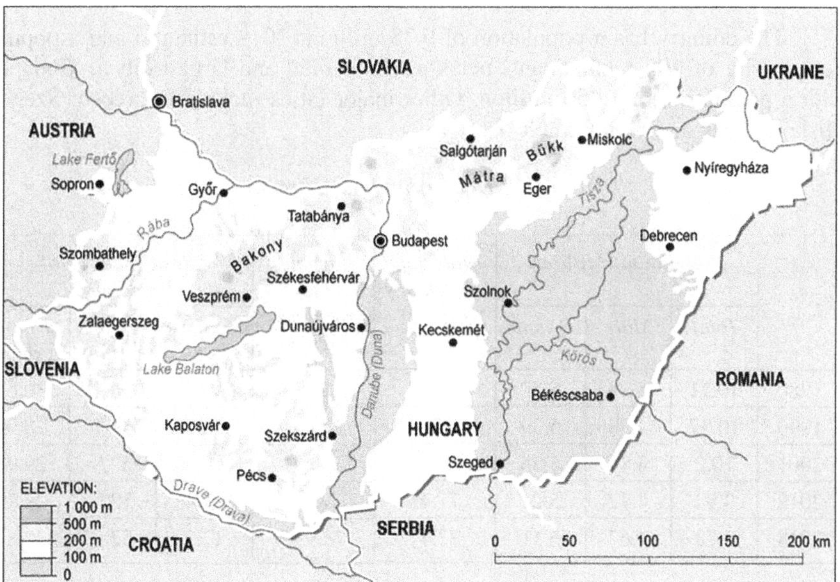

Figure 1 Map of Hungary
Source: Cserlajos (Public domain), via Wikimedia Commons.

2. Hungary is a predominantly flat country; areas reaching the heights of 300 m or more over sea level cover less than 3% of the surface. The highest point in the country is Kékes (1,014 m) in the Mátra Mountains in Northern Hungary. The landscape of Hungary is defined by its two main rivers, the Danube (length in Hungary: 417 km) and Tisza (length in Hungary: 596 km). Hungary has three major geographic regions: the Great Plain (Alföld) located east to the Danube River; Transdanubia, a hilly area west to the Danube with some mountain ranges and the largest lake (Balaton) in Central Europe; and the North Hungarian Mountains.

3. Hungary has a temperate continental climate with cold winters and warm to hot summers. The average yearly rainfall is about 600 mm; the western parts usually receive more rain while severe droughts may occur in the east.

4. Hungary's most important natural resource is arable land. Although soil quality varies extremely, around 70% of its total territory is suitable for agricultural activities. The country has a remarkable thermal water cave system and one of the largest thermal lakes (Hévíz) in the world. Other than that, Hungary has few domestic sources of energy and raw materials.

II. Demography and Cultural Composition

5. The country has a population of 9.78 million (2018 estimate) and a population density of 105.1 inhabitants per km^2. Its capital and largest city is Budapest with a population of 1.750 million. Other major cities include Debrecen, Szeged, Miskolc, Pécs and Győr (Table 1).

Table 1 Demography of Hungary

	Population (Million)			*Male Life Expectancy (Years)*	*Female Life Expectancy (Years)*	*Residence (% of Population)*		
	Total	*Male*	*Female*			*Budapest*	*Other Urban*	*Non-urban*
1980	10.71	5.19	5.52	65.5	72.7	19.2	50.2	30.6
1990	10.37	4.98	5.39	65.1	73.7	19.4	51.7	28.9
2001	10.2	4.85	5.35	68.2	76.5	17.3	52.8	29.9
2012	9.93	4.72	5.21	71.45	78.38	17.4	52.9	29.7
2018	9.78	4.67	5.11	72.4*	78.99*	17.9	52.5	29.6

*2017 Data – *Source*: Hungarian Central Statistical Office.

6. Hungary is composed of one dominant cultural-linguistic community, the Hungarians as well as thirteen officially recognised nationalities.[1] According to the

1. Act No. CLXXIX of 2011 on the rights of nationalities, Annex 1.

2011 official census data,[2] 83.7% of the population claimed to be Hungarian. The largest minority groups were the Romani (3.1%) and the Germans (1.3%).[3] Other officially recognised minorities include the Slovaks, Romanians, Croats, Serbs, Ukrainians, Polish, Bulgarians, Greek, Ruthenes, Armenians and Slovenes. A significant Chinese community also resides in Hungary that is officially not recognised as a nationality due to its lack of at least a century-long history in the country.

7. According to the 2011 census data 45.4% of the population in Hungary are atheist, non-religious or did not declare its religious affiliation. Religion in Hungary has been dominated by different forms of Christianity, the most important denominations being Roman Catholicism (37.1%), Calvinism (11.6%), Lutheranism (2.2%) and Greek Catholicism (1.8%). Orthodox Christianity is also present in the country mainly among certain minorities (Romanians, Serbs, Ukrainians and Ruthenes). Hungary used to be home to a significant Jewish community that at its peak made up more than 6% of the population. Most of the Hungarian Jewish community was exterminated during the Holocaust and many survivors decided not to return or leave the country after World War II and the 1956 revolution.

III. Political System

8. The political and legal system of Hungary is based on the Fundamental Law that entered into force on 1 January 2012 and has been amended on seven occasions.[4] Since 1990, Hungary is a multi-party democracy and a parliamentary republic. Hungary became a member of the Council of Europe in 1990, OECD in 1996, NATO in 1999 and the European Union (EU) on 1 May 2004 where it joined the Schengen Area in 2007.

9. The head of the state is the President of the Republic elected by the National Assembly for a once renewable five-year term. The President fulfils mainly ceremonial functions. He is the commander-in-chief of the armed forces and nominates the Prime Minister taking into account the outcome of the general elections. The President may dissolve the National Assembly only under strictly defined circumstances (inability to elect the Prime Minister or to adopt the state budget). He does not have veto powers but before promulgation may refer adopted laws for constitutional review to the Constitutional Court or may send them back to the National Assembly for reconsideration.[5]

10. The highest political representative and legislative body in Hungary is the unicameral National Assembly. Its 199 members are elected for a four-year term using a mixed system where 106 members are elected in individual constituencies

2. 2011 census data is available at http://www.ksh.hu/nepszamlalas/?lang=en.
3. Respondents could declare more than one ethnicity, so the sum of ethnicities is higher than the total population. On the other hand, 14.7% of the population did not declare their ethnicity.
4. An official English translation of the Fundamental Law with the amendments incorporated is available at http://www.kormany.hu/en/ministry-of-justice/information-in-the-public-interest.
5. Fundamental Law Arts 6 (4)–(5), and 9–14.

and 93 members are elected from national party lists (where a 5% election threshold is applied) or minority lists (where the election threshold is around one-fourth of the votes needed to obtain a seat on a national party list). If an officially recognised nationality is not represented in the National Assembly through a minority list, a spokesman on its behalf may participate in the proceedings of the National Assembly without voting rights. Hungarian citizens without a residence in Hungary may vote for national party lists only.[6]

11. The National Assembly elects the Prime Minister and may remove him by a motion of no-confidence (on its own initiative) or by a vote of no-confidence (on the Prime Minister's initiative). The National Assembly exerts control over public finances through the State Audit Office and monitors compliance with human rights standards through the Commissioner for Fundamental Rights. The National Assembly in its exercise of budgetary powers is assisted by the Fiscal Council. The Council's chairman is appointed by the President of the Republic and its members are the Governor of the Hungarian National Bank and the President of the State Audit Office. The Fiscal Council makes comments on the draft Central Budget, on the planning and execution of the budget, the use of public funds and the state of public finances.[7]

12. Executive powers, in general, are vested in the Government (i.e., the council of ministers) headed by the Prime Minister. Ministers are nominated by the Prime Minister and appointed by the President of the Republic. The Government is responsible to the National Assembly and ministers are responsible to the National Assembly and the Prime Minister. The Government and its members may issue decrees when so authorised by acts of the National Assembly or in areas not regulated by acts. The Government's territorial organs of general competence are the Government Offices for Budapest Capital and for the counties.[8] The National Assembly may decide to establish autonomous regulatory organs for the exercise of executive powers in certain areas.[9] Currently, there are two autonomous regulatory organs[10] operating: the National Media and Infocommunications Authority[11] and the Hungarian Energy and Public Utility Regulatory Authority.[12] Since Hungary has not yet adopted the euro as official currency, executive powers related to monetary policy are vested in the Hungarian National Bank, the central bank of Hungary.[13] Presidents of independent regulatory organs and the Governor of the Hungarian National Bank may issue decrees.

6. Act No. CCIII of 2011 on the election of the members of the National Assembly.
7. Fundamental Law Arts 1–7, 21, 30, and 43–44.
8. Fundamental Law Arts 15–22.
9. Fundamental Law Art. 23.
10. A third autonomous regulatory organ, the Hungarian Financial Supervisory Authority also existed until 1 Oct. 2013 when its functions were taken over by the Hungarian National Bank.
11. Act No. CLXXXV of 2010 on media services and mass communication.
12. Act No. XXII of 2013 on the Hungarian Energy and Public Utility Regulatory Authority.
13. Fundamental Law Art. 41.

13. Hungary is a unitary country and its territorial administration is based on 19 counties (*megye*) and Budapest Capital (NUTS 3 level). Counties are divided into districts (6–18 districts per county), 174 districts (*járás*) in total (LAU 1 level). Budapest Capital is divided into 23 districts (*kerület*). There are 3,154 municipalities in Hungary (LAU 2 level) of which 328 have city status including Budapest Capital and 23 cities with county rights. For regional development planning purposes seven NUTS 2 level regions and three NUTS 1 level regions were also created. Municipalities, districts of Budapest Capital and counties are self-governing entities with their own elected assemblies. Municipalities and districts of Budapest Capital also directly elect their mayors for a five-year term. Municipalities are authorised to adopt decrees that are binding within their territorial jurisdiction. The legality of these decrees may be reviewed by the Curia. The legality of the activities of municipal governments is monitored by the county and Budapest Capital Government's Offices.[14] Besides local governments, Hungary maintains self-governance structures for recognised nationalities.

14. The latest general elections to the National Assembly were held in April 2018. As a result, the party alliance of Fidesz – Hungarian Civic Union (*Fidesz*) and the Christian Democratic People's Party (KDNP) obtained 133 seats out of 199 (66.83%). The right-wing Movement for a Better Hungary (*Jobbik*) came in second with 26 seats (13.07%). The coalition of the centre-left Hungarian Socialist Party (MSZP) and Dialogue (*Párbeszéd*) obtained a total of 20 seats (10.05%). Democratic Coalition (DK), the party of former Prime Minister Mr Ferenc Gyurcsány won 9 seats (4.52%), and the green Politics Can Be Different (LMP) holds 8 seats (4.02%). The liberal Together (*Együtt*) has one representative in the National Assembly. There is also an independent MP and a representative of the German nationality elected on a minority list in the National Assembly.[15] The Fidesz – KDNP alliance has governed the country since 2010 under the leadership of Mr Viktor Orbán as Prime Minister. The President of the Republic, Mr János Áder, elected in 2012 and re-elected in 2017, is also a former MP and MEP for Fidesz.

15. The latest general elections for mayors and municipal assemblies were held in October 2014. Most of the elected mayors and municipal councilmen were independent as party politics do not penetrate the public life of villages and smaller towns. On the other hand, national political parties play a determining role in municipal elections in larger cities and counties. The dominance of the Fidesz – KDNP alliance can be felt here as well. It holds a majority in all nineteen county assemblies and the assembly of Budapest Capital. Mayors supported by Fidesz – KDNP were elected in twenty cities with county rights (out of twenty-three). The mayors of Budapest Capital and seventeen districts in the capital (out of twenty-three) are affiliated to Fidesz – KDNP.

14. Fundamental Law Arts 31–35.

15. For official results of previous elections *see* the website of the National Election Office: http://valasztas.hu/dyn/pv18/szavossz/hu/start.html.

§2. Economic System

16. Hungary is an Organisation for Economic Co-operation and Development (OECD) high income mixed economy with a GDP per capita of EUR 20,334 on purchasing power parity in 2017. Hungary posted a GDP growth of 4.1% on a year in 2017 and 2.3% in 2016. Hungary is an export-oriented economy heavily dependent on foreign trade. Hungary's external trade surplus was EUR 5.56 billion in 2018 mostly due to trade with other EU Member States. Hungary's most important trade partner is Germany (followed by Austria), around a quarter of its external trade and 51% of its trade surplus in goods is realised in relation to Germany (Figure 2).[16]

17. Hungary ranks 48th on the World Economic Forum 2018 Global Competitiveness Index making it the fifth least competitive Member State of the EU preceding only Bulgaria, Romania, Croatia and Greece.[17] As far as economic freedom is concerned, Hungary is a moderately free country according to the 2019 Heritage Foundation economic freedom index ranking alongside Belgium, Poland, Portugal, Slovenia, Spain and Slovakia.[18] Roughly the same assessment was given by Fraser Institute's 2018 Economic Freedom Ranking where Hungary was placed in the second quartile with the same score as Iceland.[19]

Figure 2 GDP Per Capita on Purchasing Power Parity and Annual GDP

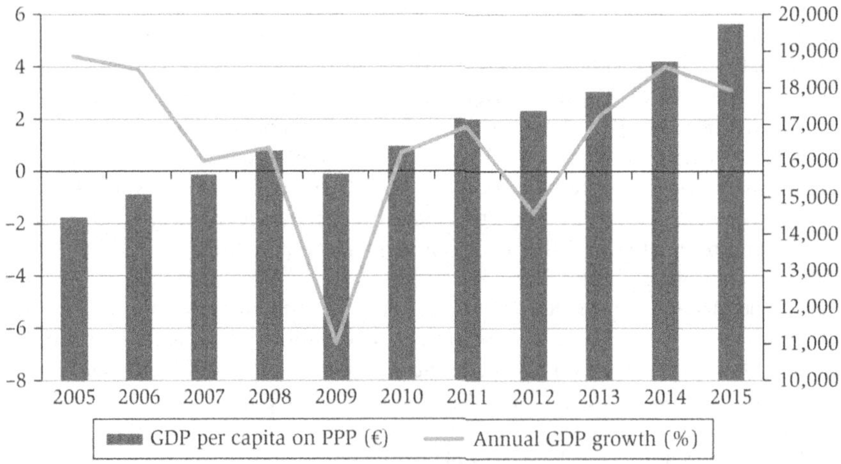

Growth in Hungary from 2007 to 2017

Source: Hungarian Central Statistical Office.

16. All data by the Hungarian Central Statistical Office (http://www.ksh.hu/?lang=en) unless indicated otherwise.
17. The report is available at: https://www.weforum.org/reports/the-global-competitveness-report-2018.
18. *Source*: http://www.heritage.org/index/.
19. *Source*: https://www.fraserinstitute.org/studies/economic-freedom .

18. In 2018 there were 1,908,808 registered economic entities in Hungary of which 1,757,489 for-profit entities but only around one-third of registered economic entities are actually operating. Around 70% of actually operating economic entities are individual enterprises and employ not more than one person. The number of entities with 250 or more employees is less than 1,000 but they account for 41% of the annual net income and 67% of export revenues.

19. In 2018 71.9% of the working age (15–64 years) population was economically active and 69.2% was employed. Unemployment stood at 3.7% down from 4.2% in 2017 and 5.1% in 2016. 32.4% of the employees worked in the industrial sector, 62.8% in services and around 4.8% in agriculture. Hungary's Human Development Index was 0.838 according to UNDP's 2018 Human Development Report; the country ranks 45th globally and falls into the category of very high human development (Figure 3).[20]

Figure 3 Development of Economic Activity Rate, Employment Rate and Unemployment Rate in Hungary from 2008 to 2018 (Working Age Population, 15–64 Years)

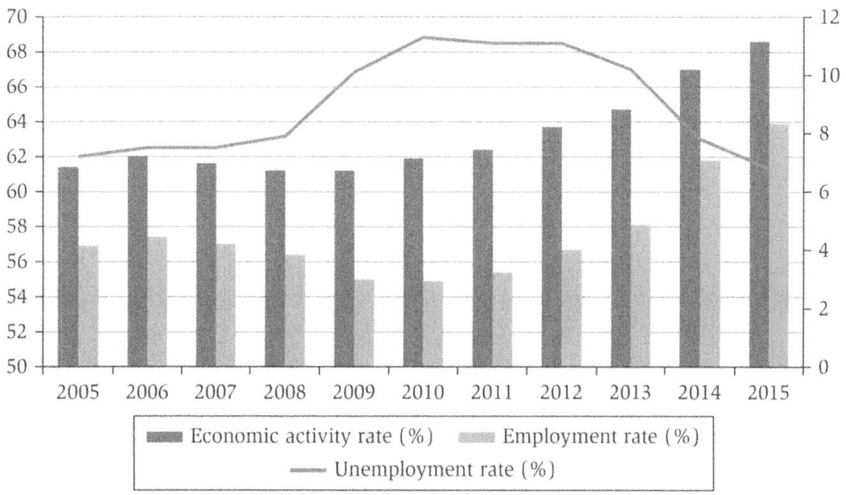

Source: Hungarian Central Statistical Office.

20. The average gross monthly salary of employees was HUF 329,943 in 2018 (approximately EUR 1,030) and has been increasing by 8%–49% annually in the previous three years. Salaries are on average 20% higher in the private sector than in the public sector and show high disparities for different sectors and educational groups.

20. *Source*: http://report.hdr.undp.org/.

21. Hungary maintains its own currency, the Hungarian forint (HUF).[21] At the moment Hungary does not meet all the Maastricht euro convergence (Figure 4). There is no national target date for the adoption of the euro; official statements suggest that Hungary might be able to technically fulfil all the convergence criteria in the medium term but the political will to actually adopt the euro seems fragile. In 2016 the inflation was a mere 0.4% (after a 0.1% deflation in 2015) but started rising sharply in 2017, and stood at 2.7% in January 2019. The Hungarian National Bank pursues a medium-term inflation target of 3%. The central bank base rate is 0.9% since May 2016, down from 1.65% in May 2015 and 2.4% in May 2014. A floating exchange rate system is maintained since February 2008. Since 2016, the exchange rate has fluctuated in the range of HUF 310–320/EUR 1 and HUF 265–295/USD 1.[22]

21. According to Article K of the Fundamental Law the official currency of Hungary shall be the forint.
22. *Source*: Hungarian National Bank, http://www.mnb.hu/en.

Figure 4 Compliance with Selected Maastricht Euro Convergence Criteria in

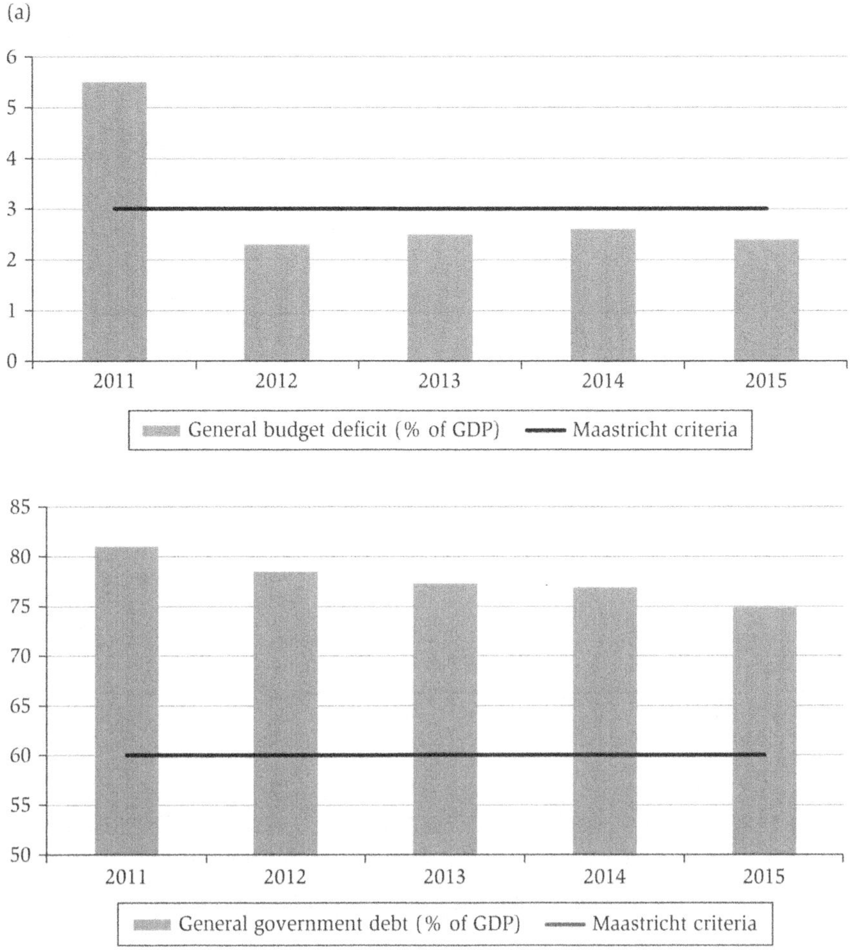

Hungary from 2014 to 2018

(b)

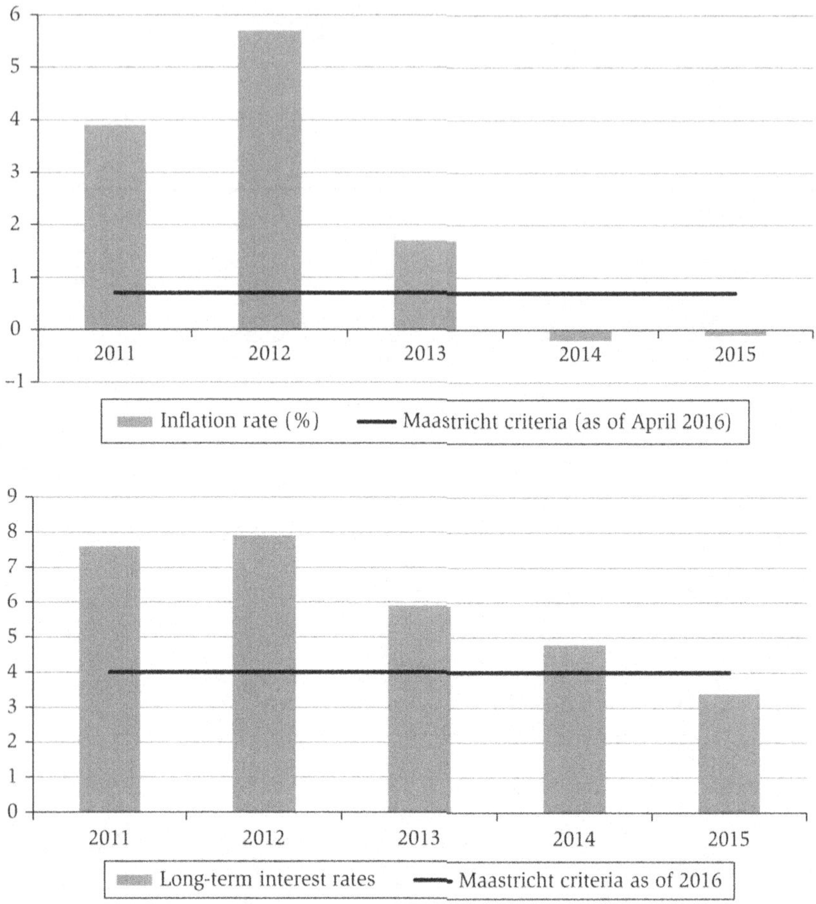

Sources: Hungarian Central Statistical Office, European Central Bank.

22. The tax system of Hungary is composed of a number of general direct and indirect taxes as well as particular taxes levied on certain products or businesses. The personal income tax is a flat rate tax that stands at 15% since 2016 (reduced from 16%).[23] Tax on company profits is significantly reduced starting from 2017 and is set at a flat rate of 9% (previously it was 10% or 19% depending on the amount of profits realised).[24] The general Value Added Tax (VAT) rate is 27% since

23. Act No. CXVII of 1995 on the personal income tax.
24. Act No. LXXXI of 1996 on the company profit tax and the dividend tax.

2012 making it one of the highest tax rate in the EU, preferential rates are maintained however for certain services (18% for restaurant services, 5% for Internet services and distant heating) and certain basic foodstuff (5% for pork, chicken, milk and eggs).[25] Special taxes are levied on insurance policies[26] and financial institutions.[27] Employers also pay a number of contributions and a social contribution tax after employees.[28] Excise duties are levied on tobacco products, alcoholic beverages and refined fuel.[29]

§3. The Legal System

23. The legal system of Hungary is a civil law system. While heavily influenced by Austrian and German law, it has always maintained its peculiar characteristics based on national legal culture and legal traditions. With the exception of brief periods in history, Hungary has always been ruled according to its own laws, rules and customs even under foreign occupation or as part of a larger political entity.

24. Even though codification is a relatively new phenomenon in Hungarian legal history (the first comprehensive written Constitution was adopted in 1949 and the first fully codified Civil Code in 1959), Hungarian law is now written law adopted by appropriate legislative and regulatory bodies and applied by courts of justice and other judicial or administrative organs. The Hungarian legal system is based on a strict hierarchy of norms. The Fundamental Law of Hungary and its amendments occupy the top of this hierarchy. The Fundamental Law and its amendments are adopted by the National Assembly by two-thirds of its members.[30] Cardinal acts are acts regulating areas of crucial legal importance and so designated by the Fundamental Law (e.g., on citizenship, political parties, nationalities, military service). Cardinal acts are adopted by the National Assembly by two-thirds of its members present. Regular acts adopted by the National Assembly may not be in conflict with cardinal acts. Besides acts, generally binding rules of conduct may be laid down in government decrees, prime ministerial decrees, ministerial decrees, decrees of the Governor of the National Bank of Hungary (NBH), decrees of the heads of autonomous regulatory organs and municipality decrees.[31] Between 1949 and 1989 the Presidium of the People's Republic of Hungary was authorised to adopt decree-acts (i.e., decrees having the legal force of acts) when the National Assembly was not in session. Such decree-acts may no longer be adopted but existing decree-acts remain in force and regulate important aspects of commercial law.[32]

25. Act No. CXXVII of 2007 on the general value added tax.
26. Act No. CII of 2012 on the insurance tax.
27. Act No. LIX of 2006 on the special tax and contribution to ameliorate the balance of public finances.
28. Act No. CLVI of 2011 on the amendment of certain tax legislation and related acts.
29. Act LXVIII of 2016 on the excise duties.
30. Fundamental Law Art. S.
31. Fundamental Law Art. T.
32. For Example, Decree-Act No. 13 of 1979 on private international law.; replaced from 1 Jan. 2018 by Act No. XXVIII of 2017 on private international law.

25. The Constitutional Court is the main organ entrusted with safeguarding the provisions of the Fundamental Law. The Constitutional Court is composed of fifteen judges elected by the National Assembly with a two-thirds majority for a non-renewable term of 12 years. The Constitutional Court may review the constitutionality of laws and judicial decisions and may also rule on the compatibility of laws with international treaties. *In abstracto* constitutional review may be initiated by the Government, one-fourth of the members of the National Assembly, the President of the Curia (Supreme Court), the Prosecutor General and the Commissioner for Fundamental Rights. *In concreto* constitutional review may be initiated by the judge who has doubts as to the constitutionality of a legal rule to be applied in the case before him. Individual constitutional complaints may also be filed by the concerned part against a judicial decision or a legal rule applied in a particular case.[33]

26. The Hungarian judiciary is organised in a four-tier system. District courts (111) have general first instance jurisdiction in civil and criminal matters.[34] Regional courts (20) have first instance jurisdiction in serious criminal cases, in civil litigation over the value of HUF 30 million as well as in some special civil matters (e.g., press correction claims).[35] Regional courts also have appellate jurisdiction for cases decided by district courts.[36] Regional courts of appeal (5) have appellate jurisdiction for cases decided by regional courts as first instance courts and serve as third instance courts for criminal cases decided by regional courts on appeal.[37] Administrative and labour courts (20) are attached to regional courts and are responsible for administrative review and handling labour disputes.[38] The company registry in Hungary is managed by company registry courts attached to regional courts.[39] The Curia (Supreme Court) decides appeals from regional courts of appeal.[40] The Curia is responsible for review procedures that may be initiated on points of law against final decisions and is entrusted with the task of ensuring the uniformity of the application of law.[41]

27. The administration of the judiciary is managed by National Office for the Judiciary (NOJ). The President of NOJ is elected by the National Assembly by a two-thirds majority from among the judges for a nine-year term. The activities of

33. Fundamental Law Art. 24; Act No. CLI of 2011 on the Constitutional Court.
34. CP Art. 22 (1); Act No. XIX of 1998 on Criminal Procedure (Crim. P.) Art. 15.
35. CP Art. 23 (1); Crim. P. Art. 16 (1).
36. CP Art. 10 (2) a); Crim. P. Art. 13 (2) a).
37. CP Art. 10 (2) b); Crim. P. Art. 13 (2) b); Crim. P. Art. 13 (3) a).
38. CP Art. 22 (2).
39. FA Art. 1.
40. CP Art. 10 (2) c); Crim. P. Art. 13 (2) c; Crim. P. Art. 13 (3) b).
41. CP Art. 10 (3); Crim. P. Art. 419.

NOJ are under the control of the National Judicial Council (NJC). The NJC is composed of the President of the Curia and fourteen elected judges representing all levels of the judiciary. Judges in Hungary are appointed by the President of the Republic on the initiative of the President of NOJ or the President of the Curia (if appointment is to the Curia).[42]

28. The internal structure of courts is quite divergent. At district courts groups may be formed with the participation of judges dealing with similar cases. In addition to groups consisting of panels, higher level courts may establish departments. Regional courts have criminal, civil, economic, and administrative-labour departments; regional courts of appeal have only criminal and civil departments. The Curia consists of a criminal, a joint civil and economic as well as an administrative-labour department.[43] All courts are headed by a president. Presidents of regional courts and regional courts of appeal are appointed by the President of NOJ; presidents of district courts and administrative and labour courts are appointed by the president of the regional court to which they are attached.[44] Company registry courts are not institutionally separate courts; they are organised as groups within regional courts.

29. First instance courts are composed of a sole professional judge who is assisted in exceptional cases (e.g., serious criminal cases or labour disputes) by two lay assessors. In criminal cases where the number of defendants or the complexity of the case so require a panel of two professional judges and three lay assessors may proceed at first instance.[45] Lay assessors are nominated by citizens, Non-governmental Organisations (NGOs) and local governments and elected for a term of four years by the municipal (for district courts) or county council (for regional courts) corresponding to the seat of the court. Assessors for labour disputes are nominated by employee and employer organisations. As regards juvenile criminal cases, at least one of the assessors must be a primary or secondary school teacher; they are nominated by the staff of the schools located in the jurisdiction of the relevant courts. Lay assessors are remunerated and enjoy the same procedural rights and obligations as professional judges.[46]

30. Second and third instance courts as well as review panels are composed of three professional judges with the possibility of referring complex criminal and review cases to a panel of five professional judges.[47] Legal uniformity decisions are adopted by special councils of the Curia composed of five or seven judges. A whole

42. Fundamental Law Arts 25–26; Act No. CLXI of 2011 on the organisation and management of courts of justice; Act No. CLXII of 2011 on the legal status and remuneration of judges.
43. Act No. CLXI of 2011 on the organisation and management of courts of justice Arts 18 (4), 21 (4), 22 (4), 24 (2).
44. Act No. CLXI of 2011 on the organisation and management of courts of justice Art. 128.
45. CP Art. 11 (1)–(2); Crim. P. Art. 14 (1)–(4).
46. Act No. CLXII of 2011 on the legal status and remuneration of judges Arts 212–221.
47. CP Art. 11 (4)–(5); Crim. P. Art. 14 (5).

department of the Curia may act as special council if the legal uniformity decision is adopted with a view to amend previous uniformity decisions or to settle a principal legal question.[48]

31. Hungarian court decisions do not form a binding system of precedents however legal uniformity decisions adopted by the Curia on questions of legal interpretation are binding on all courts.[49] The Curia regularly publishes some of its own rulings and selected rulings by lower courts (decisions on principles) with the intention to guide jurisprudence. The published rulings are not binding on lower courts but the Curia is expected to follow them as well as other guidelines adopted by its departments.[50]

32. The Prosecution Service in Hungary is independent from the executive branch and is headed by a Prosecutor General elected for a nine-year term from among the prosecutors on the proposal of the President of the Republic by the National Assembly with the votes of two-thirds of its members. Prosecutors are appointed by the Prosecutor General. The Prosecution Service supervises criminal investigations and penal enforcement, represents the State in criminal proceedings and as a guardian of public interest exercises other functions and powers laid down in the Fundamental Law or other acts (e.g., may initiate court proceedings for claims arising from void contracts if those contracts are against the public interest; may act to enforce compliance with consumer protection legislation if the violation affects a large number of consumers or causes significant damage).[51]

48. Act No. CLXI of 2011 on the organisation and management of courts of justice Arts 34–35.
49. Fundamental Law Art. 25 (3).
50. Act No. CLXI of 2011 on the organisation and management of courts of justice Arts 31–32.
51. Fundamental Law Art. 29; Act No. CLXIII of 2011 on the Prosecution Service.

Part I. Commercial Law

Chapter 1. Concepts and Sources of Commercial Law

33. The 'civilistic' is in use as the concept of civil law (or private law) and its related branches of law (there is the commercial law among these). The commercial law became a relatively independent area of law of civilistic.[52]

34. In Hungary there is not a unified viewpoint in connection with the notion of commercial law: its place in the Hungarian legal system is a question under debate. In the legal literature somebody denies the existence of this independent branch of law,[53] somebody admits its being.

35. Kecskés László means to imply that the thinking of commercial law is senseless in subjective terms of merchant and in objective accordance with the business transactions, he only considers the commercial law view important in the sense of formal law.[54] Also, Nochta Tibor attaches importance to the commercial law view in the regulation of private law.[55] Lábady Tamás is of the opinion that there is no need for commercial law because of the private law received a commercial law attitude by the new and monistic Hungarian Civil Code.[56]

36. Eörsi Gyula thought that the commercial law is a *lex specialis* from the aspect of private law.[57] Asztalos László believed that the private law and the commercial law duplicate horizontally the legal regulation of economic life and the commercial law is an independent branch of law;[58] Boóc Ádám and Sándor István are of the same mind as Asztalos: they think that the commercial law is the law of merchant on the subjective ground and the law of business transactions on the

52. L. Kecskés, 'A civilisztika és a civilisztikai gondolkodás rétegei', *Jura* 1, 2015, 43, 44.
53. Z. Novotni *Polgári jog, A gazdasági társaságok és a gazdálkodás egyéb jogalanyainak joga*, Miskolc: Miskolci Egyetemi Kiadó, 1992, 10–11.
54. Kecskés, *supra* n. 52.
55. T. Nochta, 'A magánjog kereskedelmi jogias szemléletéért', *Jura* 2, 2004, 102–103; T. Nochta *Társasági jog*, Budapest – Pécs: Dialóg Campus Kiadó, 2007, 24.
56. T. Lábady, *A magánjog általános tana*, Budapest: Szent István Társulat, 2013, 34.
57. Gy. Eörsi, *Összehasonlító polgári jog (Jogtípusok, jogcsoportok és a jogfejlődés útjai)*, Budapest: Akadémiai Kiadó, 1975, 173.
58. L. Asztalos, *Polgári jog, Általános rész, Személyek*, Budapest: Tankönyvkiadó, 1988, 18.

objective base.[59] Others mean that the commercial law is existing in Hungary since the first Commercial Act, which gave commercial qualification from subjective and objective aspects.[60] Bíró György and Lenkovics Barnabás looked on commercial law as special private law and agreed with the horizontal duplication theory.[61] Jobbágyi Gábor is of the opinion that the commercial law was separated from the private law and became an independent branch of law.[62] Some think that inside of private law the commercial law is developed as the professional law of merchants.[63] Szalma József also agrees with the separation of commercial law and he distinguishes the status law: the legal status of enterprises and the dynamic law: the commercial contracts inside of commercial law.[64] Bárdos Péter and Menyhárd Attila consider the commercial law as mixed professional law, with private and public law elements.[65] In my opinion the commercial law is an independent branch of law inside of private law and the private law is the background legal field of commercial law.

37. The sources of commercial law are branching out and it is impossibility or absurdity to make an inventory of sources of commercial law.

38. The sources of commercial law consist of private and public law norms, which can be:

- Civil Code (Act V of 2013);
- Commercial Act/Act on Trade (Act CLXIV of 2005);
- Firm Act (Act V of 2006);
- as '*Gewerbeordnungen*': acts on enterprising (Act CXV of 2009 on Private Entrepreneurs and Sole Proprietorships, Act CXXXII of 1997 on Hungarian Branch Offices and Commercial Representative Offices of Foreign-Registered Companies, Act CCXXXVII of 2013 on Credit Institutions and Financial Enterprises, Act C of 1990 on Local Business Tax, Act LXXXI of 1996 on Corporate and Dividend Tax, etc.);
- rules related to particular legal relationships and institutes (e.g., membership of different chambers, name-board, official permits, skilled professions, registration, accountancy, organizations, physical place of business activity, etc.);
- provisions for enterprises of foreigners;
- international agreements and conventions;
- norms of the EU;

59. Á. Boóc & I. Sándor, *Előadásvázlatok a polgári jog általános tanaiból,* Budapest: Patrocinium, 2012, 17.
60. J. Barta, Z. Fazakas et al., *A kereskedelmi szerződések alapvető szabályai,* Budapest: Patrocinium, 2015, 15, 22; Act XXXVII of 1875 §§ 258–260.
61. Gy. Bíró & B. Lenkovics, *Általános tanok (Magyar polgári jog),* Miskolc: Novotni Kiadó, 2000, 21.
62. G. Jobbágyi, *Magyar polgári jog I., Általános rész, Emberi személy, Családjog, Szellemi alkotások joga,* Budapest: Szent István Társulat, 2013, 16.
63. M. Balásházy, K. Pázmándi & T. Sárközy, *Business law,* Budapest: Typotex, 2008, 21.
64. J. Szalma, 'A polgári és a kereskedelmi jog kapcsolata az új Ptk. fényében', *Jogtudományi Közlöny* 10, 2014, 460.
65. P. Bárdos & A. Menyhárd, *Commercial Law,* Budapest: HVG Orac, 2008, 16.

– customary law;
– judicial practice and so on.

39. Act V of 2013 – the new Hungarian Civil Code – implies the majority of commercial law (in the Books 3 and 6) on the basis of the monistic principle of codification. The new Hungarian Civil Code has three levels in the Book 3: general and common provisions of legal persons related to business associations, cooperative, grouping, fund and society; general and common rules of business associations (concerning together general partnership, limited partnership, limited liability company and stock company); the special rules of each company. The general character of provisions of the Book 3 of the new Hungarian Civil Code related to business associations are dispositive, and the rules only exceptionally are cogent: the legal entities must not depart from the rules of Civil Code, or deviation is permitted only in one direction. The Book 6 of Hungarian Civil Code is divided into parts of common provisions relating to obligations, common rules on contracts, express contracts, non-contractual liability for damages, securities and other facts establishing obligations, with dispositive regulation.

40. The Fundamental Law of Hungary declares the following:

> Inviolable and inalienable human rights shall be respected and it shall be the primary obligation of the State to protect these rights. Hungary shall recognize the fundamental human rights, exercised either individually or collectively with other members of the community. The rules relating to fundamental rights and obligations shall be laid down in an act of Parliament. A fundamental right may only be restricted in order to enforce another fundamental right or to protect a constitutional value, to the extent that is absolutely necessary and proportionate to the objective pursued, and with respect to the essential content of the relevant fundamental right. Legal entities established on the basis of an act of Parliament shall also have these fundamental rights, and they shall also be bound by those obligations which, by their nature, are applicable not only to human beings.[66] Everyone shall have the right to freely choose his or her job or profession, and the freedom to conduct a business. Everyone shall have a duty to contribute to the enrichment of the community through his or her work, performed according to his or her abilities and faculties.[67] Everyone shall be equal before the law, every person shall have legal capacity. Hungary shall guarantee the fundamental rights to everyone without discrimination based on any ground such as race, colour, sex, disability, language, religion, political or any other opinion, ethnic or social origin, wealth, birth or any other circumstance whatsoever. Women and men shall have equal rights. Hungary shall promote equal opportunities and social convergence by means of introducing

66. Article I.
67. Article XII (1).

special measures. Hungary shall introduce specific measures to protect families, children, women, the elderly and the disabled.[68] Everyone residing lawfully in the territory of Hungary shall have the right to move freely and to freely choose his or her place of residence.[69]

68. Article XV.
69. Article XXVII (1).

Chapter 2. The Economic Operators

§1. Personal Status of Merchants

41. In terms of Act CXV of 2009 (about private entrepreneurs and sole proprietorships) natural persons shall have the right to pursue an economic activity – normally provided for remuneration – on own account, in the territory of Hungary, under the right of establishment according to the Act on the general provisions relating to the taking up and pursuit of the business of service activities, on a regular basis under economic exposure with a view to making a profit.[70] The rules of the Act on Private Entrepreneurs and Sole Proprietorships shall not apply to: the activities of small-scale agricultural producers as defined in the Personal Income Tax Act; the activities of veterinary service practitioners; legal practices; the activities of independent patent agents; the activities of notaries public; the activities of independent court bailiffs.[71]

42. The following may pursue the activities of *private entrepreneurs*: Hungarian nationals; nationals of any Member State of the EU or any State that is a party to the Agreement on the European Economic Area (EEA), and persons enjoying the same treatment as nationals of States who are parties to the Agreement on the EEA by virtue of an agreement between the European Community and its Member States and a State that is not a party to the Agreement on the EEA with respect to establishment; persons – other than those mentioned in the foregoing – exercising the right of free movement and residence in the territory of Hungary in accordance with the Act on the Admission and Residence of Persons with the Right of Free Movement and Residence; persons who have been granted immigrant or permanent resident status under the Act on the Admission and Residence of Third-Country Nationals, persons holding a residence permit for the purpose of gainful employment, family reunification or for the pursuit of studies, as well as exiles and stateless persons holding a residence permit granted on humanitarian grounds.[72]

43. The following *may not pursue the activities of private entrepreneurs*: minors, and any person who is under guardianship or conservatorship; any person who has been sentenced to imprisonment by final court verdict without probation: for any crime against the integrity of public life, for any crime against international justice, for any economic crime, for any crime of corruption, for any violent crime against property, for any crime against property, for any crime against intellectual property rights, for any crime relating to counterfeiting currencies and philatelic forgeries, for any crime against public finances, for money laundering, for any economic and business crime, for any crime against consumer rights and any violation of competition laws, or illicit access to data and any crime against information systems until relieved from the detrimental consequences attached to prior convictions; any person who has been sentenced to imprisonment for a term of over one year

70. Section 2 (1).
71. Act CXV of 2009 s. 2 (2).
72. *Ibid.*, s. 3 (1).

without probation for a premeditated crime, until relieved from the detrimental consequences attached to prior convictions; any person who is a member of a sole proprietorship or a business association subject to unlimited liability.[73]

44. A natural person shall be allowed to have one private entrepreneurial status at any given time.[74] The *notification* for the starting up and termination of private entrepreneurial activities, and application for private entrepreneur's licenses may be submitted electronically through the customer port of entry, or at the Authority (*Közigazgatási és Elektronikus Közszolgáltatások Központi Hivatala*, Central Office for Administrative and Electronic Public Services).[75] With a view to starting up the activities of private entrepreneurs, the applicant natural person is required to submit a notification to the body in charge of the register; this notification shall be made at the Authority, or through the customer port of entry, using the standard form prescribed for this purpose (electronic notification).[76] The body in charge of the register shall assign a register number to the private entrepreneur admitted, and shall send the notification containing data entered into the register (notice) to the notifier, or shall have it delivered through the Authority.[77] The body in charge of the register shall, at the time of delivery of the notification, notify the state tax authority, the Central Statistics Office and the Authority.[78] Private entrepreneurial activities may be started up on the day of registration.[79] Notification of the starting up of private entrepreneurial activities, the notification of changes, and the notification of suspension and termination of private entrepreneurial activities is exempt from fees and duties.[80]

45. At the private entrepreneur's request, the Authority shall provide a private entrepreneur's *license*. The license may be requested at the time of notification of private entrepreneurial activities, or any time during the pursuit of such activities; including when a license is requested on account of changes in the relevant data. A license is not necessarily required for the taking up and pursuit of private entrepreneurial activities.[81]

46. Private entrepreneurs shall be subject to unlimited *liability* for any and all obligations arising from or in connection with their activities to the extent of their personal resources. Private entrepreneurs are authorized to pursue different activities, and pursue them in any number of permanent *establishments and branches*. The real estate property used for the private entrepreneur's main office, permanent establishment or branch must be owned outright by the private entrepreneur, or that

73. *Ibid.*, s. 3 (2).
74. *Ibid.*, s. 3 (3).
75. *Ibid.*, s. 4 (2).
76. *Ibid.*, s. 5.
77. *Ibid.*, s. 7 (3).
78. *Ibid.*, s. 7 (5).
79. *Ibid.*, s. 7 (6).
80. *Ibid.*, s. 8.
81. *Ibid.*, s. 10 (1), (3), (5).

the private entrepreneur is legally entitled to use. The private entrepreneur must take an active part in the activity for which he is licensed, on the understanding that he may hire employees as contributors.[82]

47. Where authorization by the competent authority is prescribed mandatory by law, not including the decrees of municipal governments, to engage in a certain *economic activity*, the private entrepreneur may only start up and pursue the activity in question when in possession of such authorization. Where an activity is subject to professional qualification, the private entrepreneur may engage in such activity if able to meet such qualification requirements; unless an exemption is provided by law, not including the decrees of municipal governments, if the private entrepreneur fails to meet the qualification requirements, he may pursue such activities if there is at least one person among his employees participating in the activity in question under contract for an unfixed duration, who satisfies the qualification requirements (compliance with qualification requirements shall be maintained on an ongoing basis while carrying out the activities).[83]

48. In all *business correspondence* private entrepreneurs are required to indicate the designation '*egyéni vállalkozó*' (private entrepreneur) (or its abbreviated form 'e.v.') and their register number next to their name (signature).[84]

49. In the event of the private entrepreneur's death, the widow of the private entrepreneur, or his/her heir if there is no widow or under the widow's consent, may *take over the private entrepreneur's business operations*, subject to notifying the Authority in person of such private entrepreneurial activities, within ninety days of the occurrence of such reason.[85]

50. Private entrepreneurs may *suspend* their private entrepreneurial activities for a minimum period of one month and a maximum period of five years.[86]

51. Right for the pursuit of the activities of private entrepreneurs shall *cease* on the strength of the Act on Private Entrepreneurs and Sole Proprietorships: upon the private entrepreneur notifying the Authority or the holder of the register concerning the termination of his activities, on the day of notification; if the private entrepreneur has established a sole proprietorship, or has become the principal of a sole proprietorship, on the day preceding the operative date of the resolution of registration, or if the private entrepreneur has obtained the sole proprietorship's capital by way of transfer, on the day of transfer; on the day of the private entrepreneur's death; on the day when the court ruling on placing the private entrepreneur under guardianship or conservatorship becomes final; if the tax authority has withdrawn the private entrepreneur's tax number, on the day when the resolution on withdrawal

---

82. *Ibid.*, s. 15 (1), (2), s. 16 (1), (6).
83. *Ibid.*, s. 15 (3), s. 16 (2).
84. *Ibid.*, s. 16 (4).
85. *Ibid.*, s. 17 (1).
86. *Ibid.*, s. 18 (1).

becomes final; in the case of the occurrence of any of the grounds for disqualification, or when conflict of interest is identified; if the private entrepreneur failed to notify further pursuit or termination of private entrepreneurial activities by the time, on the first day after five years from the first day of suspension.[87]

52. The Authority shall *prohibit* the pursuit of private entrepreneurial activities: if the requirements for taking up private entrepreneurial activities are no longer satisfied or any grounds for exclusion apply concerning the pursuit of private entrepreneurial activities, specifically if the private entrepreneur has no registered office or principle activity; if the private entrepreneur is not lawfully engaged in either of the activities.[88]

53. The body in charge of the register shall ex officio *remove from the register* any private entrepreneur whose right for the pursuit of private entrepreneurial activities ceased to exist, upon receipt of notice from the competent authority, effective as of the day when the right is lost, and shall inform the private entrepreneur thereof. The body in charge of the register shall forthwith notify the state tax authority, the Central Statistics Office and the Authority electronically concerning the private entrepreneur's removal from the register, indicating the date of removal as well.[89]

54. A *sole proprietorship* is an entity without legal personality established by a natural person listed in the register of private entrepreneurs; it is brought into existence when entered into the firm registry. Sole proprietorships shall have legal capacity, they may obtain rights and undertake commitments under their corporate names, such as acquire property, conclude contracts, and may sue and be sued.[90]

55. Sole proprietorships shall fall within the scope of the FA, however, the provisions of the FA shall apply subject to the exceptions set out in the Act on Private Entrepreneurs and Sole Proprietorships. In matters not regulated in the Act on Private Entrepreneurs and Sole Proprietorships concerning sole proprietorships and the principals of sole proprietorships, the general provisions on legal persons and the common provisions relating to business associations of the Hungarian Civil Code shall apply.[91]

56. Subject to the exceptions set out in the Act on Private Entrepreneurs and Sole Proprietorships, sole proprietorships shall have only *one principal* (founder). Any one natural person may only have one sole proprietorship in the capacity of principal (founder).[92] A sole proprietorship may not be set up by way of transformation, and for reasons other than business operations.[93] A sole proprietorship and

87. *Ibid.*, s. 19 (1).
88. *Ibid.*, s. 19 (3).
89. *Ibid.*, s. 19 (4).
90. *Ibid.*, s. 20 (1), (2).
91. *Ibid.*, s. 20 (3), (6).
92. *Ibid.*, s. 20 (4).
93. *Ibid.*, s. 25 (1).

its principal may not be a member with unlimited liability in a business association.[94] Private entrepreneurs whose activities are suspended temporarily may not establish a sole proprietorship during the period of suspension.[95]

57. The *charter document* for the formation of a sole proprietorship shall be drawn up in an authentic instrument by a notary public, or in a private document countersigned by a lawyer and signed by the principal (founder). The charter document may be signed at the earliest on the day following the date of registration in the register of private entrepreneurs. Sole proprietorships may use the standard contract form to draw up their charter document; in this case, the charter document may contain only the provisions set out in the standard form.[96] The charter document shall function as the basic document governing the operations and finances of the sole proprietorship, and it may be freely established by the principal within the framework of the Act on Private Entrepreneurs and Sole Proprietorships and other legislation, however, any derogation from the Act on Private Entrepreneurs and Sole Proprietorships is allowed only if expressly permitted by law.[97] The charter document shall specify: the name and address of the sole proprietorship; the sole proprietorship's founder, showing his/her surname and forename, mother's name, home address and register number assigned in the register of private entrepreneurs; the sole proprietorship's main business activity and all other activities; the subscribed capital of the sole proprietorship, the financial contribution of its principal as well as how and when the subscribed capital is made available; the duration of the sole proprietorship, if established for a limited period of time; the name (corporate name), registered office (address) of the auditor, if applicable; an indication if interim dividends are paid.[98]

58. The foundation of a sole proprietorship shall be notified to the competent Court of Registry for *registration* and publication within thirty days from the signature of the charter document. The principal shall be responsible for notifying the Court of Registry – by way of electronic means – concerning the foundation of the sole proprietorship, any amendment of the charter document, the rights, facts and data contained in the firm registry and changes therein, as well as any other data required by law. The principal shall bear liability toward the sole proprietorship for any damage resulting from the incorrectness of the data, rights or facts notified, or from any delay in filing or failure to file the notification.[99]

94. *Ibid.*, s. 27 (2).
95. *Ibid.*, s. 21 (4).
96. *Ibid.*, s. 21 (1), (2).
97. *Ibid.*, s. 21 (3).
98. *Ibid.*, s. 21 (4).
Ibid., s. 21 (1), (2).
Ibid., s. 22 (1).
99. *Ibid.*, s. 24 (1), (4), (5).

59. The sole proprietorship shall be considered established when admitted into the firm registry, effective as on the day of admission. Sole proprietorships may not commence operations before admitted into the firm registry.[100]

60. Sole proprietorships are founded with the *subscribed capital* indicated in the charter document. If the sole proprietorship's subscribed capital exceeds two hundred thousand HUF, the subscribed capital may comprise cash and in-kind contributions (the founder shall indicate the amount of capital contribution in the application for registration). If the sole proprietorship's subscribed capital does not exceed two hundred thousand HUF, it must be provided in the form of cash contribution. Cash and non-cash contributions are to be made available at the time of foundation.[101]

61. Sole proprietorships are required to indicate the designation '*egyéni cég*' (sole proprietorship) (or its abbreviated form 'ec.') in the *name* of the sole proprietorship.[102]

62. The sole proprietorship shall be primarily *liable* for its obligations with its assets; if the assets of the sole proprietorship do not cover an obligation, the principal shall bear unlimited liability with his personal resources. Where the right for the pursuit of private entrepreneurial activities ceases for reasons of foundation of a sole proprietorships, up to the time of termination of the entitlement, the natural person and the sole proprietorship shall be subject to unlimited and joint and several liability for the private entrepreneur's commitments. The provisions of the Hungarian Civil Code pertaining to limited liability companies shall also apply to payments made from the sole proprietorship's capital to the order of the principal, subject to membership.[103]

63. The sole proprietorship's principal shall have decision-making powers in all matters conferred under the competence of the supreme body by any legislation pertaining to sole proprietorships. The management of the sole proprietorship shall be entrusted to an executive employee, or may be carried out by the principal under his membership in the sole proprietorship. If the sole proprietorship is managed by its principal, the principal shall function as the company's legal representative vis-à-vis third parties, and in front of the court and other authorities. In this case the principal shall represent the sole proprietorship in writing. The principal shall conduct the management of the sole proprietorship with due care and diligence as generally expected from persons in such positions and give priority to the interests of the sole proprietorship. In the event of any imminent threat for the sole proprietorship's insolvency, the principal shall conduct the management of the sole proprietorship having regard to creditors' interests. If the founder of the sole proprietorship failed to meet the conditions prescribed for private entrepreneurs, the

100. *Ibid.*, s. 24 (1), s. 25 (2).
101. *Ibid.*, s. 26.
102. *Ibid.*, s. 27 (1).
103. *Ibid.*, s. 27 (1), (3), s. 29.

company shall be considered to have failed to operate in compliance with regulations pertaining to the company's structure and operations. The capital contribution of a sole proprietorship may only be transferred to a private entrepreneur.[104]

64. In the event of the *principal's death*, the widow of the principal, or his/her heir if there is no widow or under the widow's consent, or upon being placed under guardianship or conservatorship by final court ruling, the principal's legal representative acting in his name and on his behalf may take over the sole proprietorship by replacing the principal, provided that he/she meets all requirements prescribed by the Act on Private Entrepreneurs and Sole Proprietorships and that the competent Court of Registry is notified accordingly within thirty days from the date of occurrence of the underlying reason. If the principal has more than one heir, all heirs may be recognized as principals of the company for a period of not more than three months, on condition that they specify in the notification the person placed in charge for handling the tasks conferred upon the executive officer or representative by the relevant legislation pertaining to sole proprietorships. The three-month time limit shall be calculated: from the death of the testator, if no probate is held; from the operative date of the grant of probate adopted in probate proceedings with full effect; from the date when the judgment of the court becomes final, in the event of inheritance proceedings.[105]

65. Sole proprietorships *may be transferred into business associations* under the relevant provisions laid down in the Hungarian Civil Code. In the process of transformation sole proprietorships are required to abide by the relevant provisions of the Accounting Act pertaining to transformations.[106]

66. A sole proprietorship shall *terminate* if: the period of time specified in the charter document expires or any other condition of termination is realized; the principal has adopted a decision for the company's termination without succession; the principal has adopted a decision for the company's termination with succession (transformation); declared terminated by the Court of Registry; the Court of Registry orders its cancellation ex officio; terminated by decision of the court in the course of liquidation. The provisions governing liquidation, dissolution, involuntary de-registration and bankruptcy proceedings shall also apply to sole proprietorships.[107]

67. The Act CLXIV of 2005 on Trade shall apply to trading activities and to the control of these activities.[108] Generally any person who wishes to engage in trading activities in the territory of Hungary shall notify the authority for trade and commerce in advance thereof. *Traders* (any person engaged in trading activities) shall have the right to choose the means of their trading activities according to the rules

104. *Ibid.*, s. 30.
105. *Ibid.*, s. 32.
106. *Ibid.*, s. 33.
107. *Ibid.*, s. 34.
108. Section 1.

set out in the Act on Trade.[109] An act or a decree adopted by the Government acting within its original legislative competence, and a government decree adopted by authorization granted in the Act on Trade, may contain provisions to prescribe the supply of certain products described therein to be carried out solely by way of either of the means of trading listed below or may restrict or ban the supply of such products by way of certain specific means of trading:[110]

- in-store trading activities: a building, an independent section of a building or an area constructed or used for trading activities, including any building or building section used primarily for warehousing and storage where trading activities are also pursued;[111]
- trading activities via mobile retail outlets: a vehicle converted for retail trading activities, whether self-propelled or towed by a motor vehicle;[112]
- trading activities in shopping centres: mean a multi-purpose building or multiple buildings consisting of a complex of commercial units, mostly shops, representing permanently established merchandisers of different type, and offering – additionally – various types of entertainment and leisure services to visitors;[113]
- trading activities in markets and fairs: 'market' shall mean a building or multiple buildings, or an area consisting of a complex of commercial units used for retail trading activities on a permanent or regular basis, typically daily or occasionally weekly and under 'fair' shall be understood a building or multiple buildings, or an area consisting of a complex of commercial units used for retail trading activities typically in a specific season of the year, or in connection with specific events or calendar days;[114]
- street sales: retail trading activities performed on public land, or in places which are open to the general public;[115]
- direct sale: the sale of goods within the framework of retail trading activities directly at the place of manufacture or production;[116]
- sales negotiated away from business premises: the activity of a trader or any other person acting in the trader's name or on his behalf that results in the supply of goods or services to consumers under contracts which are concluded during an excursion organized by the trader, or during a visit by a trader to the consumer's home or place of work, where the visit does not take place at the express request of the consumer;[117]
- retail via mail order houses: any commercial activity where the seller conveys commercial communication to prospective customers, which indicates the characteristics of the product and the price in a way to enable the consumer to make

109. Section 3 (1), (2), s. 2 (11).
110. Act CLXIV of 2005 s. 3 (4).
111. *Ibid.*, s. 2 (27.
112. *Ibid.*, s. 2 (17.
113. *Ibid.*, s. 2 (3.
114. *Ibid.*, s. 2 (19 and (29.
115. *Ibid.*, s. 2 (14.
116. *Ibid.*, s. 2 (15.
117. *Ibid.*, s. 2 (28.

an informed transactional decision to make a purchase, and delivers (by themselves or by others) the product selected and ordered on the strength of this commercial communication to the address indicated;[118]
- supply of goods by way of vending machines;
- supply of goods on means of transport: retail sales activities carried out in railroad dining cars and cafeterias, on coach lines, in the restaurant or cafeteria of passenger boats and on commercial flights.[119] Some other conditions for performing trading activity are the following: the evidence in proof of the origin of the products, the training and qualification decreed by the minister in charge of trade and commerce, the customer complaint book, the authorization, etc.[120]

68. The Act CCXXXVII of 2013 on Credit Institutions and Financial Enterprises shall apply to financial services, financial auxiliary services, bank representation activities and voluntary institutional protection performed, and to deposit insurance arrangements provided in the territory of Hungary; mixed-activity holding companies and companies other than financial institutions with which a financial holding company or credit institution subject to supervision on a consolidated basis has close links.[121] *Financial services* shall mean the pursuit of the following activities of a financial nature on a commercial scale, in HUF and other currencies: taking deposits and receiving other repayable funds from the public; credit and loan operations; financial leasing; money transmission services; issuance of electronic money; issuance of paper-based cash-substitute payment instruments (e.g., traveller's checks and bills printed on paper) and the provision of the services related thereto, which are not recognized as money transmission services; providing surety facilities and guarantees, as well as other forms of banker's obligations; commercial activities in foreign currency, foreign exchange – other than currency exchange services – bills and checks on own account or as commission agents; financial intermediation services; safe custody services, safety deposit box services; credit reference services; purchasing receivables.[122] *Financial auxiliary services* shall mean the pursuit of the following services of a financial nature on a commercial scale, in HUF and other currencies: currency exchange activities; operation of payment systems; money processing activities; financial brokering on the interbank market; activities for the issue of negotiable credit tokens; credit consultancy services.[123] Unless otherwise provided for by law, the financial services and financial auxiliary services may be performed subject to authorization issued under the Act on Credit Institutions and Financial Enterprises by the NBH acting exclusively within its function as supervisory authority of the financial intermediary system ('Authority').[124] Credit institutions and financial enterprises are recognized as *financial institutions.*[125] *Credit institution* means a financial institution whose business *inter alia* includes to

118. *Ibid.*, s. 2 (4.
119. *Ibid.*, s. 2 (13a.
120. *Ibid.*, s. 5 (1), (3), (4), s. 4 (5).
121. Section 1 (1) a) and d).
122. Act CCXXXVII of 2013 s. 3 (1).
123. *Ibid.*, s. 3 (2).
124. *Ibid.*, s. 3 (3).
125. *Ibid.*, s. 7 (1).

take deposits or other repayable funds from the public (not including the issue of bonds to the public as specified in the relevant legislation), and to grant credits and loans. The following activities may be pursued by credit institutions only: taking deposits and other repayable funds from the public in excess of their own funds, without a guarantee or without any surety facilities provided by a credit institution or the State for guaranteeing repayment; currency exchange services.[126] *Financial enterprise* signifies: a financial institution authorized to perform one or more financial services and to engage in the operation of payment systems; a financial holding company.[127]

69. Banks and specialized credit institutions may only operate in the form of companies limited by shares or branches, credit institutions set up as cooperative in the form of cooperatives, or company limited by shares which is a bank or specialized credit institution, and financial enterprises in the form of companies limited by shares, cooperatives, foundations or branches. Companies limited by shares, limited liability companies, cooperative and branches, other than financial institutions, may also engage in money processing activities.[128]

70. The investments of *foreigners* in Hungary shall enjoy full protection and security. The *investments of foreign nationals* in Hungary shall mean the share of a foreign national in the assets of a business association, grouping or cooperative society that is established in Hungary by virtue of membership (shareholder relationship, partnership interest), furthermore, in the assets of the Hungarian branch or commercial representation of a non-resident company, and of the independent enterprise of a foreign national, and of supranational forms in EU: European Economic Interest Grouping (Act XLIX of 2003), *Societas Europaea* (Act XLV of 2004), European Cooperative Society (Act LXIX of 2006). The *right of establishment of foreign nationals* shall be understood the actual pursuit of an economic activity on own account, in the territory of Hungary for an indefinite period, performed on a regular basis under economic exposure with a view to making a profit by way of a business facility, fixed establishment, office, commercial establishment or other similar place, fixed equipment or machinery, designed or used exclusively for this purpose.[129]

71. The foreign nationals shall have the right of establishment in the territory of Hungary for the pursuit of an economic activity on own account, on a regular basis under economic exposure with a view to making a profit in the following *forms of business operations*:

– in a self-employed capacity on own account, in the form of private entrepreneurship or sole proprietorship in accordance with specific other legislation;

126. *Ibid.*, s. 8 (1), (2).
127. *Ibid.*, s. 9 (1).
128. *Ibid.*, s. 11 (1), (6).
129. Act XXIV of 1988 on the Investment of Foreigners in Hungary s. 1 (1), s. 2 b) and c).

- by way of a branch or commercial representation in accordance with specific other legislation;
- by way of resident business association, grouping or cooperative society in which the foreign national holds a share.[130]

72. The foreign natural persons shall have the right of establishment to take up and pursue – in a self-employed capacity – an economic activity on own account, on a regular basis under economic exposure with a view to making a profit under the conditions applicable to Hungarian citizens if established in an EEA Member State, or this entitlement and national treatment is afforded by law or international treaty. When acting in a self-employed capacity, foreign nationals are required to comply with the vocation requirements and other conditions prescribed by law for resident persons pertaining to the economic activity in question. When acting in a self-employed capacity, foreign nationals are required to observe the regulations pertaining to residents in their contracting practices and to obtain the necessary permits and authorizations where one is required. In the application of the regulations governing the acquisition of real estate properties, when acting in a self-employed capacity, foreign nationals shall be recognized as foreign natural persons. Undertakings operating with foreign participation may take part in the foundation of other business associations and cooperatives, may themselves found other business associations, and may acquire holdings in existing business associations and cooperatives. Legal supervision of economic associations with foreign participation shall be exercised by the court which maintains the firm registry (Court of Registry).[131]

73. Of the forms of business establishment in Hungary available to foreigners, the Act CXXXII of 1997 on Hungarian Branch Offices and Commercial Representative Offices of Foreign-Registered Companies shall govern the general conditions and rules for the establishment, operation and termination of branch offices and direct commercial representative offices of foreign-registered companies in Hungary.[132] The foreign-registered company is a legal person or organization without legal personality which conducts entrepreneurial activities as its principle activity and whose registered office is located outside the territory of Hungary, and other entrepreneurs who have a company abroad or are included in a business registration.[133]

74. Branch Offices of Foreign Companies in Hungary is an *organizational unit* of a foreign company, without legal personality, vested with financial autonomy and registered as an independent form of company in Hungarian firm registry as a branch office of a foreign company.[134] A foreign company shall be entitled to conduct entrepreneurial activities through its branch office or offices registered in Hungary pursuant to the provisions of the Act on Hungarian Branch Offices and

130. Act XXIV of 1988 s. 3 (1).
131. Act XXIV of 1988 s. 3/B, s. 4, s. 5.
132. Section 1 (1).
133. Act CXXXII of 1997 s. 2 a).
134. *Ibid.*, s. 2 b).

Commercial Representative Offices of Foreign-Registered Companies. In the course of such activities, the branch office shall proceed in legal relations with the authorities and with third parties in connection with the branch office, unless prescribed by law to the contrary, and in the relationships with other branch offices of the foreign company. A branch shall have *legal capacity*, it may obtain rights and undertake commitments under its corporate name on the foreign parent company's behalf, such as acquire property, conclude contracts, and may sue and be sued. A branch office may have business premises (locations) in more than one city (community).[135] A branch office is regarded as *establish*ed upon having been entered in the firm registry and may commence entrepreneurial activities following such registration. The authorized signatories may proceed in the name and on behalf of the branch office following submission of the application for registration; however, the affix 'under registration' shall be indicated on all correspondence and shall be attached to the company's name (pre-branch office). *Prior to registration*, the branch office may not engage in any activities subject to official authorization (including activities relating to foundation and the licensing of business premises). If the branch office's application for registration is rejected, it may not acquire additional rights and may not undertake new commitments, and it shall terminate all activities. The foreign parent company shall be subject to unlimited liability for the branch office's debts arising from commitments.[136] Responsibility for the *notification* of the establishment of a branch, and the rights, facts and data recorded in the firm registry and any changes therein, as well as any other statutory information lies with the person or persons authorized to sign on behalf of the branch. The branch office may be *represent*ed by persons who are employed under contract or assigned, or persons with domestic residence who are under a long-term service contract.[137] Unless otherwise provided for in the Act on Hungarian Branch Offices and Commercial Representative Offices of Foreign-Registered Companies, a foreign company shall, in respect of the establishment and operation of its branch office, receive the same treatment as a domestic economic organization.[138] A branch office may not perform representation activities on behalf of a foreign company. A foreign company may only dispose over assets and rights acquired *under the branch office's company name*, and liabilities assumed under its own company name upon dissolution of the branch office or during the insolvency proceedings described in the Act on Hungarian Branch Offices and Commercial Representative Offices of Foreign-Registered Companies, and during proceedings initiated abroad in connection with assets and rights obtained and liabilities assumed under the branch office's company name.[139] The foreign company shall continuously provide the *assets* required for the operation of the branch office and the settlement of its liabilities. The foreign parent company and the branch office shall be subject to unlimited joint and several *liability* for the debts of the branch office. In respect of the execution of liabilities incurred in connection with the activities of a branch office, all assets of the foreign

135. *Ibid.*, s. 3.
136. *Ibid.*, s. 4.
137. *Ibid.*, s. 6.
138. *Ibid.*, s. 9 (1).
139. *Ibid.*, s. 10 (1), (2).

company in Hungary may be subject to such execution.[140] Branch offices, unless otherwise provided for by law, shall be treated as residents for foreign exchange purposes.[141] The *employees* of a branch are bound to the foreign company by way of a contract, where employer's rights shall be exercised by the foreign company through the branch.[142] The *insolvency* of the branch office shall be declared, in the event that the foreign company or the branch office has not paid non-disputed or acknowledged debts within sixty days of due date, or execution proceedings conducted in Hungary against such party were unsuccessful.[143] A branch office shall be considered *dissolved* upon removal from the company registration records. A *request for the cancellation* of a branch office shall be submitted to the Court of Registry within sixty days following a decision made by the foreign parent company in regard to this. Upon request, the Court of Registry may remove a branch office from the firm registry if all of the following conditions are fulfilled:

- the foreign company has no public debts in Hungary in relation to the operation of its branch office;
- the branch office has published an announcement of its dissolution in the Firm Gazette, whereby creditors have been invited to register their claims within thirty days, yet no such claim has been received or the creditor's claim has been satisfied or secured;
- there are no regulatory or court proceedings (including arbitration proceedings) in progress in Hungary against the foreign company related to activities performed by its branch office, or the branch office or the foreign company has provided security in respect of monetary claims, in proceedings which are in progress;
- there are no insolvency proceedings in progress against the foreign company or the branch office.[144] The Court of Registry shall act ex officio to remove the branch office from the firm registry in the cases specified in the Firm Act. The Court of Registry, if banning a branch office from further operation by judicial supervisory action, shall publish an announcement in the Firm Gazette inviting creditors to report their claims at the branch office within thirty days. The Court of Registry shall declare the branch office dissolved, and remove it from the firm registry, if no such claims are registered, or if the creditors' claims have been satisfied based on the notice.[145]

75. Foreign companies may establish permanent, direct *commercial representative offices* in Hungary.[146] A commercial representative office is an *unincorporated organizational unit* of a foreign company, established upon entry into the firm registry, which may commence its operations after such *registration*. The provisions of

140. *Ibid.*, s. 11 (1), (3).
141. *Ibid.*, s. 13.
142. *Ibid.*, s. 18 (2).
143. *Ibid.*, s. 22 (2).
144. *Ibid.*, s. 23 (1), (2).
145. *Ibid.*, s. 23 (5).
146. *Ibid.*, s. 25.

the Firm Act shall be applied in respect of the entry into the registration and registration requirements for commercial representative offices, including the judicial supervisory competence of the Court of Registry, and public company information, whereby reporting to the Court of Registry of the establishment of a commercial representative office, the rights, facts and data recorded in the firm registry and any changes therein, as well as such information required by law shall be the responsibility of the person(s) authorized to sign on behalf of the commercial representative office. The commercial representative office may be *represent*ed by persons employed under contract or assigned, or persons under long-term service contract with domestic residence.[147] A commercial representative office shall, on behalf of the foreign company mediate contracts in the name of the foreign parent company, participate in the preparation of contracts, perform information, advertisement and promotional *activities*. The commercial representation may enter into contracts in the name and on behalf of the foreign parent company in connection with the operation of the representation. Commercial representative offices may not engage in business activities in their own name, and may not provide lawyer's services or foreign legal counselling services as set forth in other laws.[148] The *employees* of a commercial representative office are in legal relationship with the foreign company; employer's rights shall be exercised by the foreign company.[149] A commercial representative office is considered *dissolved* upon being removed from the firm registry of the Court of Registry. A *request for cancellation* shall be submitted to the Court of Registry within sixty days following a decision made by the foreign parent company in regard to this. Upon request, the Court of Registry may *remove* a commercial representative office from the firm registry in the event that:

- the foreign company has no public debts in Hungary in relation to the operation of its commercial representative office;
- the commercial representative office has published an announcement of its dissolution in the Firm Gazette, whereby creditors have been invited to register their claims within thirty days, yet no such claim has been received or the creditor's claim has been satisfied or secured;
- there are no regulatory or court proceedings (including arbitration proceedings) in progress in Hungary against the foreign company related to activities performed by its commercial representative office.[150] The Court of Registry shall act ex officio *to remove* the commercial representative office from firm registry in the cases specified in the Firm Act. The Court of Registry, if banning a commercial representative office from further operation by judicial supervisory action, shall publish an announcement in the Firm Gazette inviting creditors to report their claims at the commercial representative office within thirty days. The Court of Registry shall declare the commercial representative office dissolved, and remove

147. *Ibid.*, s. 26 (1), (2), (3).
148. *Ibid.*, s. 27 (1), (2), (4).
149. *Ibid.*, s. 29 (2).
150. *Ibid.*, s. 30 (1).

it from the firm registry, if no such claims are registered, or if the creditors' claims have been satisfied based on the notice.[151]

§2. Partnerships and Corporations

76. Three groups of legal entities can be distinguished in the Hungarian Private Law: the natural persons, the legal persons and associations with limited legal capacity.[152]

77. All persons shall have legal capacity; all persons shall be entitled to have rights and obligations. Unilateral statements limiting legal capacity shall be null and void.[153]

78. All legal persons shall have legal capacity; they shall be entitled to have rights and obligations. The legal capacity of legal persons shall cover all rights and obligations that do not inherently pertain solely to individual human beings.[154]

79. Legal persons may be established in a form defined by law, for the pursuit of activities and objection which are not prohibited by law; any instrument of constitution made in violation of this provision shall be null and void. Persons shall have freedom of establishment of a legal person by means of a contract, charter document or articles of association, and shall themselves decide on the legal person's organizational structure and operational arrangements.[155]

80. A legal person shall have its own name and seat, shall have assets separate from its members and founders, and shall have a management and representative body.[156]

81. The legal persons by Hungarian Civil Code are the following: the State, the cooperative societies, *the companies (the general partnership, the limited partnership, the limited liability company and the stock company),* the associations, the foundations and the groupings.[157]

151. *Ibid.*, s. 30 (4).
152. With application: T. Papp, *Corporations and Partnerships Hungary, International Encyclopaedia of Laws,* Suppl. 81, Alphen aan den Rijn: Wolters Kluwer, 2015, 29–38; T. Papp, *Law of Business Enterprises,* In: Business Law in Hungary, ed. I. Sándor, Budapest: Patrocinium, 2016, 245–266.
153. Section 2:1 CC.
154. Section 3:1 (1), (2) CC.
155. Section 3:1 (4), 3:4 (1) CC.
156. Section 3:1 (5) CC.
157. Sections 3:63–3:406 CC.

82. The general rules relating to legal persons shall apply where the Civil Code does not provide otherwise in connection with certain types of legal persons. The general rules relating to legal persons shall also apply to legal persons of the types not governed under the Civil Code.[158]

83. The associations with limited legal capacity set out by the Hungarian Civil Code are the civil associations and the condominiums. Where legal personality is conferred by civil law upon any organization lacking the legal status of legal persons, the general rules relating to legal persons shall also apply to those entities.[159]

84. Under a *civil law partnership*[160] agreement the parties (members) undertake to cooperate in order to achieve their common goals and to make capital contributions necessary for achieving said common goals, and to bear the risks of their activities collectively.

85. Each member shall provide capital contributions in equal proportions. Capital contribution may be provided in the form of money, a marketable thing of value or intangible property, or any other form of service, such as – in particular – work performed in person.

86. As regards the assets contributed, the ones that cannot be consumed will be used collectively, and the ones that can be consumed will be owned jointly. The ownership share of assets given into common ownership may not be disposed of by a member individually.

87. Should a member fail to provide the contribution agreed upon in the contract, either of the other members shall have the right to demand performance as contracted.

88. The profits and losses from common activities shall be distributed among members in proportion to their capital contributions. Any agreement excluding any member from receiving a share of the profits or from covering the losses shall be null and void (the prohibition of *societas leonina*). If the members' responsibility for covering losses derogates from the ratio previously agreed upon based on a contract concluded with a third party, they shall settle accounts with each other as laid down in the contract.

89. If any member is engaged in any conduct which seriously endangers the success of collective activities or the achievement of the purpose of the partnership, either of the other members shall have the right to demand the member to cease such conduct.

---

158. Section 3:3 (1), (2) CC.
159. Sections 6:498–6:513, 5:85, 3:3 (3) CC.
160. Sections 6:498–6:513 CC.

90. Members shall be entitled to manage the partnership's affairs collectively. Members may also provide that authorization for management is granted to a certain member or members. Non-members shall not be granted management rights. Management shall be carried out personally.

91. Members may grant authorization in the partnership agreement to either of the members to represent the other members in dealings with third parties.

92. Each member shall have access to management processes, that is to say they shall have the right to inspect the related documents and books. Any agreement of parties to the contrary shall be null and void.

93. If the partnership agreement is terminated, the creditor of any member shall be entitled to lay claim to the partner's share of the settlement of final accounts.

94. The termination of the civil law partnership agreement:

- the partnership agreement concluded for an indefinite period may be terminated by either of the members with a three months' notice;
- the partnership agreement may be terminated without notice where justified by substantial reasons;
- the partnership agreement shall be terminated upon the death or dissolution of a member (the surviving members may decide to carry on the agreement without the deceased or dissolved member).

95. The partnership agreement may provide that a member may be excluded from the partnership by unanimous decision of the other members in the event where either member has the right to terminate with immediate effect for a reason attributable to the member to be excluded; accounts shall be settled with the excluded member.

96. If the partnership agreement is terminated accounts shall be settled among the members. Any prior agreement for the exclusion of settlement shall be null and void. In the process of settlement, common assets shall be distributed among the members in proportion to their capital contribution. The assets made available for collective use shall be returned to their owners.

97. The place of civil association among the other associations:

Aspects	*Civil Association*	*General Partnership*	*Cooperative Society (Grouping)*	*Limited Liability Company*	*Company Limited by Shares*
Legal capacity	– defective	✓, legal person	✓, legal person	✓, legal person	✓, legal person
Proceedings in their own name	–	✓	✓	✓	✓

Aspects	*Civil Association*	*General Partnership*	*Cooperative Society (Grouping)*	*Limited Liability Company*	*Company Limited by Shares*
Separated assets	– (joint property)	'✓' (it is relative because of the secondary unlimited, joint and several liability of members)	–/✓ (it may be established without initial capital)	✓	✓
Permanent organization	–	–	✓	✓	✓
Object	cooperation	joint engagement in business operations	cooperation and coordination, possibly economic activity	joint engagement in business operations	joint engagement in business operations
Formation	–	✓	✓	✓	✓
Formalities	–	✓	✓	✓	✓
Registration	– (contract without formalities and registration)	(memorandum of the founders +)	association in registration into	(document and firm registry)	undersigned by
Performance of contribution by members	compulsory	compulsory	Possible/ compulsory (at carrying out economic activity)	compulsory	compulsory
Possibility of single-member company (relations without obligation)	–	–	–	✓	✓
Personal cooperation	possibility	possibility	in form of accessory consideration	in form of accessory consideration	may not be defined at stock companies
Prohibition of *societas leoninas*	✓	✓	explicit – implicit ✓	(because of business share with special rights)	(e.g., because of preferential shares)

Aspects	*Civil Association*	*General Partnership*	*Cooperative Society (Grouping)*	*Limited Liability Company*	*Company Limited by Shares*
Liability of members	primary, joint and several, in proportion to the members' capital contribution	secondary, unlimited, joint and several	secondary (sometimes primary – if the grouping does not have assets-) unlimited, joint and several	generally – only exceptionally	generally – only exceptionally
Right of organization	each member shall be entitled to manage affairs collectively	all the members shall be entitled to the management of the partnership	management by members is a possibility	management by members is a possibility	it is not typical
Transferability of the members' proportion	– (non-transferable the ownership stake)	✓	✓	it may be limited/ excluded	✓
Separation of termination of association and membership	it is not separated	✓	✓	✓	✓
Termination of membership as obligation	✓ (by notice)	✓ (by notice)	similar (by withdrawal)	–	–
Method of amendment of contract/ memorandum of association	novation	by unanimous decision	by unanimous decision/qualified majority	generally by qualified majority, exceptionally unanimous decision	by qualified majority
Breach of contract	among members	between the company and the member(s), and among members	between the company and the member(s), and among members	between the company and the member(s), and among members	between the company and the member(s), and among members
Control of legal operation	–	✓ judicial	✓ supervisory	✓ competence of	✓ firm court

98. Business associations[161] are legal persons established for the pursuit of business operations with financial contribution provided by its members, where each member has a right to a share of the profit and an obligation to participate in covering the losses.[162]

99. The object of the company may be engagement in joint business operations, or other than making profit.

100. Non-profit companies may be established and operated in any corporate form. A business association shall be recognized as a non-profit business association, and as such shall be authorized to use the designation 'non-profit' in its corporate name, if the instrument of constitution specifically indicates that the profit from the business association's operations may not be distributed among the members, for it shall be retained by the company's purposes.[163]

101. The corporate name of a non-profit company shall contain the designation 'non-profit' with the corporate form.[164]

102. A non-profit business association may be established also by decision of the supreme body of a registered business association to continue operating in the form of a non-profit business association.[165]

103. A non-profit business association may be granted public-benefit status; the designation 'public-benefit organization' shall be granted upon request, upon foundation or subsequently, by the Court of Registry. Non-profit business associations may include their public-benefit status in their corporate name.[166]

104. Where a non-profit business association of the status of a public-benefit organization is terminated without succession, the assets remaining after settlement of all debts from the company's own funds available at the time of termination may be distributed among members, not exceeding the value of the share of members in the company's capital at the time they were provided. Assets in excess of this value shall be allocated by the Court of Registry to objectives of public interest according to the provisions set out in the instrument of constitution. In the absence of such provisions, the remaining assets shall be allocated to the national Cooperation Fund.[167]

105. From the point of view of the legal entity the companies may be classified as legal persons and each company has legal capacity under their corporate names.

161. T. Papp, *Company Law*, Szeged: Lectum Kiadó, 2011, 42–48.
162. Section 3:88 (1) CC.
163. Sections 9/F (2), (3) FA.
164. Section 9/F (1) FA.
165. Section 9/F (3) FA.
166. Section 9/F (4) FA.
167. Section 9/F (6) FA.

106. On the basis of the cooperation of members the companies may be distinguished as partnerships or as capital mergers. The partnerships are founded on the common activities of members, on the mutual trust, on the personal cooperation. The capital mergers are forms of a great number of members and with great capital, for making profit.

107. On the ground of the number of members the companies may be established and operated by one legal entity (single-member company) or by more (at least two) legal entities; only the limited liability company and the company limited by shares may be functioned as single-member company.

108. From the aspect of the member's liability the companies may be separated where:

- the members are liable secondary, unlimited, joint and several for the debts of the company (the members of general partnership, and the general partner of the limited partnership);
- the members are not generally – only exceptionally – liable for the obligations of the company (the limited partner of the limited partnership, the members of the limited liability company and the shareholders).

109. The companies may be established only with *initial capital*; by the partnerships the Civil Code does not determine minimum amount of the initial capital, but the companies with legal personality may be formed only with minimum subscribed capital (the minimum amount is HUF 3,000,000 in case of a limited liability company, HUF 5,000,000 in case of a private company limited by shares and HUF 20,000,000 in case of public company limited by shares).

110. In accordance with registration of companies the partnerships, the limited liability companies and the private company limited by shares may be corporate by model of contract (memorandum of association determined by Civil Code and Firm Act).

111. In Hungary there is a disappearing form of companies: the *joint enterprise*. After the entry into force of the Act IV of 2006 (Company Act) new joint enterprises may no longer be established. The joint enterprises registered in the firm registry or in the process of registration on the day of the Act IV of 2006 entering into force may continue to operate according to the provisions of Act CXLIV of 1997 on Business Associations in force on 30 June 2006.[168] Joint enterprises are companies founded by members who/which are, first and foremost, liable for their obligations, with their assets. If the assets of the enterprise do not cover any debts the members shall, in proportion to their contribution, bear joint liability for the debts

168. Section 333 (7) CA.

of the enterprise, as guarantors.[169] The designation 'joint enterprise' (*közös vállalat*), or its abbreviation 'kv.' shall be indicated in the company name of the enterprise.[170] The supreme body of a joint enterprise is the council of the directors. Management and representation of an enterprise shall be carried out by the director within the framework of the articles of association and the resolutions of the council of directors.[171] According to the conditions contained in the articles of association, members may also enter an enterprise following its foundation (admission).[172] Membership in joint enterprise shall terminate: if the member has not provided his contribution defined in the articles of association despite an order to this effect; upon withdrawal of the member; upon death or termination without legal successor of the member; upon exclusion of the member; if the existence of such is in violation of the law.[173] In the event of termination without legal successor of an enterprise, unless otherwise provided by the articles of association, the assets remaining after settlement of all debts shall be distributed among the members of the enterprise in proportion to their contribution.[174]

112. Historically the form of *grouping* appeared in Hungary in 1950: it was the directing organ of the state-owned companies in the socialist period. This form is not a business association but a *cooperative society*. The grouping could be founded easily (under only few legal conditions) and has simple organizational structure. The general regulations of legal person and common provisions of the business association of the Civil Code shall be applied for the grouping as well. The grouping is a cooperative society vested with legal personality, founded by its members in order to improve the efficiency of their financial management, to coordinate their economic activities, and to represent their professional interests. The *purpose* of the grouping is not to make profits for itself. The members of the grouping shall bear unlimited, joint and several liability for debts in excess of the assets of the grouping. A grouping may also pursue other service and joint economic activities (economic auxiliary activity) in support of its coordination duties.[175]

113. The grouping is a coordinate – cooperative, non-business association with legal personality. It is a non-profit society, which may be established without initial capital; in this case the members shall bear the costs of the operation of the grouping. If the grouping pursues supplementary economic activity (this is not purely non-profit grouping) the members shall provide the assets required for such activities. Whether the grouping is formed with or without initial capital, the *liability* of its members is secondary, unlimited, joint and several.

169. Act CXLIV of 1997 s. 106 (1).
170. *Ibid.*
171. Act CXLIV of 1997 s. 114 (1).
172. *Ibid.*, s. 115 (1).
173. *Ibid.*, s. 117 (1).
174. *Ibid.*, s. 120.
175. Section 3:368 CC.

114. According to the practical experiences, there are not too many material and financial instruments required by the grouping during its operation. Yet the grouping was founded in order to:

- facilitate the success of the activities of its members: for example, for organization of recreation and holiday for the workers of the members of the grouping;
- coordinate the business activities of its members: for example, for research and development, for common marketing, for the exchange of information;
- represent the professional interest of its members: for example, for activity of patent agent.[176]

115. Historically the form of *general partnership* (*közkereseti társaság*, kkt.) appeared in Hungary by the Act XVIII of 1840. This type of partnership which is suitable for family businesses and enterprises was born due to the economic necessity. This form of business association could be established easily (with only some legal conditions) and has a simple structure; in Hungary the general partnership is a popular business association. The general regulations of legal person and common provisions of business association must be applied for the general partnership as well.

116. For the legal act to create a general partnership an agreement between legal entities is necessary. The legal relationship following from the incorporation has not lost its *contractual relationship* totally, for example, all members shall be entitled to the management of the kkt., any member of a general partnership may assign his participation (rights and obligations) in the partnership to a third party only with unanimous decision. The general partnership is a personal association that can be founded by more members for business operations or for non-profit-making. The general partnership may be incorporated under both of the general registration proceedings and simplified registration proceedings (with a standard contract form), but always by electronic means.

117. The general partnership is an association with the legal status of a legal person, so it also has legal capacity under its corporate name: it may obtain rights and undertake commitments. The *legal place* of kkt. is between the civil association and the limited liability company. The general partnership is a form of small enterprises with some members, where the separation from the members' person is fundamental; the personal character, the contractual aspect and the engagements of partnership-member (e.g., the members may be sued together with the kkt.) are the strongest here.[177]

118. The *member* of a general partnership shall make available to the partnership the capital contribution necessary for its activities and undertake joint and several liability for the partnership's obligations not covered by the assets of the

176. Papp, *supra* n. 161, 362–363; BH 1992.651.; LB Cgf.II.321/1990. LB Cgf.II.30.219/1999/I.; LB Cgf.II.31.570/1991.
177. Papp, *supra* n. 161, 373.

partnership.[178] A partnership shall be primarily liable for its obligations with its assets. If the *assets* of the kkt. do not cover an obligation, the members shall bear unlimited and joint and several *liability* with their private assets for the obligations of the partnership. Without prejudice to their subsidiary liability, members may also be sued together with the partnership. Decisions in favour of the plaintiff may be passed and enforcement may be carried out in connection with the assets of the partnership without the members being involved in the proceedings. The liability of a new member for the obligations originating prior to his admission to the kkt. shall be identical to all other members; any agreement of the members to the contrary shall be null and void with respect to third parties.[179]

119. The kkt. is founded with an *initial capital* consisting of capital contributions that are not predetermined by the Civil Code; the founders may ascertain the amount of initial capital (*theoretically* two legal entities are necessary to establish a general partnership, they perform HUF 5 each, namely the general partnership may be founded with capital contributions of value in all HUF 10). At the registration of the general partnership the Court of Registry is not entitled to examine whether the initial capital is enough for the operation of kkt.: the scope of judicial oversight of the Court of Registry shall not cover the management of firms, nor their business decisions in terms of economic feasibility.[180]

120. Following the registration of the kkt., the member has a participation (rights and obligations) in partnership, and the value of this is equal with the capital contribution of the member at the time of the foundation of the kkt. This participation in the general partnership does not embody any interest or right.

121. At least two members are required for the foundation of partnerships. The Hungarian branch of foreign companies, the direct commercial representative office of foreigners in Hungary, the civil association, the condominium and the pre-company are not entitled to found partnership or to participate in its operation.[181] A natural person may be a member with unlimited liability in only one business association at any given point in time. Minor may not be a member with unlimited liability in a business association. A general partnership or limited partnership may not be a member with unlimited liability in business association.[182] The cooperative, the budgetary agency and the local government may only be a member with limited liability in a business association, so not in the kkt.

122. The general partnership must have an *object* permitted by law. The kkt. may be established to carry out a business or non-profit activity. Certain specific economic activities may be restricted by law to be pursued only in specific business association forms; for example, the activity of pharmacies may be carried out –

178. Section 3:138 CC.
179. Section 3:139 CC.
180. Act V of 2006 s. 74 (4).
181. Papp, *supra* n. 161, 28.
182. Section 3:90 (1), (2), (3) CC.

beside the sole proprietor – in a form of limited partnership. The activity-specific authorization is rarely necessary to the form of partnerships. A business association may engage in the pursuit of an activity that is rendered conditional upon specific qualifications by law, if the company's member bound by personal involvement, or at least one person employed by the company under contract of employment or any other form of civil employment relationship is able to satisfy such qualification requirements.[183]

123. The general partnership may be only promoted in firm registration proceedings by the Firm Act. If the legal conditions – subject, object and way of establishing – are not observed by the founders of the kkt., the partnership does not come into existence. The designation '*közkereseti társaság*' or its abbreviation 'kkt.' shall be indicated in the corporate name of the general partnership.[184]

124. In accordance with the definition, function and characteristics of the initial capital the initial capital of the general partnership consists of the *capital contributions* of each member. In connection with the initial capital of the kkt. there is no legal regulation to provide the minimum amount and the composition (the proportion of capital contribution in cash and in kind) of the initial capital. The minimum amount and the type (in cash or in kind) of capital contribution are not prescribed by the Civil Code. The founders shall provide in the memorandum of association, according to their intent, about these (the amount and the composition of the initial capital, the amount and the type of the capital contribution). Making the initial capital available to the general partnership is not a condition of the registration of a kkt.; the memorandum of association provides the date of the performance of capital contributions without restriction.[185]

125. The *supreme body* of a general partnership is the meeting of members in the activity of which all members shall take part in person.[186] The meeting of members shall have powers to resolve all matters which the law or the memorandum of association confers under the competence of the kkt.'s supreme body.

126. The *management* of the general partnerships shall be conducted by one or more managing directors, delegated or elected from among the members; if no managing director has been delegated or elected, all members shall function as such. In the memorandum of association, the members may entrust one member or several members with the management, in which case the other members shall not be entitled to exercise management. Any clause of the memorandum of association to appoint a non-member to serve as a managing director, or provides for the appointment of such person shall be null and void.[187] All matters which are not decided by the meeting of members shall be resolved by the management.

---

183. Section 3:97 (2) CC.
184. Section 3:138 CC.
185. Papp, *supra* n. 161, 76.
186. Section 3:142 (1) CC.
187. Section 3:144 CC.

127. Historically the form of *limited partnership* (*betéti társaság*, bt.) appeared in Hungary together with the general partnership by the Act XVIII of 1840. The limited partnership disposes of all features of the general partnership but in contrast to kkt. it has the possibility for a member with limited liability; in Hungary the limited partnership is a very popular business association. The general provisions of legal person and common regulations of business association must be applied for the bt. as well. Unless otherwise provided in the chapter of limited partnership of the Company Act the provisions on general partnerships shall also apply to limited partnerships.[188]

128. By virtue of the memorandum of association for the establishment of a limited partnership, the members of the bt. agree to make available to the partnership capital contribution necessary for its activities, and at least one member (general partner) for the obligations is not covered by the assets of the limited partnership undertake joint and several liability with all general partners, while at least one member (limited partner) is not liable for the obligations of the limited partnership, unless the Civil Code provides otherwise.[189] The designation '*betéti társaság*' (hereinafter 'bt.') shall be indicated in the corporate name of the limited partnership.[190]

129. Through the position of the *limited partner* the capital character appears in the limited partnership: some members of the bt. only have to provide the capital contribution, namely his participation in the limited partnership may be only capital investment. The most important character of the bt. is the two kinds of membership: the general partner with unlimited (and joint and several with all other same partners) liability and the limited partner with an obligation to perform the capital contributions and on the grounds of the exceptions in the Civil Code with liability.

130. The *general partner* is liable unlimited with its own assets for the duties of the limited partnership only if the assets of the bt. do not cover the obligations of the limited partnership, so the liability of the limited partner is secondary.

131. The limited partner is obliged to perform its capital contribution and generally is not liable for the obligations of the bt. The Civil Code ascertains exceptions, when the limited partner has secondary *liability* for the obligations of the bt.:

- the limited partner is liable conditionally (if there are distributed assets of the limited partnership) and limited (up to the part due from the assets of the bt.) for the debts of pre-company and in case of the termination of the bt. without succession;
- the limited partner's liability is unlimited and joint and several for overrating of the contribution in kind and the dishonest approval of the overrating of the contribution in kind, at the abusing of the limited liability, at the change of quality of

188. Section 3:155 CC.
189. Section 3:154 CC.
190. Section 3:89 (2) CC.

membership (if from a general partner will be a limited partner) within a five-year forfeit deadline and at the conversion of a general partnership into a limited partnership, if the member(s) of the kkt. will be limited partner(s).[191]

132. In the memorandum of association the type of the membership shall be established: which member is a limited or general partner.

133. The rights and obligations of the general partner are identical with the rights and obligations of the member of the kkt. The organizational member's rights are different between the general and the limited partners. A limited partner may not serve as the partnership's executive officer.[192] If the partnership is left without an executive officer for the lack of any general partner or limited partner, or due to the number of members being reduced to one, until the partnership's memorandum of association is amended, or failing this until the time of dissolution without succession or until a liquidator is appointed, the member who meets the statutory requirements prescribed for executive officers shall be regarded as the partnership's executive officer. In that case, the limited partner may also serve as the partnership's executive officer. If no such member remains in the partnership, the Court of Registry shall appoint a supervising commissioner for the partnership.[193]

134. Historically the form of *limited liability company* (*korlátolt felelősségű társaság*, kft.) appeared in Hungary by the Act V of 1930. This type of company which also had the advantage of limited liability for its members was born due to the economic necessity, but it was a more flexible kind, could be established easier and it had a more simple organizational structure than a stock company. The kft. was converted into the general frame of small and medium enterprises; in Hungary the main and most popular form of company is the limited liability company. The general regulations of legal person and common rules of business association must be applied for the limited liability company as well.

135. For the legal act to create a kft. an agreement between legal entities is necessary. The legal relationship which follows from the incorporation has not lost totally its contractual relationship, for example, the business shares of the members can only be transferred to third persons only if this is not precluded or restricted by the memorandum of association and the administration of the affairs of the company and representation of the company could be carried out by one or more managing directors elected from the members. The kft. is both capital and personal association, suitable for a family business and for a large enterprise as well. The limited liability company can be founded by one single member or by more members. The kft. may be established by non-resident and resident natural persons and legal persons to jointly engage in business operations or for objectives other than making profit (*non-profit kft.*). The limited liability company may be incorporated both

---

191. Papp, *supra* n. 161, 390–391.
192. Section 3:156 CC.
193. Section 3:158 (2) CC.

under the general registration proceedings and simplified registration proceedings (with a standard contract form), but exclusively by using the electronic form of registration.[194]

136. The kft. is a full legal person, which means that it is a separate legal person with its own property, liability, organization and it has its own corporate name. The kft. has legal capacity under its corporate name: it may obtain rights and undertake commitments, such as acquiring property, concluding contracts and may sue and be sued.

137. The expression 'limited liability company' (*korlátolt felelősségű társaság*) is misleading: not the liability of the company is limited, but the liability of its member. With the exceptions set out in the Hungarian Civil Code, members of the kft. shall not be liable for the liabilities of the company, as a rule the liability of members to the company extends only to the provision of their capital contributions and to other contributions as set forth in the memorandum of association.[195]

138. *Exceptionally* the member of the kft. may have limited liability against the creditors of the company, and unlimited liability against his company and sometimes against the creditors of the kft. The *liability* of the member of the company is limited in the following cases:

- the members of the pre-company (existing form from the date of countersigning or executing in an authentic instrument of the memorandum of association until the decision of the Court of Registry) shall be held limited (to that share of the assets distributed) liable for any debts originating from commitments entered into up to the time of termination of operations of the pre-company;[196]
- if the liability of a member was limited for the obligations of the business association during the existence of the kft., the liability of the member for the obligations of the terminated company shall be limited to that share of the assets distributed upon the termination of the business association which is due to such member.[197]

139. The member of the kft. has *unlimited liability against his company* in these cases:

- any member providing a contribution in kind shall accept responsibility towards the kft. to the effect that the value indicated in the memorandum of association does not exceed the value of the contribution in kind as effective at the time of its provision; if the value of contribution in kind does not reach the value indicated

194. Papp, *supra* n. 161, 49.
195. Section 3:159 CC.
196. Section 3:101 (1), (5) CC.
197. Section 3:48 (3) CC.

in the instrument of constitution, the company may demand payment of the difference from the person having provided the contribution in kind within five years from the date of transfer;[198]

- members who were knowledge about, and consented to, a contribution in kind that a member has provided at a value higher than what it was worth at the time when provided shall, together with the person providing it, be subject to joint and several liability toward the company in accordance with the provisions on liability for damages for loss caused by non-performance of an obligation.[199]

140. The member of the limited liability company is *liable unlimitedly toward the creditors* of the company in the following cases:

- in the event of abuse of limited liability on the part of any member of a legal person, on account of which any outstanding creditors' claims remain unsatisfied at the time of the legal person's dissolution without succession, the member in question shall be subject to unlimited liability for such debts;[200]
- if any controlled member of the group is undergoing liquidation, the dominant member shall be held liable for any debt the member may have outstanding; the dominant member shall be relieved of liability if able to verify that the controlled member's insolvency did not arise as a consequence of the group's common business strategy.[201]

141. The kft. is *founded* with an initial capital consisting of capital contributions of a predetermined amount. The initial capital of the company consists of the capital contribution of the individual members. As a result of that the liability of the members is – generally – limited to their contribution, the claims of the kft. creditors will be against the company's property. The fixed minimum value of the assets must be raised initially and it must also be aiming at retaining in the business. This condition serves primarily for the protection of creditors and secondarily for the protection of members against action taken by the managing directors which might reduce the value of their business shares as long-term investments.

142. Following registration of the company, the rights and obligations of members and their share from the assets of the kft. are embodied by their business shares; *business share* means the whole of rights and obligations arising in connection with the core deposit.[202] The member's business share also means an interest in the company and is qualified as valuable, transferable right, including a bundle of capital and membership rights. The business shares of members shall be consistent with their respective capital contributions.

---

198. Section 3:10 (3) CC.
199. Section 3:99 (2) CC.
200. Section 3:2 (2) CC.
201. Section 3:59 CC.
202. Section 3:164 CC.

143. The *principle of the freedom of enterprise and association* admits and supports the right of establishing business enterprise, and it is also declared that everybody has the right to form an organization together with others or to join it in order to the protection of his economic and social interests. But this constitutional principle is not enforced without limits: a company cannot be established by anyone, for anything and in any way. With the exception of limited liability companies and public or private limited companies, at least two members are required for the foundation of a business association. The Hungarian branch of foreign companies does not have the right to found a company or to participate in its operation.[203] The direct commercial representative office of foreigners is without legal capacity; therefore it may not carry on business activity. The civil association and the condominium – by reason of limited subjectivity defined to object – may not form a company. The pre-company may not establish a company or participate as a member in it,[204] because only the registered company with full subjectivity conforms to requirements of company's foundation.[205] The cooperative, the budgetary agency and the local government can only be a member in a company with limited liability.

144. The kft. must have an *object* permitted by law. The limited liability company may be established to engage in joint business operations for objectives of making profit or of non-profit character. Certain specific economic activities may be restricted by law in order to be pursued only in specific company forms; for example, the activity of the patent agent may be carried out only by kft. in form of joint business. Certain economic activities may begin in possession of authorization (activity-specific authorization); for example, telecommunication. A business association may engage in the pursuit of an activity that is rendered conditional upon specific qualifications by law, if the company's member bound by personal involvement, or at least one person employed by the company under contract of employment or any other form of civil employment relationship is able to satisfy such qualification requirements.[206]

145. The limited liability company may only be promoted in firm registration proceedings by Act V of 2006 (on Public Company Information, Company Registration and Winding-up Proceedings). If the legal conditions (subject, object and mode of establishing) are not observed by the founders of the kft., the company does not come into existence. The designation '*korlátolt felelősségű társaság*', or its abbreviation 'kft.', shall be indicated in the corporate name of the limited liability company.

146. *Capital contributions* are provided by the members, in cash and in kind, to comprise the capital of the company. The capital contributions of members may be of varying value, but the value of each contribution may not be less than HUF 100,000. The members shall determine the value of their own contributions in kind

203. EBH 2003.887; BH 2003.420.
204. Section 3:101 (2) c) CC.
205. EBH 2003.883; BH 2003.471.
206. Section 3:97 (2) CC.

and they shall be approved by the other members.[207] Each member shall have one core deposit; where several persons have agreed to provide a core deposit collectively, their liability for providing such core deposit shall be joint and several. The members have to make capital contribution available to the kft. by reason of principle of real (effective) performance:[208] the members are required to fulfil capital contributions may not be exempted for such completion and any offsetting of payments with company is not permitted. During the existence of the company members may not reclaim the capital contributions which they have provided from the company, apart from capital reduction.

147. The *initial capital* of the kft. consists of the capital contributions of the individual members. The amount of initial capital may not be less than HUF 3,000,000. The movements of initial capital can indicate the increase of this (it means the subsequent capital allotment of kft. or the converting of capital structure of the limited liability company) or the reduction of this (it means the decreasing of company assets).

148. The *business share* means the whole of rights and obligations arising in connection with the core deposit. Business shares shall come to existence upon the company's registration. The business shares of the members shall be consistent with their respective capital contributions. Identical membership rights shall be attached to equivalent business shares.[209] One business share may be owned by several persons. These persons shall be treated as a single member from the standpoint of the company; their rights may only be exercised by their joint representative, and they shall bear joint and several liability for the obligations of the members.[210]

149. The *supreme body* of a kft. is the members' meeting. The members' meeting shall have exclusive competence for the approval to conclude contracts which take place between the company and one of its members, its managing director, supervisory board member, auditor, or their close relatives.[211]

150. The administration of the company's affairs and the kft.'s representation shall be carried out by one or more *managing directors* elected from the members or third persons. The duties of the managing director are as follows: representing the company; administrative working (e.g., convening the members' meeting); exercising of employer's rights; informing the members; keeping the business secrets; drawing up minutes; taking book of resolutions; keeping the register of members; organizing of selling the member's business share.[212]

151. The *single-member kft.* is a limited liability company having only one member. The single-member limited liability company is not an association in a real

207. Section 3:161–3:163 CC.
208. A. Kisfaludi, *Company Law*, Budapest: Complex Kiadó, 2007, 352, 355.
209. Section 3:164 CC.
210. Section 3:165 (1) CC.
211. Section 3:188 (2) CC.
212. Papp, *supra* n. 161, 435–439.

sense (it does not operate with the participation of two members); the company and the member are not separated organizationally and pecuniary from each other. These specialities of the single-member kft. establish the different rules from the limited liability with more members, for lack of specific provisions the requirements of kft. with more members shall be applied for the single member-limited liability company.[213]

152. Historically, the form of *stock company* (*részvénytársaság*, rt.) appeared in Hungary with the Act XVIII of 1840. The rt. is a stock corporation, where the person of members is indifferent, only the capital investment (the capital contributions of the members) is important. The main feature of the stock company is the anonymity and this is the only company that issues securities about the membership. The general rules of legal person and the common regulations of business association of Civil Code must be applied also for the stock company as well.

153. The stock company is the general legal frame of large enterprises. The legal act creating the rt. is necessarily an agreement between legal entities, but the legal relationship that follows from the incorporation has totally lost its contractual characteristics. The rt. is a capital association, which may be founded by a single member or by more members as well. The stock company may be established by nonresident and resident natural persons and legal persons to jointly engage in business operations or for objectives other than making profit (non-profit rt.).[214]

154. The stock company is a business association founded with a share capital (subscribed capital) consisting of shares of predetermined number and face value; in the case of which the obligation of members (shareholders) to the stock company extends to the performance of the nominal value or the issue price of shares. The stock company may be established privately and it may operate in the form of private or public limited company. Public and private limited companies may change their operating form, but it does not mean the transformation of the limited company.[215]

155. The *public limited company* shall mean any company whose shares are listed on a stock exchange. The *private limited company* shall mean a company whose shares are not listed on any stock exchange. It is not allowed to solicit shareholders or to collect capital for a private limited company by public invitation. A decision adopted by at least a three-quarters majority of the general meeting is required to change the corporate form of a stock company; such decision shall enter into effect in the case of conversion of a private limited company into a public limited company upon the admission of the company's shares for trading on a stock

213. G. Károlyi, 'Az egyszemélyes társaságokról', Jogtudományi Közlöny 9, 1999, 397; Papp, *supra* n. 161, 443–444.
214. Papp, *supra* n. 161, 444.
215. Section 3:210. 3:211, 3:249 CC.

exchange, and vice versa, upon the delisting of the company's shares in the case of conversion of a public limited company into a private limited company.[216]

156. The rt. is a full legal person, which means that it is a separate legal person, with its own property, liability, organization and corporate name. The stock company has legal capacity under its corporate name: it may obtain rights and undertake commitments, such as acquiring property, concluding contracts and may sue and be sued. The stock company is liable for its obligations with its own assets, the members of the 'rt.' do not have liability for the debts of the company, with the exceptions set out in the Civil Code; the obligation of a member in the stock company is only to provide the nominal value/issue price of shares. Exceptionally the Civil Code establishes *liability* for the members of the stock company:

- if, at the time of transfer, the value of contribution in kind does not reach the value indicated in the instrument of constitution, the stock company may demand payment of the difference from the person having provided the contribution in kind within five years from the date of transfer;[217]
- members who were knowledgeable about, and consented to, a contribution in kind that a member has provided at a value higher than what it was worth at the time when provided shall, together with the person providing it, be subject to joint and several liability toward the company in accordance with the provisions on liability for damages for loss caused by non-performance of an obligation;[218]
- the members of a stock company dissolved without succession shall be held liable up to their respective shares for the debts of the dissolved company outstanding.[219] In the event of dissolution of a business association without succession, claims that remain outstanding on the basis of the obligations of the business association that will cease to exist may be enforced within a five-year preclusive period against the former members of the business association;[220]
- if any controlled member of the group of corporation is undergoing liquidation, the dominant member shall be held liable for any debt the member may have outstanding; the dominant member shall be relieved of liability if able to verify that the controlled member's insolvency did not arise as a consequence of the group's common business strategy.[221]

157. The rt. shall be founded with an *initial capital* consisting of a predetermined amount. The initial capital of the company consists of the capital contributions of the individual shareholders. The share capital – the initial/subscribed capital – is the amount of the face value of all shares. The share capital of a private limited company may not be less than HUF 5 million, the share capital of a public limited company may not be less than HUF 20 million.[222] The fixed minimum value of the

216. Section 3:211 (1), (2), (3) CC.
217. Section 3:10 (3) CC.
218. Section 3:99 (2) CC.
219. Section 3:48 (3) CC.
220. Section 3:137 (1) CC.
221. Section 3:59 CC.
222. Section 3:212 (2) CC.

assets of the company must be raised initially with one of the intentions being retaining the business. These conditions serve primarily for the protection of creditors and secondarily for the protection of shareholders against the action made by the management board which might reduce the value of their shares as long-term investments.

158. In accordance with the limit on the freedom of enterprise and association, a stock company cannot be *establish*ed anyhow by anybody and for anything. At least one shareholder is required for the foundation of stock company. The rules for non-residents are the following:

- the Hungarian branch of foreign companies has not got right to found a company or participate in its operation;
- the direct commercial representative office of foreigners in Hungary is without legal capacity, therefore it may not carry on business activity;
- the civil association and the condominium may not form a company by reason of limited and to object fixed legal capacity;
- the pre-company may not establish a company or participate as a member in it, because only the registered company with full subjectivity has possibility for it;
- the cooperative, the budgetary agency and the local government may only be member with limited liability in a company.[223]

159. The rt. must have an *object* permitted by law. The stock company may be established to engage in joint business operations for objectives of making profit or of non-profit character. Certain specific economic activities may be restricted by law to be pursued only in specific company forms; for example, the public warehouse and financial institution may be operated in the form of stock company among business associations. Other certain economic activities may be begun in possession of authorization (activity-specific authorization); for example, service of district heating.[224] A stock company may engage in the pursuit of an activity that is rendered conditional upon specific qualifications by law, if the company's member bound by personal involvement, or at least one person employed by the company under contract of employment or any other form of civil employment relationship is able to satisfy such qualification requirements.[225]

160. The stock company may be promoted only in company registration proceedings by Act V. of 2006 (Firm Act). The private limited company may be incorporated in both the general registration proceedings and simplified registration proceedings with a standard contract form, but always electronically. The public limited company may be incorporated only in the general registration proceedings in electronic way. If the founders of the rt. do not observe the legal conditions (subject, object and way of establishing), the company does not come into existence. A

---

223. Papp, *supra* n. 161, 28.
224. *Ibid.*, 47.
225. Section 3:97 (2) CC.

private limited company is established upon the commitment of the founders to subscribe for all shares of the company (private foundation). The founders shall provide for the foundation of the private limited company and their obligation to subscribe for the shares, as well as for the organization of the company in the articles of association. Shareholders and capital may not be solicited for the foundation of a stock company by way of public invitation.[226] The designation 'részvénytársaság' (limited company) and an indication as to whether it is private or public, that is to say, the abbreviation 'zrt.' or 'nyrt.' shall be indicated in the corporate name.

161. The *supreme body* of a limited company is the general meeting. The administrative duties of limited companies are handled by the *management body*, consisting of at least three members, all natural persons. The articles of association of private limited company may provide that a management board is not required, and the rights conferred in the Civil Code upon the management board shall be exercised by the chief executive officer (general director).[227] The management board shall exercise its rights and perform its duties as an independent body. The management body shall elect its chairman from among its members.[228]

162. The *initial capital* of the private limited company consists of the shares of the members and the amount of the initial capital is the sum of the nominal value of all shares. The initial capital of the private limited company may not be less than HUF 5 million. The Civil Code does not determine proportion of the capital contributions in cash and in kind in connection with the initial capital of the private limited company; so a zrt. may be established only by contributions in kind. The initial capital is the part of the assets of the private limited company, but with respect to the contributions the given shares are in the property of the shareholders and they may provide freely with the shares.[229]

163. The share capital of the private limited company is specified by the number and the nominal value of shares; if the shareholders want to alter the share capital, they have to amend the numbers or the nominal value (or combining these) by a technique established in the Civil Code. The *share* is an equity security representing membership rights in the issuing stock company, they are registered, have a nominal value and are tradable.[230] One share may have several owners, who shall be treated as a single shareholder in respect of the limited company; their rights may only be exercised by their joint representative and they shall bear joint and several liability for the obligations of shareholders.[231]

164. Two categories of share may be distinguished: the *printed share certificate* and the *dematerialized share*. The main characteristic of the printed security is that

226. Section 3:249 CC.
227. Section 3:282 (1), 3:283 CC.
228. Section 3:282 (2), (3) CC.
229. BH 2003. 209.
230. Section 3:213 (1) CC.
231. Section 3:213 (2) CC.

the document is represented physically and may be possessed. The dematerialized share shall mean an electronic instrument that has no serial number and whose identifiably contains all the material information of securities, which are created, recorded, transmitted and registered electronically as defined in specific other legislation. In connection with dematerialized shares, the shareholder's name and other data required for identification are contained in the securities account maintained by a securities broker on behalf of the shareholder. The printed share certificates may be converted into and recorded as dematerialized shares, and vice versa, dematerialized shares may be converted into printed securities. The shares of public limited company may be issued in the form of dematerialized shares.[232] The shares may be *offered publicly or privately*; the shares of private limited company may not be offered publicly.

165. The stock company may issue *different types of shares*: ordinary shares, preference shares, employees' shares, interest-bearing shares, redeemable shares. Within the category of preference shares, shares may belong to different classes of shares according to the shareholder rights to which the preference pertains, and within the same class of shares. Shares of different content or shares representing different membership rights may be issued. Within one category or class of shares, several series of shares may be issued.

166. The provisions pertaining to private limited company shall apply to any matters not regulated in connection with public limited company. Any limited company whose shares are listed on a stock exchange shall be recognized as a public limited company (nyrt.).[233] Shareholders and capital may not be solicited for the foundation of a limited company by way of public invitation,[234] so a public limited company may be established only by way of transformation, merger or division. The shares (including interim shares) of public limited company may only be of the dematerialized type.[235]

167. Where a private limited company has decided to *convert* into a public limited company, the company's preference shares attaching privileges for the appointment of executive officers or supervisory board members, and its preference shares with the right of pre-emption, as well as any preference shares collectively embodying preferential rights other than dividend preference with preferential right to any liquidation surplus, shall be converted into preference shares or ordinary shares that can be issued by public limited company as well, before the time being listed on the stock exchange.[236]

232. Section 3:214 CC.
233. Section 3:211 (1) CC.
234. Section 3:249 CC.
235. Section 3:214 (2) CC.
236. Section 3:235 CC.

168. The public limited company may be founded by means of share subscription through a public procedure, according to the conditions laid down in the statutory provisions on securities. The public limited company may be established by public offering: it shall mean when securities are offered to any investors without any pre-selection process, conveying sufficient information on the terms of the offer and on the securities so as to enable the investors to take investment decisions on an informed basis. The public limited company may be formed also by way of the offering of privately issued securities for sale to the general public, the admission of such securities to trading on a regulated market or their registration in a multilateral trading facility. The share capital of a public limited company may not be less than HUF 20,000,000.

169. In public limited companies the *general meeting* shall have exclusive jurisdiction to lay down the guidelines and framework for a long-term salary and incentive scheme for executive officers, supervisory board members and executive employees.[237] When the articles of association provides it, it shall be controlled by the *board of directors* under the one-tier system instead of the management board and the supervisory board; in this case, the board of directors shall discharge the duties of the management board and the supervisory board conferred upon them by law.[238] The public limited company shall set up an *audit committee* consisting of three members elected by the general meeting from among the independent members of the board of directors or the supervisory board, where applicable.[239] At least one member of the audit committee shall have competence in accounting or auditing.[240]

170. The *single-member stock company* is a company having only one member (shareholder). The single-member stock company is not an association in a real sense: the company and the shareholder are not separated organizationally and pecuniary from each other. These specialities establish different rules from the stock company with more members (shareholders); for lack of specific provisions the requirements of stock company with more members shall be applied for the single-member stock company.[241]

171. *Corporate Governance*:[242] the management board of a public limited company shall present to the annual general meeting the company governance and management report prepared according to the rules applicable to the actors of the given

237. Section 3:268 (2) CC.
238. Section 3:285 (1) CC.
239. Section 3:291 CC.
240. Section 3:291 (2) CC.
241. Papp, *supra* n. 161, 504–505.
242. Á. Auer, 'A felelős társaságirányítás hatása a jogi személyek elméletére', *Jogtudományi Közlöny* 4, 2013, 193–202.

stock exchange.[243] The report shall be approved by decision of the general meeting. The general meeting's resolution and the approved report shall be posted on the website of the stock company.[244]

172. A *cooperative* (*szövetkezet*) is a legal person established with a capital made up of the members' contributions; it operates under the principle of open membership and variable capital with the objective of lending assistance to its members so as to satisfy their economic and societal needs, where the obligation of its members toward the cooperative covers the provision of capital contribution and their personal involvement as provided for in its statutes. Members shall not bear liability for the cooperative's obligations. The activities of cooperative may include sales, purchases, production and services.[245]

173. The number of *members* that are not natural persons in a cooperative may not exceed 20% of the total number of members; the legal person members of a cooperative set up as a cooperative shall be ignored when calculating the number of members that are not natural persons. The number of members of the cooperative refusing personal involvement in operations may not exceed one-quarter of all members. The capital contribution provided by any one member in a cooperative may not exceed 15% of the capital; the capital contribution provided by members that are not natural persons may not exceed 1/3% of the capital. Members may not be solicited by public invitation.[246]

174. The *statutes* of a cooperative shall also function as its instrument of constitution. The statutes shall be adopted upon the unanimous declaration of intent of at least seven persons. When adopted, the statutes shall be signed by all founding members. The statutes may be signed on behalf of a member by his representative holding an authorization fixed in an authentic instrument or in a private deed representing conclusive evidence. The statutes shall be drawn up in a notarial document, or in a private document countersigned by a lawyer or the legal counsel of a founder.[247]

175. The formation of a cooperative shall be notified to the Court of Registry within thirty days from the date when the statutes is executed in a notarized document or countersigned by a lawyer or legal counsel.[248]

176. *Capital contribution* may also be provided in the form of receivables, if it is acknowledged by the debtor or based on a final court ruling. Commitments of members for performing work or for any other personal involvement or service shall not be accepted as a form of non-monetary capital contribution. Each member is

243. Section 3:289 (1) CC.
244. Section 3:289 (2) CC.
245. Section 3:325 CC.
246. Section 3:326 CC.
247. Section 3:331 (1), (2), (3) CC.
248. Section 3:329 (1) CC.

required to make available at least 30% of his cash contribution before the application for registration is submitted, together with all of his asset contributions. The members of the cooperative refusing personal involvement in operations shall make available their cash contribution in full before the application for registration is submitted.[249]

177. The *assets* placed in the fellowship fund by decision of the general meeting from which to provide benefits to members and their family members may not be distributed among the members.[250]

178. The *supreme body* of a cooperative is the general meeting, which consists of all members.[251] Cooperative shall be managed by the administrative body consisting of at least three members.[252] If the cooperative has less than fifteen members, the statutes may provide for the *office of director* of operations in lieu of the administrative body, vested with the same powers as the administrative body.[253] *Executive officers* of cooperative are the chairman and members of the administrative body or the director of operations.[254] The *supervisory body* of a cooperative is comprised of three members.[255] The *auditor* of a cooperative may be an individual auditor or an audit firm shown in the register of auditors.[256]

179. Apart from the general cases of dissolution of a legal person without succession, a cooperative shall be dissolved without succession if the number of its members drops below seven, and the cooperative does not apply for the registration of an adequate number of new members at the Court of Registry within a preclusive period of six months from that time.[257]

180. Special rules for the *enterprises of state and local governments* on the base of six aspects:

(1) *Special prohibitions of further association*: Such companies owned in 100% by state or local government, which was founded for performing public duties, mustn't establish another company for these public duties.[258] The state and the self-government mustn't found such company and mustn't get share in such company which is not transparent.[259] Non-profit company with majority control of state/self-government is permitted to create an other non-profit company with majority control of state/self-government – apart from recycling

249. Section 3:332 (1), (2) CC.
250. Section 3:334 (1) CC.
251. Section 3:335 (1) CC.
252. Section 3:343 (1) CC.
253. Section 3:345 CC.
254. Section 3:346 (1) CC.
255. Section 3:349 (1) CC.
256. Section 3:351 (2) CC.
257. Section 3:367 CC.
258. Act CXCVI of 2011 on National Assets s. 8 (6).
259. Act CXCVI of 2011 s. 8 (1).

activity – but this new non-profit company mustn't establish further companies.[260] These provisions also have to apply to the acquisition of share in other business associations by enterprises owned by state or local government.[261]

(2) *Special issues relating to assets*: The share of company providing public service and with majority control of state may be available as contribution in kind or on the ground of other transferring legal title only for companies owned in 100% by state/self-government.[262] The share of company providing public and parking service, with majority control of local government and of Balaton Shipping Private Company Limited by Shares may be available as contribution in kind or on the ground of other transferring legal title only for companies owned in 100% by state/self-government.[263] These mean limited transferability of shares of state/self-government in companies. The share in companies owned by state/self-government mustn't be an object of assets management.[264] In connection with the share in companies owned by state, which is a part of national assets and important from the national economy, only the minister pointed out by act, or a central budgetary agency or an economic enterprise owned in 100% by state may exercise the owner's rights.[265] To the increase of capital at company owned in more than 50% by state/self-government which reduces the proportion of state/self-government:
- the consent of the exerciser of owner's rights is necessary;
- over HUF 2,000,000 the resolution of government of Hungary or municipal council is required;
- between HUF 5,000,000 and HUF 2,000,000,000 the resolution of the minister, who is responsible for supervision of state assets or municipal council, is needed.[266] In the name of the state only the Hungarian National Trustee Private Company Limited by Shares and the Hungarian Development Bank Private Company Limited by Shares may give credits and loans to the companies with majority control of state.[267] The reasonable undertaken business risks are determined by company activity and its background, the market surroundings.[268]

(3) *Special rules of organization*: Among the state-owned companies, at the private limited companies the operative organ usually is the general manager and if the importance, size, type of operation of the company is explained itself, then the operative organ is the board of directors (with three to five members);[269] the legislator allows only the two-tier/dualistic system, but not the one-tier/monistic system for organization of state-owned companies.[270] At the

260. *Ibid.*, s. 8 (8), (9).
261. *Ibid.*, s. 8 (1), (8), (9).
262. *Ibid.*, s. 4 (6).
263. *Ibid.*, s. 5 (8).
264. *Ibid.*, s. 8 (7).
265. *Ibid.*, s. 7/A (3).
266. *Ibid.*, s. 8 (10).
267. *Ibid.*, s. 45 (1).
268. BH 2004. 372.
269. Act CXXII of 2009 s. 3 (1).
270. About this *see* more details in: T. Papp, 'Corporate governance – felelős társaságirányítás', *Acta*

state-owned companies is obligatory to form supervisory board with three members (over HUF 200,000,000 between three and six members).[271]

(4) *Special provision for decision*: At the companies with majority control of state/self-government, the competence of supreme body includes the foundation, the termination of economic association, the acquisition and the transfer of shares in economic association.[272]

(5) *Special regulation of transparency*: The state-owned company shall publish the name, the function and the allowances of its executive officers and of its supervisory board members.[273] The head of the state-owned company shall be liable for the publication of these data, for its continuous availability and for the authenticity of publication.[274]

(6) *Special shareholder's rights*: At the state-owned company providing fundamental services, the state may exercise the right of option to purchase shares which are not its property in the interest of safety of supply, of supplying duties, of increasing efficiency, of national economic strategy.[275] Any shareholders at the state-owned company may request that the shareholder exercised the right of option to purchase shall buy his shares (the selling right).[276]

Juridica et Politica, Tomus LXXIII, Fasciculus 1–64, Szeged: 2008, 639–653.

271. Act CXXII of 2009 on More Economical Operation of State-Owned Companies s. 4 (1).
272. Act CXCVI of 2011 s. 8 (14).
273. Act CXXII of 2009 s. 2 (1).
274. *Ibid.*, s. 2 (1).
275. *Ibid.*, s. 7/A (1).
276. *Ibid.*, s. 7/F (1).

Chapter 3. Economic Institutions

§1. Professional Organisations, Chambers of Commerce

I. Free Choice of Profession

181. Article XII of the Fundamental Law of Hungary stipulates that:

> Everyone shall have the right to freely choose his or her work, occupation and freely engage in entrepreneurial activities.

182. The Fundamental Law, however, does not guarantee employment or access to a specific profession and does not exclude the requirement of membership in professional chambers for the exercise of some professions. Professions that may only be exercised by members of professional chambers are as follows:

Profession	*Chamber*	*Relevant Legislation*
Health care professionals	Chamber of Hungarian Health Care Professionals	Act XCVII of 2006 on chambers operating in the area of healthcare
Medical doctors and dentists	Hungarian Medical Chamber	
Pharmacists	Hungarian Chamber of Pharmacists	
Auditors	Chamber of Hungarian Auditors	Act LXXV of 2007 on the Chamber of Hungarian Auditors, the activities of auditors and the public oversight of auditors
Attorneys	Hungarian Bar Association	Act XI of 1998 on attorneys
Architects	Chamber of Hungarian Architects	Act LVIII of 1996 on the professional chambers of architects and engineers
Engineers (related to construction and urban planning and development)	Hungarian Chamber of Engineers	
Notaries	Hungarian Chamber of Civil Law Notaries	Act XLI of 1991 on civil law notaries
Expert witnesses (court experts)	Hungarian Chamber of Expert Witnesses	Act XXIX of 2016

Patent attorneys	Hungarian Chamber of Patent Attorneys	Act XXXII of 1995 on patent attorneys
Veterinary physician	Hungarian Veterinary Chamber	Act CXXVII of 2012 on the Hungarian Veterinary Chamber and the provision of veterinary services
Plant protection and phytosanitary engineers	Hungarian Chamber of Plant Protection and Phytosanitary Engineers	Act LXXXIV of 2000 on the Hungarian Chamber of Plant Protection and Phytosanitary Engineers
(Professional) hunter	Hungarian Hunters' National Chamber	Act XLVI of 1997 on the Hungarian Hunters' National Chamber
Farmers, agricultural cooperatives or companies with agriculture as their main activity	Hungarian Chamber of Agriculture	Act CXXVI of 2012 on the Hungarian Chamber of Agriculture

183. For some professions the law allows for the establishment of voluntary membership professional chambers, e.g., private security services (Act CXXXIII of 2005). Other professions may establish professional associations for the promotion of their interests, e.g., National Association of Hungarian Accountants or Association of Hungarian Insurance Brokers.

184. Professional chambers are organised on a territorial basis with regional branches electing and maintaining a national umbrella organisation. Members are directly attached to regional branches. The functions and activities of professional chambers are far from uniform but usually cover the following main areas:

- maintenance of an official register of members authorised to exercise the profession;
- examination and/or continuous training of members;
- professional supervision and quality assurance;
- conducting disciplinary or ethical procedures;
- consulting the legislator on issues related to the profession.

II. Hungarian Chamber of Commerce and Industry

A. *History*

185. Chambers of commerce have been operating in Hungary since the 1850s. Originally, these chambers operated on the basis of regional autonomy and there was not any national umbrella organisation allowed to coordinate their activities and assist in interest representation. Membership was compulsory for all traders, craftsmen as well as companies and enterprises. The autonomy of the chambers was terminated in 1940 by the appointment of government commissioners as executives. The chambers were briefly restored in 1945 but were dissolved in 1948 without legal successors. Subsequently, an institution under the name of Hungarian Chamber of Commerce was created but it was a chamber in name only: membership was by appointment (until 1968 only entities conducting external trade were included) and its budget was provided by the State. In 1985, it was transformed into the Hungarian Chamber of Economy that actually engaged in coordination and interest representation. After 1989, its regional committees gradually developed into autonomous chambers based on voluntary and open membership.

186. Based on a legislation adopted in 1994, chambers of commerce were reorganised on the level of counties and Budapest Capital as public law bodies and their representatives established the Hungarian Chamber of Commerce and Industry as a national umbrella organisation. Under the 1994 legislation membership in county chambers was compulsory but this requirement was abolished from 2000.

B. *Regional Chambers*

187. The current legislation on chambers of commerce is Act No. CXXI of 1999 on economic chambers that has been frequently and comprehensively amended. Even though the title of the act refers to economic chambers in general, the act specifies that only chambers of commerce and industry may be established as economic chambers covering activities related to trade, industry and craftsmanship.[277] Regional chambers of commerce and industry may be established by at least ten economic entities (companies, cooperatives, individual entrepreneurs, affiliate companies or branch offices of foreign companies) other than farmers, agricultural cooperatives or companies with agriculture as their main activity. Regional chambers may be established in Budapest Capital, county seats and cities with county rights. Regional chambers may operate local offices.[278] As of 2018, there are twenty-three regional chambers of commerce and industry operating in Hungary – in Budapest Capital, in the nineteen county seats as well as in the cities of Dunaújváros, Nagykanizsa and Sopron.

277. Act No. CXXI of 1999 on Economic Chambers (ECA) Art. 3 (3).
278. ECA Art. 4.

188. Membership in regional chambers of commerce and industry is open to all economic entities (as specified above) with their registered seats in the chamber's geographic area of competence. A request for membership may be denied only in case of an economic entity that has been expelled from the chamber less than one year before the application due to repeated or grave violations of membership obligations.[279] Members have the right to benefit from the services provided by the chamber, to hold offices and be elected as a representative of the regional chamber to the General Assembly of HCCI. Members are required to pay a membership fee that is determined by the regional chambers and is calculated on the basis of the net income of the entity.[280] The total membership of regional chambers now amounts to 43,000 entities mainly composed of large companies.

189. The main organ of a regional chamber is the General Assembly that is composed of representatives elected by the members of the chamber. In the process of the election of representatives all members have a single vote. The number of representatives is determined in each department (*see* below) according to the relative economic strength of the department by the Statute of the chamber. The General Assembly adopts and amends the Statute and other regulations of the chamber, elects its officials (president, vice presidents, secretary general, secretary, chairman of the ethical committee and chairman of the supervisory committee), determines its budget and decides on the accession to or secession from a regional chamber. The General Assembly is convened at least once a year and must be convened on the request of at least one-fifth of the representatives.[281]

190. The president is the external representative of the chamber. The president or the Statute of the chamber may delegate his responsibilities to a vice president, the secretary general or the secretary. The management of the chamber in the period between General Assemblies is conducted by a Presidium composed of the president, the vice presidents and other representatives determined by the Statute of the chamber. All officials of the chamber must be members, shareholders or employees of economic entities that are members of the chamber. Detailed rules of incompatibility apply.[282] Officials are elected for a four-year term; they may be re-elected or recalled.[283]

191. The ethical committee:

- monitors compliance with ethical rules and legal obligations related to unfair commercial practices and competition; may issue and publish warnings to entities in breach;
- may issue and publish warnings to members in breach of intellectual property regulations;

279. ECA Art. 8 (4)–(5).
280. ECA Art. 8 (2)–(3).
281. ECA Arts 17–18.
282. ECA Art. 27.
283. ECA Art. 33.

- may issue and publish warnings to members conducting activities against the interests of consumers; may initiate the suspension of economic activities of such members and may take legal action to enforce consumer claims;
- cooperates with the consumer protection authority and the GVH.[284]

192. The supervisory committee:

- monitors the legality of the chamber's activities and the reasonability of its expenditures;
- arranges for an annual independent audit of the chamber's finances;
- provides an opinion on the annual budget and its discharge;
- convenes the General Assembly if the president fails to do so or fails to comply with the supervisory committee's call to restore the lawful activities of the chamber.[285]

193. Regional chambers are required to establish three departments according to the activities of their members: commerce, industry and craftsmanship. Other departments may be established according to the Statute of the chamber.[286]

194. The main tasks of regional chambers are as follows:

195. In the field of economic development regional chambers:

- promote the development of business infrastructure;
- contribute to the preparation of strategic economic policy decisions and regional development strategies;
- provide information on domestic and foreign regulations related to economic activities;
- coordinate economic information and promotion activities, organise fairs, exhibitions, conferences and other events;
- provide assistance in the application process for EU grants;
- participate in adult education, organise and conduct master (advanced vocational) trainings and examinations.[287]

196. In the field of security and reliability of business transactions regional chambers:

- issue and certify certificates of origin, other certificates and documents;
- compile and publish commercial terms;
- monitor compliance with ethical rules, competition, intellectual property and consumer protection regulations;
- set up consumer conciliation bodies;

284. ECA Art. 24 referring to ECA Art. 10 (1) c)–f).
285. ECA Arts 22–23.
286. ECA Art. 26.
287. ECA Arts 9–9/A.

- assist in quality assurance and shipping damages claims related to international transactions;
- may initiate judicial supervisory action or the termination of individual entrepreneurship.[288]

197. In the field of general interest representation regional chambers:

- formulate proposals and recommendations for laws, programmes and measures to promote the public interest in the area of economic development, security and reliability of business transactions and fair commercial practices;
- collect, analyse and publish statistical data related to economic trends.[289]

198. Even though membership in regional chambers is optional, there are some obligations vis-a-vis regional chambers that apply to all economic entities regardless of membership:

- all economic entities must pay an annual contribution of HUF 5,000 to support public interest activities of chambers; 90% of the contribution belongs to respective regional chambers, 10% is transferred to HCCI; members may deduct the contribution from their membership fees;
- all economic entities that are required to register in the company registry or other registries must also register with the respective regional chambers; based on this registry and using other available public registers chambers maintain a comprehensive public database on economic entities in the region including *inter alia* public debt, tax arrears, refusal to comply with recommendations of the consumer conciliation body, exclusion from public procurement procedures, breach of competition or consumer protection rules, and net income;
- all economic entities engaged in the construction business must also register in the registry of construction enterprises with HCCI directly or through a regional chamber and pay an administrative fee.

C. HCCI as a National Umbrella Organisation

199. The main organ of HCCI is the General Assembly that is composed of representatives elected by regional chambers. The General Assembly adopts the Statute and Code of Ethics of HCCI, elects its President as well as members of the supervisory and ethical committee.

200. HCCI is structured in different colleges (departments) based on economic sectors (e.g., food, construction, tourism) as well as functional areas (e.g., research and development, EU funds, international relations). HCCI also has sections

288. ECA Art. 10.
289. ECA Art. 11.

devoted to bilateral economic relations (e.g., Hungarian-Chinese, Hungarian-German, Hungarian-Russian) and participates in joint chambers of commerce (Hungarian-Slovakian, Hungarian-Ukrainian and Hungarian-Serbian Chamber of Commerce and Industry).

201. HCCI:

- is consulted on draft laws related to national economy;
- maintains relations with foreign chambers and international economic organisations;
- coordinates information activities abroad and for foreign entities in Hungary;
- promotes foreign trade;
- adopts ethical standards related to fair commercial practices;
- adopts uniform standards for registries maintained by regional chambers;
- distributes budgetary allocations among regional chambers;
- establishes and operates a court of commercial arbitration.[290]

202. The Prosecution Service is entrusted with monitoring the legality of the chambers' (regional and HCCI) activities. The monitoring extends to the legality of the chambers' Statutes and regulations as well as to the conformity of the chambers' activities with laws and regulations. The supervision of the Prosecution Service does not extend to activities of the Court of Arbitration organised by HCCI and cases that are subject to judicial or administrative procedures.

§2. Commercial Courts and Commercial Arbitration

203. There are no special commercial courts in Hungary. Commercial cases are heard by regular courts where economic departments (at regional courts), civil departments (at regional courts of appeal) and joint civil and economic departments (at the Curia and smaller regional courts) are established.

204. Hungarian law[291] allows for the settlement of commercial disputes through arbitration, including international commercial arbitration. Consumer disputes, review of decisions by the public administration and certain special claims (personal status, labour disputes, enforcement of personality rights, executory procedures, retention of possession) may not be subject to arbitration. As a main rule, Hungarian legislation regulates arbitration procedures in cases where the seat of the

290. ECA Art. 12 (1).
291. Act No. LX of 2017 on arbitration (ARA).

arbitration tribunal is located in Hungary, however, some provisions[292] are applicable to international arbitration as well – unless international treaties provide otherwise. Hungary is a party to the 1958 New York Convention on the recognition and enforcement of foreign arbitral awards.[293]

205. The Hungarian law on arbitration closely follows the 2006 UNCITRAL Model Law on International Commercial Arbitration and it even contains a provision that it shall be interpreted in accordance with the explanatory note attached to the Model Law.[294]

206. The jurisdiction of an arbitral tribunal is established by an arbitration clause or an arbitration agreement concluded in writing between the parties. An arbitration clause or agreement excludes the jurisdiction of regular courts unless the regular court seized determines that the arbitration clause or agreement is not concluded, void, ineffective or impossible.

207. The parties enjoy great freedom in deciding the composition and procedure of the arbitral tribunal. The law provides for only a few mandatory rules (e.g., the number of arbitrators must be uneven,[295] an arbitrator must be at least 24 years of age),[296] some general principles (equality of the parties and the right to be heard)[297] and default rules that apply in absence of contrary agreement by the parties (e.g., appointment and challenge of arbitrators). Regular courts may intervene in the arbitration proceedings only on request of the arbitral tribunal or a party and if so authorised by law,[298] e.g.:

- if a party or the arbitrators fail to appoint an arbitrator, the other party request the court to do so, except for permanent courts of arbitration where appointment is done by the Presidium according to the Rules of Proceedings;[299]
- if a party unsuccessfully challenged an arbitrator, he may request the court to decide on the challenge;[300]
- if an arbitrator becomes unable to perform his functions or fails to perform his functions without undue delay and refuses to withdraw and the parties are unable to agree on the termination of his mandate, any party may request the court to decide on the termination;[301]

292. Lack of jurisdiction by regular courts except for interim and safeguard measures, request to a regular court to assist in taking evidence, and recognition and enforcement of arbitral awards.
293. Promulgated in Hungary by Decree-Act No. 25 of 1962.
294. ARA Art. 3 (3).
295. ARA Art. 11 (1).
296. ARA Art. 12 (7) a).
297. ARA Art. 29.
298. ARA Art. 6.
299. ARA Art. 12 (3).
300. ARA Art. 14 (4).
301. ARA Art. 15 (1).

- if the arbitral tribunal made a ruling on its jurisdiction as a preliminary question, any party may request the court to decide the matter;[302]
- the arbitral tribunal or one of the parties with the approval of the tribunal may request assistance from a court in taking evidence;[303]
- courts may grant interim measures on the request of a party before or during the arbitral proceedings.[304]

208. When a person is approached in connection with his possible appointment as an arbitrator, he shall disclose any circumstances likely to give rise to justifiable doubts as to his impartiality or independence. An arbitrator, from the time of his appointment and throughout the arbitral proceedings, shall without delay disclose any such circumstances to the parties unless they have already been informed of them by him. An arbitrator may be challenged if circumstances exist that give rise to justifiable doubts as to his impartiality or independence, or if he does not possess qualifications agreed to by the parties. A party may challenge an arbitrator appointed by him, or in whose appointment he has participated, only for reasons of which he becomes aware after the appointment has been made.[305] If the arbitrator does not withdraw or the parties do not agree on the termination of his mandate, the arbitral tribunal decides on the challenge.[306]

209. The arbitral tribunal may order interim measures on the request of a party in order to preserve evidence or assets, maintain or restore the status quo or prevent action that is likely to cause harm to the arbitration process.[307] The tribunal may require the party requesting an interim measure to provide security in connection with the measure.[308] The tribunal may also adopt preliminary orders in which case it orders interim measures without prior disclosure to the other party. After the adoption of a preliminary order the concerned party may file an objection against the order. A preliminary order expires twenty days after it was issued, however, the tribunal may issue an interim measure to adopt or modify the preliminary order after the concerned party was given notice and an opportunity to present its case.[309]

210. Interim measures are enforceable along the same line as arbitral awards. The court, however, in addition to the grounds of refusal to enforce the final award, may refuse enforcement of an interim measure if:

- the party requesting the interim measure failed to provide appropriate security;
- the arbitral tribunal suspended or terminated the interim measure;

302. ARA Art. 17 (3).
303. ARA Art. 40.
304. ARA Art. 10.
305. ARA Art. 13.
306. ARA Art. 14 (3).
307. ARA Art. 18.
308. ARA Art. 23.
309. ARA Arts 20–21.

– the interim measure is incompatible with the powers conferred upon the tribunal.[310]

211. Preliminary orders are binding on the parties but may not be subject to enforcement by courts.[311]

212. The arbitration is terminated by the award of the tribunal or an order if the claimant fails to submit his claim, withdraws his claim (unless the defendant objects thereto), the parties agree to the termination of the proceeding or the tribunal finds that the continuation of the proceeding is unnecessary or impossible.[312] The arbitral award is final; there is no appeal. The parties, however, may within thirty days of its communication request the correction or interpretation of the award as well as an additional award as to claims presented in the procedure but omitted from the award.[313] Within one year after communication of the award, a party may request the novation of the procedure if new facts or evidence arise that may result in a more favourable award for the party concerned and the party was not at fault in previously not referring to the fact or evidence in question.[314]

213. The arbitral award has the same legal force as a final court Judgment and may be enforced accordingly. The court may refuse the enforcement of the award if the award violates public policy (*ordre public*) or the dispute may not have been subject to arbitration.[315]

214. A party may request the regional court at the seat of the arbitral tribunal to set aside the arbitral award. Such request may be submitted within sixty days of the communication of the award exclusively on the following grounds:

– one of the parties was incapable;
– the arbitration clause was void;
– the party was not given proper notice of the appointment of the arbitrator or of the arbitral proceedings or was otherwise unable to present his case;
– the award deals with a dispute not contemplated by or not falling within the terms of the arbitration agreement, or contains decisions beyond the scope of the agreement;
– the composition of the arbitral tribunal or its procedure was not in accordance with the agreement of the parties;
– the subject matter of the dispute may not have been subject to arbitration;
– the award is against public policy (*ordre public*).[316]

310. ARA Art. 27.
311. ARA Art. 21 (6).
312. ARA Art. 45.
313. ARA Art. 46.
314. ARA Arts 48–52.
315. ARA Art. 54.
316. ARA Art. 47.

215. On a reasoned request by one of the parties, the court may suspend the procedure to set aside the award for ninety days to allow the arbitral tribunal to resume the arbitral procedure and eliminate the grounds for setting aside. If the award is set aside, the arbitral proceedings may be recommenced with the appointment of the arbitrators. If an arbitral award is set aside, the arbitrators are not entitled to an arbitration fee. In repeated arbitral proceedings, the parties are exempt from administrative fees.[317]

216. In Hungary there are three permanent courts of arbitration established by law:

- the Permanent Arbitration Court attached to the HCCI (HCCI PAC);[318]
- the Permanent Court of Arbitration for Sport attached to the Hungarian Olympic Committee;[319] and
- the Permanent Court of Arbitration attached to the Hungarian Chamber of Agriculture.[320]

217. HCCI PAC may proceed in commercial disputes between the parties. In this context, the term 'commercial' applies to all disputes commercial, economic, contractual and non-contractual.[321]

218. The general decision-making body of the HCCI PAC is the Presidium consisting of seven members. The President and further two members are delegated by HCCI, and the other members are appointed by the Hungarian Energy and Public Utility Regulatory Authority, the Budapest Stock Exchange (BSE), the Hungarian Bank Association, and the Hungarian Bar Association. The Presidium adopts the PCA's Rules of Proceedings and its Roll of Arbitrators. The Roll consists of a general section and two specialised sections for energy-related disputes and financial and capital market related disputes. The general section includes at least sixty arbitrators, while the special sections include thirty additional arbitrators each. Arbitrators on the roll must have passed the Bar examination and have at least ten years of relevant professional experience.

219. Proceedings at HCCI PAC are confidential according to its Rules of Proceedings. The law, however, requires HCCI PAC to publish anonymous extracts of all awards and final orders on its website in searchable format after six months following the termination of the proceedings.[322]

---

317. ARA Art. 57 (2).
318. The Permanent Court of Arbitration of the Money and Capital Markets and the Permanent Energy Arbitration Court ceased their activities on 31 Dec. 2017. Pending cases are conducted and closed by the HCCI PAC.
319. This Court of Arbitration has jurisdiction in disputes between sports associations and their members as well as in disputes related to transfers, disciplinary matters and licences.
320. This Court of Arbitration has jurisdiction in disputes related to agricultural activities, land ownership and use.
321. ARA Art. 3 (1) 1, 7.
322. ARA Art. 62 (2) b).

Chapter 4. General Obligations of Economic Operators

220. The Central Office for Administrative and Electronic Public Services (Közigazgatási és Elektronikus Közszolgáltatások Központi Hivatala; as '*body in charge of the register*') shall:

- operate the register of private entrepreneurs;
- operate the IT systems for registration and administration;
- carry out regulatory inspections;
- discharge other duties conferred under its competence by law.[323]

221. The district offices of Budapest and county government agencies (as 'Authority') shall:

- under nation-wide jurisdiction relating to notifications for the starting up and termination of private entrepreneurial activities;
- set up a customer port of entry for any client submitting the notification in person, who does not have a customer port of entry;
- provide information relating to the activities of private entrepreneurs, for the pursuit of private entrepreneurial activities, and on economic activities for which professional qualification is required, and which are subject to authorization by the relevant authority or to notification;
- carry out the duties connected to the issue and registration of private entrepreneur's licenses;
- carry out regulatory inspections under jurisdiction by reference to the private entrepreneur's address;
- discharge other duties conferred under its competence by law.[324]

222. The body in charge of the register shall enter the following information in the *register of private entrepreneurs* in order to be able to identify them through their register number and for reasons of distinguishing private entrepreneurs, moreover to improve the transparency of the activities of private entrepreneurs and to promote their lawful operation:

- the private entrepreneur's natural identification data, home address, nationality and the date of admission into the register of private entrepreneurs;
- the private entrepreneur's main activity and scope of activities;
- the private entrepreneur's registered office and the address of his permanent establishment(s) and branch(es);
- if the activities of the private entrepreneur are suspended, the first and last day of suspension;
- the private entrepreneur's tax number and its current status, furthermore, if the private entrepreneur's tax number is suspended or withdrawn, the termination of

323. Act CXV of 2009 s. 3/A (1).
324. *Ibid.*, s. 3/A (2).

suspension, also if these resolutions are annulled, abolished, amended, supplemented or withdrawn, and the operative dates of these resolutions;
- the private entrepreneur's statistical code and register number;
- if the private entrepreneurs has a license, the license number, place date of issue, name of the issuing authority, an indication if the license has been replaced or if a replacement was refused, if the license has been withdrawn or annulled;
- the date of removal, including the reasons;
- if in the event of the private entrepreneur's death his widow or heir takes over the private entrepreneur's business operations;
- if in the event of the private entrepreneur being placed under guardianship or conservatorship, the private entrepreneur's business operations are taken over by his legal representative, indicating also the legal representative's natural identification data and home address;
- the notifications made and the related notices in the electronic document storage system.[325]

223. The objective of monitoring the activities of private entrepreneurs is to ascertain the authenticity of the register of private entrepreneurs and to ensure the lawful operation of private entrepreneurs. Within thirty days following the date of registration, an also within the framework of a control plan and on an ad hoc basis the Authority shall check whether the activities and operations of the private entrepreneur are in compliance with the relevant regulations.[326]

224. Sole proprietorships shall fall within the judicial supervisory competence of the Court of Registry in accordance with the provisions of the FA. The rights, facts and data constituting a part of the register which relate to sole proprietorships and the principals of sole proprietorships are considered public information.[327]

225. Trade registers: The *authority for trade* and commerce shall maintain a register on:

- traders;
- authorized and notified commercial establishments, and on the business hours of commercial establishments;
- notified shopping centres and local farmers' market, and on the authorized fairs and markets;
- licensed tour guides;
- providers of equine services;
- operators pursuing accommodation activities;
- providers of long-term accommodation and timeshare services;
- notified tour operators and travel agents.[328]

---

325. *Ibid.*, s. 11 (1).
326. *Ibid.*, s. 19/A (1), (2).
327. *Ibid.*, s. 24 (2), (3).
328. Act CLXIV of 2005 s. 6/G.

226. The Authority (NBH) shall be responsible for exercising supervision on *credit institutions* registered in Hungary.[329]

227. The *register of official firm records* shall consist of the *firm registry* and any enclosures for the verification of data contained in the firm registry, as well as other documents that the firm is required by law – in the public interest and in order to ensure the safety of transactions and the protection of creditors' interests – to submit. All data (current and previous) of the firm registry and firm documents – including those submitted by way of electronic means and the firm documents converted into electronic format – shall be made available to the public. Following the successful conclusion of tax registration procedures conducted under the Act on the Rules of Taxation, any application for registration, which has been submitted but not yet processed, and its enclosures are also considered public knowledge, whereas the registry shall contain an indication that the registration of the firm, or any change in its data of record (amendment notification), is in progress. Documents of judicial oversight proceedings shall also be made available to the public in accordance with the Firm Act.[330]

228. *Publicity of firm records* shall be ensured by the Court of Registry, the firm information service, and by way of publication in the Firm Gazette (*Cégközlöny*).[331]

229. Firm documents shall be made available at the Courts of Registry to the general public for inspection and for taking notes free of charge. Official copies of firm records, certificates of incorporation and firm certificates may be requested from the firm registry. An official copy of firm records contains all data and information (current and deleted) in the firm registry, while a certificate of incorporation contains current data only; a firm certificate is an official certificate of specific data which has been requested from the firm registry (current and/or deleted), and attests to the fact that some specific entry or data is not or was not included in the firm registry.[332]

230. The firm information service shall provide information – upon request – concerning any data (current or previous) from the firm registry, and concerning any data contained in an application for registration (amendment notification) which are recorded electronically pending registration. This public service is available to any party. The database of the firm information service is analogous with the electronic database of the Courts of Registry. The firm information service is also authorized to issue the authentic instruments.[333] Data from the various firm registries may also

329. Act CCXXXVII of 2013 s. 172, s. 2 (3).
330. Act V of 2006 s. 10 (1), (2).
331. *Ibid.*, s. 11; Papp, *supra* n. 161, 35.
332. Act V of 2006 s. 12 (1); Papp, *supra* n. 161, 35.
333. Act V of 2006 s. 13 (1); Papp, *supra* n. 161, 36.

be requested from the firm information service in the form of categorized firm information. The firm information service shall provide free access to certain information from the firm registry on its website with a view to the protection of creditors (www.e-cegjegyzek.hu).[334]

231. The responsibilities of the general courts, acting as the Court of Registry shall include the following:

- conducting firm registration (amendment notification) proceedings and – if the ruling is in favour of the request and also ex officio in the cases specified by the Firm Act – the registration or cancellation of data, rights and facts relating to a firm into or from the firm registry;
- the entry and removal of the particulars pertaining to the former executive officers and directors of a firm that has been removed from the firm registry by virtue of specific other legislation;
- disclosure of information from the firm registry and on firm documents;
- conducting judicial oversight proceedings – ex officio or upon request – with a view to ascertain the authenticity of registers of official firm records and for the lawful operation of firms;[335]
- adjudging petitions relating to the exercise of minority rights and the protection of creditors' interests as specified in the Hungarian Civil Code and other acts governing specific forms of firms, and as laid down in regulations of the EU;
- decision on the granting of public-benefit status, and on the registration of public-benefit status in the firm registry, or on removal therefrom;
- dealing with other matters conferred by law under the competence of the Court of Registry.[336]

232. The responsibilities of the firm information service shall include:

- to promote the enforcement of the requirement of publicity of firm records, and access to data and firm documents contained in the firm registry;
- to operate the system designed to support administration by way of electronic means in registration proceedings and other non-judicial proceedings regulated in another act;
- to maintain a legal department to provide counselling and legal advice to micro and small enterprises relating to firm formation and termination – by way of modern information technology means and equipment – in a clear and easily understandable language in a user-friendly environment, free of charge.[337]

334. Act V of 2006 s. 14 (1), s. 15 (1); Papp, *supra* n. 161, 36.
335. *See* Papp, *supra* n. 152, 96–100.
336. Act V of 2006 s. 1 (1).
337. *Ibid.*, s. 1 (2).

233. In Hungary the *associations and foundations* are controlled by the state attorney, by the register court and by the tax revenue office.[338]

234. The *chambers* also are keeping records about their members; in Hungary the following chambers can be found: agrarian, veterinarian, of court executor, medical working, medical, of building contractor, pharmaceutical, commercial and industrial, of auditor, notarial, of forensic expert, of patent agent, of hunter, engineering (also plant-protecting), of restorer, of private detective (personal and financial defensive), of attorney and of tax adviser. The Coalition of Hungarian Professional Chambers holds together this chambers and their operations.

235. The *opening of a bank account* is regulated by Hungarian Civil Code and by the standard service agreement of banks. Under a *current account contract* the parties shall assume an obligation to record and settle their enforceable monetary claims arising from a specific relationship in a consolidated account.[339] Under a *deposit account contract* the deposit holder is entitled to deposit a specific amount of money to the bank, and the bank undertakes to accept the sum of money offered by the deposit holder and to repay the same amount at a later date with interest.[340]

---

338. *See* more Z. Csehi, *Civil Associations and Foundations*, In: Business Law in Hungary, ed. I. Sándor, Budapest: Patrocinium, 2016, 223–244.
339. Section 6:391 CC.
340. Section 6:390 (1) CC.

Chapter 5. Business Assets, Goodwill and Commercial Property Rights

§1. Business Assets

236. Private entrepreneurs shall be subject to unlimited liability for any and all obligations arising out of or in connection with their activities to the extent of their personal resources.[341]

237. Sole proprietorships are founded with the subscribed capital indicated in the charter document. If the sole proprietorship's subscribed capital exceeds two hundred thousand HUF, the subscribed capital may comprise cash and in-kind contributions. The founder shall indicate the amount of capital stock in the application for registration. If the sole proprietorship's subscribed capital does not exceed two hundred thousand HUF, it must be provided in the form of cash contribution. Cash and non-cash contributions are to be made available at the time of foundation. Where the right for the pursuit of private entrepreneurial activities ceases for reasons of foundation of a sole proprietorships, up to the time of termination of the entitlement, the natural person and the sole proprietorship shall be subject to unlimited and joint and several liability for the private entrepreneur's commitments. The provisions of the Hungarian Civil Code pertaining to limited liability companies shall also apply to payments made from the sole proprietorship's capital to the order of the principal, subject to membership. The capital stock of a sole proprietorship may only be transferred to a private entrepreneur.[342]

238. The foreign company shall continuously provide the assets required for the operation of the *branch office* and the settlement of its liabilities. The foreign parent company and the branch office shall be subject to unlimited joint and several liability for the debts of the branch office. In respect of the importation of tangible assets, the provisions of customs law and customs proceedings and such governing the transportation of goods across the country's borders, as well as the regulations on international trade pertaining to goods subject to foreign trade licensing, shall be applied. In connection with the execution of liabilities incurred in connection with the activities of a branch office, all assets of the foreign company in Hungary may be subject to such execution.[343,344] The *initial capital* is the summary of capital contributions of each founder at the establishment of the *company*, the start-up capital of the company.[345] Founders and members are required to provide capital contribution for the foundation of the company and also in cases where membership rights

341. Act CXV of 2009 s. 15 (1).
342. *Ibid.*, s. 26, s. 27 (3), s. 29, s. 30 (7).
343. Act CXXXII of 1997 s. 11.
344. From 168. until 182. on the ground of Papp, *supra* n. 152, 56–59.
345. Papp, *supra* n. 161, 72.

are otherwise acquired (founders' responsibility). Capital contributions made available to the business association are not recoverable, and equivalent compensation may not be demanded.[346]

239. The initial capital has more functions:

- it is an operational condition, it is necessary to begin, and carry on the business activity;
- it is a safety reserve, the basis for satisfaction of the company's creditors;
- it is conducive to the realization of the business purpose of the company.[347]

240. At the *general partnership and limited partnership* there is not any limit for the minimum of the initial capital, but at the limited companies there are provisions for it: the minimum degree of the subscribed capital is HUF 3,000,000 in case of the *limited liability company*,[348] HUF 5,000,000 in case of the *private company limited by shares*[349] and HUF 20,000,000 in case of the *public company limited by shares.*[350]

241. The initial capital is composed of the *contribution in cash and in kind* of the founders (members). The Civil Code does not determine the proportion of the contributions in cash and contributions in kind; so the company may be established only by contributions in kind/in cash.

242. The *contribution in cash* may be fixed in the memorandum of association in any currency (imposition), and may be performed to the current bank account of the company (settlement), which is determined in the memorandum of association and can be found in the firm register.

243. The time of the discharge of the contributions in cash is different at the forms of the companies:

- in connection with the *general partnership and limited partnership* the Civil Code does not determine the time of performance of the contributions in cash, the date determined by members in the memorandum of association shall be kept;
- at the *limited liability company*, where according to the memorandum of association a member is required to provide less than half of respective contribution in cash before the application for registration is submitted, or if the memorandum of association provides for a time limit of over one year from the time of registration of the company for making available the part of the contribution in cash

346. Section 3:9 (1) CC.
347. Papp, *supra* n. 161, 72.
348. Section 3:161 (4) CC.
349. Section 3:212 (2) CC.
350. *Ibid.*

that was not paid before the application for registration is submitted, the company shall not be allowed to pay any dividend insofar as the unpaid profit calculated relative to the member's core deposits according to the provisions on the payment of dividends reaches the initial capital together with the contribution in cash which the members have already paid up;[351]
- at the *private company limited by shares* the amount of the contribution in cash at the time of foundation may not be less than 30% of the share capital;[352]
- the *stock company* may be registered only if, prior to the submission of the application for registration: the founders who agreed to provide contributions in cash have paid at least 25% of the nominal value or accounting par value of the shares which they have committed to subscribe for in the articles of association.[353]

244. The subject of the *contribution in kind* shall have financial value and shall be transferable.[354] The founder or member may provide contribution in kind by transferring ownership rights of tangible or intangible assets to the business association. Contribution in kind may also be provided in the form of receivables, provided that it is acknowledged by the debtor or if it is based on a final court ruling. Commitments of members for performing work or for any other personal involvement or service shall not be accepted as a form of capital contribution.[355] (Sections 3:10 (2), 3:99 (1) CC).

245. In the *general partnership, limited partnership and limited liability company* the member (who performs it) determines the value of the contribution in kind and the other members accept it; here the application of an auditor/expert is only a possibility. In case of the *stock company* the report of the auditor/expert is an obligatory appendix of the articles of association; no auditor's report is required if the shareholder who has provided the contribution in kind has an audited financial report prepared within three months to date in relation to the date when the contribution was provided, if it contains the value of the contribution, or if the contribution is comprised of assets whose price is listed on the stock exchange.[356]

246. If, at the time of transfer, the value of contribution in kind does not reach the value indicated in the instrument of constitution, the company may demand payment of the difference from the person having provided the contribution in kind within five years from the date of transfer. Members who were knowledgeable about and consented to, a contribution in kind that a member has provided at a value higher than what it was worth at the time when provided shall, together with the person providing it, be subject to joint and several liability toward the company in accordance with the provisions on liability for damages for loss caused by nonperformance of an obligation.[357]

---

351. Section 3:162 CC.
352. Section 3:212 (3), (2) CC.
353. Section 3:252 (1) a) CC.
354. LB Cgf.31.217/1994; LB Cgf.VII.32.060/1999/3; LB Cgf.II.30.656/1991.
355. Section 3:10 (2), 3:99 (1) CC.
356. Section 3:251 CC.
357. Sections 3:10 (3), 3:99 (2) CC.

247. At the *general and limited partnerships* the contribution in kind shall be made available to the company at the time specified in the memorandum of association.[358] In the *limited liability company*, if the value of contributions in kind at the time of foundation reaches or exceeds half of the initial capital, it shall be made available to the company in its entirety before the time of submission of the application for registration. If the contribution in kind was not made available to the company in its entirety at the time of foundation, the remaining contribution in kind shall be provided by the time specified in the memorandum of association; where the memorandum of association provides for a time limit of more than three years from the time of registration, the part exceeding the three-year period shall be null and void.[359] At the *single-member limited liability company* the founder shall put the contribution in kind at the company's disposal in its entirety before the application for registration is submitted.[360] The *stock company* may be registered only if – prior to the submission of the application for registration – the contributions in kind have been made available to the company, with the exceptions if the value of the contribution in kind is less than 25% of the share capital.[361] Shareholders shall pay up the nominal value or accounting par value of the shares to the stock company in full within one year from the date when the stock company is registered, and shall place contributions in kind at the stock company's disposal in whole within three years from the date of registration.[362] At the single-member stock company the founder shall put the contribution in kind at the company's disposal in full before the application for registration is submitted.[363]

248. If a member fails to provide his contribution as undertaken in the memorandum of association by the prescribed time limit, the management of the company shall call such member, with the applicable consequences indicated, to provide the contribution within a period of thirty days. In the event of non-compliance within the thirty-day time limit, the membership shall be terminated on the day following the expiration of such time limit; the management of the company shall notify the former member of the termination of his membership. The former member shall be held liable for damages caused to the company by virtue of his failure to provide the contribution in accordance with the provisions on liability for damages for loss caused by non-performance of an obligation.[364]

249. The *change of amount of initial capital* (increase or reduction) is possible by the amendment of the memorandum of association with the unanimous decision of kkt.'s members.[365] The degree of capital of *general partnership* and of capital

358. Papp, *supra* n. 161, 79.
359. Section 3:163 CC.
360. Section 3:208 (1) CC.
361. Section 3.252 (1) b) CC.
362. Section 3:252 (3) CC.
363. Section 3:208 (1) CC.
364. Section 3:98 CC.
365. Section 3:143 (4) CC.

contributions of each member may be changed only by mutual consent, but not unilaterally.[366] Creditors of members may not demand to recover their claims from the partnership's assets.[367] The business association's profits and losses shall be distributed among the members in proportion to their capital contributions. Any clause of the instrument of constitution for the exclusion of any member from the profits or from the bearing of losses shall be null and void (prohibition of *societas leonina*).[368] The rules of the general partnership shall completely be applied for the financial relations of the *limited partnership*.

250. The movements of initial capital can indicate the increase of this (it means the subsequent capital allotment of kft. or the converting of capital structure of the *limited liability company*) or the reduction of this (it means the decreasing of company assets).

251. The share capital of the *private company limited by shares* is specified by the number and the nominal value of shares; if the shareholders want to alter the share capital, they have to amend the numbers or the nominal value (or combining these) by a technique established in the Hungarian Civil Code.

252. The financial standing of the *grouping* depends on whether the grouping carries out economic auxiliary activity or not:

- Grouping exclusively with coordinative (cooperative activity): In case of only coordinative – cooperative grouping the members are not obliged to provide capital contributions and the grouping may be established without initial capital. In this case the members shall bear the costs of the operation of the grouping and the memorandum of association regulates the division of operating costs among members. The founders of the grouping may decide that they perform capital contributions for the cooperative society and it is formed with assets according to the provisions of the memorandum of association. The purpose of the grouping is not to make profits in itself. If the grouping obtains profits it shall be distributed among members in equal proportions.
- Grouping with economic auxiliary activity: For conducting economic auxiliary activity assets are required and it consists of the capital contributions provided by the members. During the operation of the grouping with economic auxiliary activity the after-tax profits arising from economic activities shall be distributed among members in proportion to their capital contributions.[369]

253. The *goodwill* of a firm is a transferable right with financial value which means advantageous Judgment of corporate name, business activity and business partners of the firm.[370]

---

366. Papp, *supra* n. 161, 328.
367. Section 3:140 CC.
368. Section 3:88 (2) CC.
369. Section 3:369 (2) d) CC.
370. Vb 98/003; BH 1992. 537.

§2. Intellectual Property

254. 'The common goal of the protection of copyrights and industrial rights is to provide intellectual products with exclusive, monopoly-like protection with absolute structure.'[371,372]

255. The Hungarian Civil Code shall apply to matters falling within its scope, which are not governed by the legislation on copyright, industrial property rights and the protection of commercial secrets.[373]

256. Commercial secrecy shall also apply to technical, economic and other practical knowledge of value held in a form enabling identification, including accumulated skills and experience and any combination thereof (as '*know-how*').[374]

257. The Act LXXVI of 1999 on Copyright protects literary, academic, scientific, and artistic works.[375] All literary, academic, scientific, and artistic works are protected by *copyright*, regardless of whether they are designated in the Act on Copyright; the following in particular are considered works of this kind:

- literary works (e.g., literature, technical writings, and academic and scientific publications);
- public speeches;
- all forms of computer programs and the related documents (as 'software'), whether recorded as source code, object code, or in any other form; including user programs and operating systems;
- plays, musicals, ballets, and pantomimes;
- musical compositions with or without lyrics;
- radio and television plays;
- motion picture and other audiovisual works;
- works made by means of drawing, painting, sculpting, engraving, lithography, or in any other similar manner as well as the designs therefore;
- photographic works;
- maps and other cartographic works;
- architectural works and their plans as well as the plans for building complexes and urban architecture;
- designs for technical structures;
- applied artworks and their designs;
- costumes and scenery, and their designs;
- industrial designs;
- any database recognized as a compilation.[376]

---

371. L. Kovács, 'A szellemi alkotások múltja és jövője', *Magyar Jog* 2, 2016, 89–94.
372. A. Grad-Gyenge, *The Law of Intellectual Property,* In: Business Law in Hungary, ed. I. Sándor, Budapest: Patrocinium, 2016, 425.
373. Section 2:55 CC.
374. Act LIV of 2018 on protection of commercial secrets Section 35 (2)
375. Section 1 (1).
376. Act LXXVI of 1999 s. 1 (2).

258. A work or creation is entitled to copyright protection on the basis of its individualistic and original nature deriving from the intellectual activity of the author. Copyright protection does not depend on quantitative, qualitative, or aesthetic characteristics or any judgment of the quality of the work.[377]

259. Laws and other legal instruments of the Government, court rulings and regulatory resolutions, regulatory and other official communications and documents, standards prescribed as mandatory by law and other similar regulations do *not* fall within the scope of copyright protection. Copyright protection does *not* extend to facts and daily news items underlying announcements released in the printed press. Ideas, principles, theories, procedures, operating methods, and mathematical operations are *not* entitled to receive copyright protection. Folklore expressions cannot receive copyright protection; this provision does not concern copyright protection due the creators of individualistic and original works that have been inspired by folk art.[378]

260. The person who creates a work (author) is entitled to copyright. Copyright protection extends to the reworking, adaptation, or translation of the work of another author – without any injury to the rights held by the author of the original work – if it has an individualistic and original nature.[379]

261. If the parts of a *joint work* produced by several authors cannot be used independently, the joint authors shall be entitled to copyright protection jointly and, if there is any doubt, in equal measure. However, any of the joint authors is entitled to take independent action against copyright violations. If the parts of a joint work can be used independently as well (connected works), each author can exercise the copyright independently with regard to his/her own part. The approval of all of the authors of the original joint work is necessary for connecting a part of the originally created joint work, which consists of connected works, with another work.[380]

262. *Collective works* are those works in which the contributions of the cooperating authors are united in the resulting uniform work in such a manner that the rights of the individual authors cannot be separately determined.[381]

263. Compilations are protected by copyright if the collection, arrangement, or editing of their content is individual and original (*collection of works*). Collections of works are protected by copyright even if their parts or components are not or cannot be protected by copyright. Editors are entitled to copyright in the entire collection of works. This, however, does not concern the independent rights of the authors of the individual works and the owners of related rights that have been included in

377. *Ibid.*, s. 1 (3).
378. *Ibid.*, s. 1 (4)–(7).
379. *Ibid.*, s. 4.
380. *Ibid.*, s. 5.
381. *Ibid.*, s. 6 (2).

the compilation. The copyright protection of collections of works does not cover the components that constitute their contents.[382]

264. An author is entitled to the sum total of copyright – inherent and economic rights – from the time a work is created. Authors cannot assign or waive their moral rights or have these rights assigned to another person in any other manner. With the exceptions the following, economic rights cannot be assigned or waived (nor can these rights be assigned to any other person in any other manner):

- economic rights can be inherited, and instructions concerning economic rights can be given in the event of death;
- economic rights can be assigned or transferred in the cases and under the conditions specified in law.[383]

265. Moral rights mean: the publication of work, the designation of name, the protection of the unity of work. From the aspect of economic rights, on the basis of copyright protection, authors have the exclusive right to utilize works in whole or any identifiable part, whether financially or non-financially, and to authorize each and every use. The following, in particular, are considered uses of a work: reproduction of a work, distribution of a work, public performance, presentation to the public by broadcast or some other manner, retransmitting broadcast works to the public through an organization other than the original, adaptation and exhibition.[384] Copyright is protected during the *author's lifetime* and for *seventy years after* his/her death.[385]

266. Works that fall within the framework of *free use*[386] can be used without remuneration, and the author's authorization is not necessary for the use. Only works that have been made public can be used freely in accordance with the provisions of the Act on Copyright. Use is allowed and can be done without remuneration even on the basis of the provisions pertaining to free use only to the extent that it is not injurious to the regular use of the works and it does not damage the author's legitimate interests without justification. Furthermore, use is allowed and can occur without remuneration if it fulfils the requirements of decency and its goal is not inconsistent with the purpose of free use. The provisions pertaining to free use cannot be interpreted inclusively.[387]

267. *Database* shall mean collections of independent works, data or other materials which are systematically or methodically arranged and can be individually accessed by electronic or other means.[388]

382. *Ibid.*, s. 7.
383. *Ibid.*, s. 9 (1), (2), (3), (4), (6).
384. *Ibid.*, s. 16 (1), s. 17.
385. *Ibid.*, s. 31 (1).
386. *Ibid.*, ss. 34–41.
387. *Ibid.*, s. 33 (1)–(3).
388. *Ibid.*, s. 60/A (1).

268. Neighbouring rights: the protection of performers, the protection of producers of phonograms, the protection of radio and television organizations and the protection of producers of motion picture works.[389]

269. Collective rights management is the exercise of copyrights and rights related to copyright that cannot be individually exercised stemming from the nature or circumstances of use, as a consequence of which they are exercised through organizations established by the owners of rights to this end, regardless of whether it is prescribed by law or based on the decision of the owners of these rights. The activity of collective rights management bodies is subject to registration.[390]

270. The Act XXXIII of 1995 on the Patent Protection of Inventions provides regulation for *invention and patent.*

271. Any novel invention that involves an inventive step and is industrially applicable shall be patentable in any area of technology. The following, in particular, shall *not* be treated as inventions: a discovery, scientific theory, mathematical methods, aesthetic works, a plan, rule or procedure relating to intellectual activity, games, business management, as well as computer programs, and any display of information.[391]

272. An invention shall be deemed to be *new* if it is not a part of any existing technology. Any invention that was made available to the public before the effective date of the right of priority by means of written publication, oral representation, practical application or any other way is considered to comprise a part of an existing technology.[392] An invention appears to involve an *inventive step* if it is non-obvious to an expert relative to an existing technology.[393] An invention is deemed susceptible of *industrial application* if it can be produced or used in a branch of industry or agriculture.[394]

273. Patentable biotechnological invention: Inventions that satisfy the criteria specified above shall be patentable even if they concern a product consisting of or containing biological material or a process by means of which biological material is produced, processed or used. *Biological material* means any material containing genetic information and capable of reproducing itself or being reproduced in a biological system. Biological material which is isolated from its natural environment or produced by means of a technical process may be the subject of an invention even if it previously occurred in nature. The human body, at the various stages of its formation and development, and the simple discovery of one of its elements, including the sequence or partial sequence of a gene, cannot constitute patentable inventions.

---

389. *Ibid.*, ss. 73–84.
390. *Ibid.*, s. 85, s. 86 (1); Act XCIII of 2016 on collective rights management of copyright and neighbouring rights.
391. Act XXXIII of 1995 s. 1 (1), (2).
392. *Ibid.*, s. 2 (1), (2).
393. *Ibid.*, s. 4 (1).
394. *Ibid.*, s. 5 (1).

An element isolated from the human body or otherwise produced by means of a technical process, including the sequence or partial sequence of a gene, may constitute a patentable invention, even if the structure of that element is identical to that of a natural element.[395]

274. An invention shall be *patented* if it satisfies the requirements and it is not considered unpatentable, and the application therefor meets the conditions set out in the Act on the Patent Protection of Inventions. Inventions shall be considered *unpatentable* where their commercial exploitation would be contrary to public order or morality; however, this type of exploitation shall not be deemed to be so contrary merely because it is prohibited by law or regulation.[396]

275. *Inventor* means a person who has created an invention; the inventor or his successor in title shall be entitled to patent.[397]

276. *Service invention* means any invention created by a person in the execution of his duties stemming from employment that includes working out solutions within the domain of the invention. In connection with service inventions, patent entitlement shall be vested in the employer, as the inventor's successor in title.[398]

277. *Employee invention* means any invention created by a person who is not required to do so under his contract of employment, however, the exploitation of such invention falls within the sphere of activities of his employer. In connection with employee inventions, patent entitlement shall be vested in the inventor; the employer, however, is entitled to exploit the invention. The employer's right of exploitation is non-exclusive; the employer may not grant a license of exploitation.[399]

278. *Patent protection* shall commence upon publication of the application, with retroactive effect to the date of application. Patent protection confers exclusive rights upon the (rightful) claimant of the patent – the holder of the patent – for the exploitation of the invention.[400] The *term* of definitive patent protection shall be twenty years from the date of application.[401]

279. Under a contract of exploitation (*patent license contract*), the holder of the patent gives authorization for the exploitation of the invention, and the person enjoying exploitation rights is required to pay a fee therefor.[402]

---

395. *Ibid.*, s. 5/A.
396. *Ibid.*, s. 6 (1), (2).
397. *Ibid.*, s. 7 (1), s. 8 (1).
398. *Ibid.*, s. 9 (1), s. 10 (1).
399. *Ibid.*, s. 9 (2), s. 10 (2).
400. *Ibid.*, s. 18 (1), s. 19 (1).
401. *Ibid.*, s. 22.
402. *Ibid.*, s. 27 (1).

280. The *National Bureau of Intellectual Property* (*Szellemi Tulajdon Nemzeti Hivatala*) shall have powers to handle the following patent-related matters: granting of patents; declaration of the termination of patent protection, and the revalidation of patents; invalidation of a patent; declaration of non-infringement; interpretation of patent descriptions; registration of patent applications and patents, including maintenance and updating; providing official notice concerning patents.[403]

281. *Plant variety rights* shall be granted for varieties that are distinct, uniform, stable and new. Varieties of all botanical genera and species, including, *inter alia*, hybrids between genera or species, may form the object of plant variety rights.[404]

282. The Act XI of 1997 on the Protection of Trademarks and Geographical Indications regulates so that any sign which can be graphically represented and is suitable for distinguishing goods and services from other goods and services can be protected by *trademark*. A trademark may consist of any of the following signs: a word, combination of words, including personal names and slogans; letters, numerals; designs, graphics; flat or three-dimensional figures, including the shape of the goods or packaging; a colour, a combination of colours, a light signal, a hologram; a sound, position signs, motion displays, multimedia displays, patterns and combination of signs.[405]

283. A sign shall be *refused* trademark protection if:

- it is not capable for making a distinction, in particular, if it consists exclusively of signs or indication which may serve, in trade to designate the kind, quality, quantity, intended purpose, value, geographical origin, time of production or rendering of the service, or any other characteristic of the goods or services;
- it consists exclusively of signs or indications which have become customary in the current language or in the fair and established practices of the trade, or are devoid of any distinctive character for other reasons ;
- it is in conflict with public order or moral standards;
- it is suitable for deceiving consumers with regard to the type, quality, geographical origin or other characteristic of the goods or services;
- it was submitted for registration in bad faith.[406] In connection with the grant of trademark there are relative grounds for refusal.[407]

403. *Ibid.*, s. 44 (2).
404. *Ibid.*, s. 106 (1), (2).
405. *Ibid.*, s. 1 (1), (2).
406. Act XI of 1997 s. 2 (2), s. 3 (1).
407. *Ibid.*, ss. 4–6.

284. Legal protection of a trademark is granted to those persons who have the sign registered in accordance with the procedures set out in the Act on the Protection of Trademarks and Geographical Indications. Trademark protection commences from date of registration, and it is effective retroactively to the date of filing for registration.[408]

285. Trademark protection affords exclusive right for the proprietor of the trademark to use the trademark. Rights associated with a trademark and rights conferred by trademark protection are transferable and negotiable.[409] Trademark protection shall be *valid for* a period of ten years from the date of filing for registration; the trademark protection may be *renewed* for further periods of ten years.[410]

286. Under a licensing contract (*trademark licensing contract*) the proprietor of the trademark may grant permission for the use of the trademark and the party using the trademark assumes the obligation to pay a fee for such use.[411]

287. *Geographical signs and designations of origin* used to indicate the geographical origin of products on the market may be granted protection as geographical indications.[412] Protection of a geographical indication is *not limited in terms of time*.[413]

288. A *geographical indication* is the name of a region, specific place or, in exceptional cases, a country that is used for marking products that originate from such area – i.e., are produced, processed or prepared in the defined geographical area – and whose exceptional quality, reputation or other characteristic is essentially attributable to that geographical origin.[414]

289. A *designation of origin* is the name of a region, specific place or, in exceptional cases, a country which is used for marking products which originate from such area – i.e., products which are produced, processed or prepared in the defined geographical area – and whose exceptional quality, reputation or other characteristic is exclusively or essentially the result of the particular geographical environment and the characteristic natural and human factors of this environment.[415]

290. The Act XLVIII of 2001 on the Legal Protection of Designs determines that a *design* shall be protected to the extent that it is new and has individual character.[416]

---

408. *Ibid.*, s. 9 (1), s. 10.
409. *Ibid.*, s. 12 (1), s. 19 (1).
410. *Ibid.*, s. 11.
411. *Ibid.*, s. 23 (1).
412. *Ibid.*, s. 103 (1).
413. *Ibid.*, s. 108 (2).
414. *Ibid.*, s. 103 (2).
415. *Ibid.*, s. 103 (3).
416. Section 1 (1).

291. *Design* means the appearance of the whole or a part of a product resulting from the features of, in particular, the lines, contours, colours, shape, texture and/or materials of the product itself and/or its ornamentation. *Product* means any industrial or handicraft item, including *inter alia* parts intended to be assembled into a complex product, packaging, get-up, graphic symbols and typographic typefaces, but excluding computer programs. Complex product means a product which is composed of multiple components which can be replaced permitting disassembly and re-assembly of the product.[417]

292. A design shall be considered to be *new* if no identical design has been made available to the public before the date of priority. A design shall be considered to have *individual character* if the overall impression it produces on the informed user differs from the overall impression produced on such a user by any design which has been made available to the public before the date of priority.[418]

293. A design shall *not subsist* in features of appearance of a product which are solely dictated by its technical function. A design shall not subsist in a design which is contrary to public policy or to accepted principles of morality.[419]

294. The right to the design shall vest in the *designer*. If two or more persons have jointly developed a design, the right to the design shall vest in them jointly if there are no conflicting signs originally filed in the application for a design. The right to the design shall vest in the designer or his successor in title. A registered design shall confer on its holder the exclusive right to use it.[420]

295. Upon registration, a design shall be protected for a period of *five years* as from the date of the filing of the application. The right holder may have the term of protection *renewed* for up to four periods of five years each. In the case of renewal, the next term of protection shall commence on the day immediately following the day of expiry of the previous one. Protection may not be renewed beyond twenty-five years as from the date of the filing of the application.[421]

296. The Act XXXVIII of 1991 on the Legal Protection of Utility Models provides so that the protection may be granted to a technical invention by *utility model* relating to the construction, structure or arrangement of components, if they are new, involve an inventive step and are capable of industrial application.[422]

297. The following, in particular, shall be *excluded* from protection: aesthetic creations, plant varieties and chemical products and mixtures.[423]

417. Act XLVIII of 2001 s. 1 (2)–(4).
418. *Ibid.*, s. 2 (1), s. 3 (1).
419. *Ibid.*, s. 6 (1), s. 7.
420. *Ibid.*, s. 12 (1), (3), s. 13 (1), s. 16 (1).
421. *Ibid.*, s. 19.
422. Section 1 (1) FA.
423. Act XXXVIII of 1991 s. 1 (2).

298. A utility model shall be considered to be *new* if it does not form part of the state of the art. The state of the art shall be held to comprise everything made available to the public by means of a written description, oral representation, practical application or any other way,, before the date of priority.[424]

299. A utility model shall be considered to involve an *inventive step* if, having regard to the state of the art, it is not very obvious to a person skilled in the art.[425]

300. *Inventor* means the person who has created the utility model. The right to the utility model shall vest in the inventor or his successor in title.[426]

301. A utility model shall be protected for a period of *ten years* as from the date of the filing of the application.[427]

302. The Act XXXIX of 1991 on Protection of Topography of Microelectronic Semiconductor Products regulates the provisions for *chip*.

303. The *topography* is in any forms expressed, spatial composition of elements (among these at least one active element) and consistence (or their part) of chips, or such spatial composition of chips intended for production.[428]

304. The topography may be protected if it is *original*.[429] The topography is original if it is a product of own intellectual activity and not usual in industry.[430]

305. The protection of topography may be granted to the author and his/her successor; the author is the creator of topography.[431]

306. The protection of topography shall be *valid for a period of ten years* from the date of filing for registration.[432]

307. The rights arising from topography and protection – except of moral rights – are transferable, negotiable and chargeable.[433]

308. Under a *licensing contract* the authorized person of protection may grant permission for the use of the topography and the party using the topography assumes the obligation to pay a fee for such use.[434]

---

424. *Ibid.*, s. 2 (1), (2).
425. *Ibid.*, s. 3 (1).
426. *Ibid.*, s. 6, s. 7 (1).
427. *Ibid.*, s. 11 (1).
428. Act XXXIX of 1991 s. 1 (2).
429. *Ibid.*, s. 1 (1).
430. *Ibid.*, s. 1 (3).
431. *Ibid.*, s. 2 (1), (2).
432. *Ibid.*, s. 6 (1), (2).
433. *Ibid.*, s. 8 (1).
434. *Ibid.*, s. 8 (2).

§3. Trade Names

309. Everyone is entitled to freely practice his personality rights within the framework of the law and within the rights of others, and to not be impeded in exercising such right by others. The right to a name is a specific personality right, any violation of right to a name shall be construed as violation of personality rights.[435]

310. The name of a legal person must differ from the names of other previously registered legal persons to an extent that they should not be confused. Where the registration of several legal persons is requested under names which are identical or may be confused, the name in question may be used by the applicant having submitted the first application. The name of a legal person may not convey an unrealistic impression. The name of the legal person shall contain a designation relating to the type or form of the legal person. The type of legal person, and if the name contains an indication of the legal person's activity as well, the legal person's activity shall be fixed in Hungarian, in conformance with the rules of Hungarian grammar.[436]

311. The *trade name* expresses business, commercial and economic activity of an enterprise, and means a special value. The use of trade name does not have any influence to the original legal subjectivity and does not modify the legal quality of its user.[437]

312. The trade name is a *collective noun*: it can be the attribute of enterprise, the corporate name and the business attribute; these variations are separated from each other.[438]

313. The trade name may be:

- the object of the protection of industrial property rights, if it is a *trademark*;
- the object of the regulation of firm law, if it is a *corporate name*;
- a *business attribute* without any protection.[439]

314. The trade name may be also a geographical indication, as the trademark, but it is *not identical with the trademark*:

- the trade names distinguish among enterprises and not among goods or services;
- an enterprise may have limited number of trade name, but unlimited number of trademark;
- the period of protection of trade name is unlimited;
- the trade name does not have any qualitative function;

435. Section 2:42 (1), s. 2:43 CC.
436. Section 3:5 CC.
437. P. Havasi, 'A személyek polgári jogi védelmére vonatkozó szabályozás kritikai elemzése, javaslat az új szabályozásra', *Polgári Jogi Kodifikáció* 1, 2002, 10–18.
438. At http://cegvezetes.hu/2011/09/kereskedelmi-nevek; downloading time: 1 Aug. 2016.
439. At http://cegvezetes.hu/2011/09/kereskedelmi-nevek; downloading time: 1 Aug. 2016.

– the trade name may be granted protection as corporate name;
– the trade name is – in itself – not transferable.[440]

315. The company may appear under the corporate name:[441] it has legal capacity under its corporate name. The corporate name transmits the fundamental criteria of the company. The corporate name makes the company an individual: identifies it and simultaneously distinguishes it from other firms, and supplies information about the company.[442]

316. The corporate name of the company must contain the selected company form, and at least a lead word; the lead word is meant for better identification of the company or to help distinguish the company from other companies that are engaged in similar activities. The lead word is placed at the beginning of the corporate name. The lead word may be a foreign expression, an abbreviation or an acronym written in Roman letters.[443]

317. The corporate name of the company may contain the activity(ies) of the company, a firm attribute (it may be provided only by Act; e.g.: profit – non-profit company) and a business attribute (the company uses it in the economic life; e.g.: 'Old Jack Pub' Limited Liability Company).[444]

318. The company's *concise name* consists of the lead word and the relevant company type; namely the obligatory components of the corporate name (section 3 (3) FA). In the concise name the lead word must be included in full length, but the company form may be indicated in full or in a shortened form.

319. The corporate name (concise name) of a company must clearly differ from the name of any other company already registered in the country, and from the name reserved at the Court of Registry[445] – irrespective of the company form – and it must not suggest any misleading implications, in particular, as relating to the scope of activities and the form of the company.[446]

320. If two or more companies bear the same name, the company which first submitted its registration application shall have the right to use that name (concise name), or the company whose name had been reserved by the Court of Registry.[447]

440. At http://cegvezetes.hu/2011/09/kereskedelmi-nevek; downloading time: 1 Aug. 2016.
441. On the ground of Papp, *supra* n. 152, 52–54.
442. Papp, *supra* n. 161, 61.
443. Section 3 (1), (2) FA.
444. Papp, *supra* n. 161, 62.
445. Section 3:6 CC.
446. Section 3 (4) FA.
447. LB.Gf.II.30.224/2000/2; s. 6 (1) FA.

321. Other than the lead word, the corporate name may only consist of Hungarian words, in conformance with the rules of Hungarian grammar;[448] in a corporate name only the lead word and the type of the company may be abbreviated.[449]

322. The corporate name[450] may contain the name of the company's owner or members.

323. The corporate name shall contain the word 'non-profit' before the company form is indicated; the indication of public-benefit status is optional.

324. The corporate name may contain the words 'state' or 'national' only if the State has majority control in the company according to the Civil Code whether directly or by its organizations, or if the company falls within the category of inalienable state ownership in accordance with another Act.

325. The corporate name of the Hungarian branch of a foreign company, the commercial representative office of foreign persons, and of the Hungarian branch of a European Economic Interest Grouping shall indicate the name of the foreign parent company.

326. The names of outstanding historical figures may only be included in a corporate name by authorization of the Hungarian Academy of Sciences, and a name the rights of which are owned by others may be included in a corporate name only with the consent of the party holding such right.[451]

327. During registration proceedings the company's name (concise name) shall contain the indication '*bejegyzés alatt*' ('b.a.') ('under registration' ['u.r.']), and if the company is undergoing bankruptcy or liquidation proceedings or voluntary dissolution the company's name shall include the indication '*csődeljárás alatt*' ('cs. a.') ('under bankruptcy' ['u.b.']), '*felszámolás alatt*' ('f.a.') ('under liquidation' ['u.l.']) or '*végelszámolás alatt*' ('v.a.') ('under voluntary dissolution' ['u.v.d.']), '*kényszertörlés alatt*' ('kt.a.') ('under involuntary de-registration' ['u.i.d.']), respectively.

328. Upon receipt of an application – submitted on paper via a legal representative or by electronic means if the proper dues are paid – the Court of Registry shall check within one working day upon the receipt of the request as to whether the registers of official firm records contain any other company that has been registered or is under registration which uses that name at the time when the information is requested, or if the name selected had been reserved by any company with pending

448. LB.Gf.II.30.399/1998/6.
449. Section 3 (2) FA.
450. Sections 4, 5 FA.
451. 361/B/2003. AB határozat.

registration. If the selected corporate name can be entered into the Registers of Official Firm Records, the Court of Registry shall adopt a resolution *to reserve the corporate name*[452] indicated for the applicant for a period of sixty days and shall admit it into the electronic register of corporate names. During this period another legal entity may not be admitted into the registers of official firm records under this particular corporate name, and may not be reserved on another legal entity's behalf.

329. The Court of Registry's resolution for the rejection of registration may not be appealed or contested. If the application for registration or for changing the corporate name of the company on behalf of whom a name has been reserved is not submitted within sixty days, the reservation shall be lifted. The reservation of a name shall be automatically extended by eight days, on one occasion, past the sixty-day original deadline, in the event where the applicant's application for registration was refused, and re-submitted within eight days.

§4. OTHER ELEMENTS

330. The public interest attached to having a competitive market environment that best serves the economy and social progress, as well as the interests of the enterprises operating in observation of the requirements of integrity in business dealings as well as that of consumers, requires for the state to lay down legal facilities to ensure the fairness and freedom of economic competition; the Act LVII of 1996 on the Prohibition of Unfair Trading Practices and Unfair Competition provides the legal frame of fair competition.

331. It is prohibited to conduct economic activities in an unfair manner, in particular, in a manner violating or jeopardizing the lawful interests of trading parties, as well as competitors, or in a way which is in conflict with the requirements of business integrity.[453]

332. It is prohibited to infringe upon or jeopardize the good reputation or credibility of any competitor by communicating or disseminating untrue facts, or by misrepresenting true facts with any false implication, as well as by any other practices.[454]

333. It is prohibited to gain access to or use commercial secrecy provided for in the Hungarian Civil Code in an unfair manner, and to disclose such secrets to unauthorized parties or to make them available to the public.[455]

334. Without the express prior consent of the competitor, goods of a fungible nature or services may not be produced, placed on the market or advertised with

452. Section 6 FA.
453. Act LVII of 1996 s. 2.
454. *Ibid.*, s. 3.
455. *Ibid.*, s. 4 (1).

such distinctive appearance, packaging or marking – including the indication of origin – furthermore, any such name, marking or indication of goods may not be used by which the competitor or its goods and/or services are normally recognized.[456]

335. Any form of communication, information or the making of a representation in any form with the aim or having the effect of promoting the sale or any other manner of placing on the market of goods or services, including natural resources that can be utilized as capital goods, covering real estate properties, securities, financial instruments or rights, or in connection with this objective, the representation of the name, the trademark or the activities of a business party that directly or indirectly identifies that business party's competitor, or the goods manufactured, sold or introduced by such other business party for the same or similar purpose as those featured in the advertising is prohibited, if:

- this may result in any unfair advantage derived from the reputation of the competitor or the name, merchandise, brand name and other marking of such competitor;
- this may harm the reputation of the competitor or the name, merchandise, brand name and other marking of such competitor;
- it presents goods as imitations or replicas of goods bearing a protected trademark or trade name;
- it creates confusion among market participants, between the business party and a competitor or between the business party's trade name, goods, trademarks or other distinguishing marks and those of a competitor.[457]

456. *Ibid.*, s. 6.
457. *Ibid.*, s. 6/A.

Chapter 6. Bankruptcy and Related Institutions

§1. Overview of Insolvency Proceedings

336. For the purposes of this chapter insolvency proceedings are collective proceedings that aim at the rescue, adjustment of debt, reorganisation or liquidation of an insolvent debtor or a debtor that is likely to become insolvent.

337. An overview of different insolvency proceedings available in Hungary is provided below:

Proceeding	*Scope*	*Objective*	*Legal Base*
reorganisation procedure (*csődeljárás*)	business associations	achievement of a reorganisation settlement with the debtors	Act No. XLIX of 1991 on reorganisation and liquidation procedures (BA)
liquidation procedure (*felszámolási eljárás*)		recovery and sale of the debtor's assets, distribution of the proceedings among the creditors	
resolution (*szanálás*)	financial and investment institutions, holdings	maintain critical functions, protect the assets	Act No. XXXVII of 2014 on the development of institutions strengthening the security of certain actors in the financial system
liquidation procedure (*felszámolási eljárás*)		recovery and sale of the debtor's assets, distribution of the proceedings among the creditors	Act No. CCXXXVII of 2013 on credit institutions and financial service providers (with a reference to BA)

Proceeding	*Scope*	*Objective*	*Legal Base*
reorganisation procedure (*reorganizációs eljárás*)	insurance companies	transfer of the business as a going concern	Act No. LXXXVIII of 2014 on insurance
liquidation procedure (*felszámolási eljárás*)		recovery and sale of the debtor's assets, distribution of the proceedings among the creditors	Act No. LXXXVIII of 2014 on insurance (with a reference to BA)
debt settlement procedure (*adósságrendezési eljárás*)	local municipalities	restore the solvency of local municipalities	Act No. XXV of 1996 on the debt settlement procedure for local municipalities
personal bankruptcy procedure (*természetes személyek adósságrendezési eljárása*)	natural persons (including private entrepreneurs)	settle the debts and restore the solvency of natural persons	Act No. CV of 2015 on the debt settlement procedure for natural persons (DSNP)
reorganisation procedure (*csődeljárás*)	NGOs	achievement of a reorganisation settlement with the debtors	Act No. CLXXV of 2011 on the right to association, public-benefit status, activities and status of NGOs (with a reference to BA)
liquidation procedure (*felszámolási eljárás*)		recovery and sale of the debtor's assets, distribution of the proceedings among the creditors	

§2. Reorganisation and Liquidation

I. Common Rules

A. *Notion and Objectives*

338. There are two types of formal insolvency procedures regulated in BA:[458]

- the '*csődeljárás*' (reorganisation procedure) – with the objective to provide a moratorium for the debtor to facilitate the achievement of a settlement with its creditors; and
- the '*felszámolási eljárás*' (liquidation procedure) – with a possibility of a settlement with the creditors but with the main objective to recover the assets of the debtor, to sell them and at distribute the proceedings among the creditors – according to a rank order provided for by BA – and to remove the debtor from the company registry.

339. The intention of the legislator is to provide priority for reorganisation procedures, the primary objective of BA – according to its Preamble – is to rescue the debtor and restore its solvency.[459] This priority is confirmed by several provisions of BA, e.g., no liquidation procedure may be commenced during an ongoing reorganisation procedure.[460] The law does not require a business rescue to be pursued before a liquidation procedure may be commenced. In fact, a reorganisation procedure may be initiated only by the debtor in need of business rescue,[461] the creditors cannot force the reorganisation of the debtor; they are entitled to initiate liquidation procedures only.[462]

B. *Requirement of Insolvency*

340. The scope of reorganisation and liquidation procedures covers only insolvent debtors, i.e., debtors who failed to repay outstanding debt or will be unable to repay upon expiry.[463] There are no legal provisions for pre-insolvency procedures in addition to the formal insolvency procedures.

341. In a liquidation procedure stricter criteria apply to insolvency. For the purposes of a liquidation procedure the debtor is insolvent if:

---

458. For a detailed analysis of reorganisation and liquidation procedures *see*: L. Juhász, *A magyar fizetésképtelenségi jog kézikönyve I–II. (A Handbook of Hungarian Insolvency Law I–II.)*, HVG Orac: Budapest, 2017, 1344 p.
459. This objective is, however, rarely met in reality, *see*: R. Muzsalyi Ró, *Csődeljárások a számok tükrében (Reorganisation Procedures by the Numbers)*. Gazdaság és Jog, 2015/9, 20.
460. BA Arts 9 (3a), 10 (5).
461. BA Art. 7 (1).
462. BA Art. 22 (1) b).
463. BA Art. 3 b).

- undisputed or recognised contractual debts of at least HUF 200,000 in value are not paid after twenty days of expiry or written notice;
- obligations determined by a final court decision or payment order of at least HUF 200,000 in value are not met by the deadline;
- singular execution against the debtor has been unsuccessful;
- the debtor did not honour its payment obligations under a reorganisation or a liquidation settlement;
- in a winding-up procedure its debt exceeds its assets and its members/owners do not undertake to provide the necessary sources to pay outstanding debt upon expiry.[464]

C. Insolvency Practitioners

342. Only insolvency practitioner companies (IPCs) can be appointed as liquidators (in liquidation procedures) or administrators (in reorganisation procedures).[465] Detailed rules as to the companies available for appointment are provided by Government Decree No. 114/2006. (V.12.) on the registry of insolvency practitioner companies (RD). IPCs must apply to be included in the IPC Registry maintained by the Ministry for National Economy. Applicant companies must present a security of at least HUF 70 million.[466] The IPCs are required to engage at least two persons with professional qualifications for insolvency procedures and asset management, two lawyers, two economists and two public auditors. IPCs are not allowed to conduct any business related to real estate brokerage, lending or factoring or have a majority share in companies dealing in such business.[467] Insolvency procedures are managed by individual insolvency practitioners designated by the appointed IPCs. Insolvency practitioners represent the respective IPCs and act on their behalf. Insolvency practitioners must have a clean criminal record, at least one year of professional experience, and must not be barred by court from acting as an insolvency practitioner.[468] Detailed rules of incompatibility also apply.[469]

343. IPCs are appointed by the court where the claim to commence insolvency proceedings was filed. The appointment is based on a random, electronically managed allocation of cases with a view to availability and an even distribution of burden.[470] There is no appeal against the appointment order. The IPCs must refuse appointment in case of incompatibility and may refuse appointment if the seat of the debtor is not within the IPCs geographical area of activities as registered in the IPC Registry.[471] Creditors are not given the possibility to determine or influence the appointment decision. However, the majority of creditors in all creditors' groups

464. BA Art. 27.
465. BA Art. 27/A.
466. BA Art. 27/C (2); RD Art. 2 (3).
467. BA Art. 27/C (2)–(3).
468. BA Art. 27/A (3).
469. BA 27/A (4).
470. BA Art. 27/A (1).
471. BA Art. 27/A (5).

may request the dismissal of the insolvency practitioner without cause. They may do so only once and no later the fifteen days after the first meeting of creditors.[472]

344. Insolvency practitioners owe due care generally expected from a professional in his position. They are liable for all damages caused by breach of due care.[473] All illegal activities or inaction of an insolvency practitioner are subject to complaint. Such complaint can be filed to the court ordering the commencement of insolvency procedures by the creditors' committee, a creditor or any affected party. If the complaint is well founded, the court may strike down any decisions made by insolvency practitioner and restore the original situation or order the insolvency practitioner to issue another decision. If the insolvency practitioner does not comply with a final court order, the court appoints another insolvency practitioner and orders the dismissed practitioner to bear all costs.[474] In the absence of a complaint, the court may also dismiss the insolvency practitioner in case of serious or repeated breach of law. The dismissal may also be initiated by the creditors' committee.[475]

345. The Hungarian Association of Insolvency Practitioners also has an Ethics Committee that investigates the complaints made against insolvency practitioners by creditors or other parties concerned. According to the Ethical Rules of the HAIP, this committee has the possibility to apply sanctions to IPCs. The most serious sanction is the initiation of the removal of an IPC from the Register.

D. Creditors' Committee

346. Creditors may establish a creditors' committee in both reorganisation and liquidation procedures.[476] In a liquidation procedure, it is the duty of the liquidator to initiate the establishment of a creditors' committee with the exception of simplified liquidation procedures.[477]

347. A creditors' committee may be constituted through an agreement by at least one-third of the registered creditors representing in a reorganisation procedure at least one-half of the votes at the reorganisation settlement and in a liquidation procedure at least one-third of the registered outstanding debt of the debtor. The committee has three to seven members, creditors may appoint a chairman as well. Rules of incompatibility apply (debtor, debtor's shareholder, manager, auditor or their close relatives). The debtor, the court and the administrator or liquidator must be informed of the establishment of the committee within three working days. The committee adopts its rules of procedures within five working days of its establishment.

472. BA Art. 27/A (8).
473. BA Art. 54.
474. BA Art. 51.
475. BA Art. 27/A (7).
476. BA Art. 5/A.
477. BA Art. 39 (1).

348. Only one creditors' committee per debtor may be recognised. If more than one committee is established, the one which first communicated its establishment to the court will be recognised. If more than one communication is filed to the court at the same time, the one representing the highest number of creditors will be recognised. Creditors may join the committee at any time and their request to join cannot be refused if they assume the obligations undertaken by the founders of the committee in the founding agreement (e.g., on the advancement of costs).

349. The committee monitors the activities (including the sale of the debtor's assets) of the administrator or liquidator, represents its members in court proceedings and vis-à-vis the administrator or liquidator and exercises powers and performs tasks provided for by law. Most of these powers and tasks relate to information requests, prior consultation or approval rights in case of some crucial managerial decisions by the administrator or liquidator (e.g., the continuation of business activities by the debtor during a liquidation procedure, or the raise of salaries for employees of the debtor), or the right to file complaints related to the activities of the insolvency practitioner.

350. Creditors' votes are calculated on the basis of the amount of outstanding debt owed to them by the debtor. They have one vote after each HUF 50,000, of outstanding debt. Shareholder or affiliated creditors' votes are divided by four with the exception of creditors who acquired shares in exchange of a reorganisation loan with a value not less than the listed capital of the debtor.[478] In a liquidation procedure, votes are calculated on the same basis as in a reorganisation procedure, however, the number of votes of creditors who registered their claims more than forty days after the opening of the procedure is divided by two.[479]

351. If a committee is not formed, the creditors may appoint a creditors' representative. A representative has the same powers as a committee. The representative performs his functions according to a mandate given by the creditors.

E. Role of Courts

352. Insolvency procedures are supervised by courts. The role of the supervising court is to guarantee the legality of the procedure with a special emphasis on the enforcement of the provisions of BA.[480] The court is not involved in substantial economic and financial decisions taken by the administrator or the liquidator (e.g., the authorisation of certain transactions) or the determination of the economic content of a settlement with the creditors.[481] The court's tasks include:

– the ordering of the commencement of the procedure;

478. BA Art. 18 (5).
479. BA Art. 44 (1).
480. EBH 2011. 2332.
481. Gfv.VII.30.339/2013/5.

- the ruling on complaints related to the activities of the administrator or liquidator and to the ranking of creditors;
- the confirmation of a settlement with the creditors;
- the termination of the procedure.

II. Reorganisation

353. The objective of a reorganisation procedure is to reorganise the economic position of the debtor through the facilitation of a reorganisation settlement with its creditors with a view to enable the continuation of its business activities. This objective is further highlighted by the constant jurisprudence of Hungarian courts whereby reorganisation settlements reached by the parties are confirmed by courts only if evidence disclosed during the procedure reveals a genuine intention on behalf of the debtor to continue its business activities.[482]

A. Commencement

354. A reorganisation procedure may be initiated by the chief executive officer of the insolvent debtor. Prior approval of the highest company organ exercising the rights of founders/owners/members is required. The highest organ must adopt a formal resolution to this effect, and a protocol witnessing this decision must be attached to the request for the commencement of the reorganisation procedure. Employees, trade unions and the Works Council must be informed of the filing but they do not have prior consultation rights or the right to assent.[483] A request to open a reorganisation procedure is filed using a form with annexes to be attached as required by law – after 1 January 2015 only in an electronic format.[484] Legal representation through an attorney is compulsory for the debtor.[485] These provisions aim to facilitate a quick court decision on the commencement of the reorganisation procedure without the need for a detailed examination of the merits of the case.

355. The request for the opening of reorganisation procedure must contain in the petition form or attached:

(a) the debtor's name, registered office, registered number and tax number;
(b) a document in proof of the prior consent of the highest organ and a document in proof information of employees;
(c) the annual account (simplified annual account) and the interim financial statement prepared within three months to date, together with a written statement by the chief executive officer of the debtor that they give a true and fair view of the debtor's financial situation;

482. BH2014. 118., Kúria Gfv.VII.30.339/2013.
483. BA Art. 8 (1).
484. BA Art. 7 (5).
485. BA Art. 7 (1).

(d) a written statement by the chief executive officer of the debtor showing any major changes in the debtor's financial situation since the time the annual account or the interim financial statement referred to in (c) above had been adopted;
(e) if the debtor is a member in a recognised or de facto group of companies as governed in the Companies Act, the related contracts;
(f) a list of the debtor's creditors, a list of the debtor's liabilities and their due dates, an indication of the creditor's claims recognized and the ones disputed by the debtor, an indication of secured and unsecured creditors' claims, the contingent liabilities assumed by the debtor according to the Accounting Act, and a description of the contingent claims for which the debtor is responsible;
(g) the document in proof of payment of publication charges relating to the ordering of reorganisation proceedings and to the stay/moratorium;
(h) a statement by the chief executive officer of the debtor indicating the financial service provider or providers where the debtor has a current account, showing the account numbers as well, and the name of the investment firm where the debtor has a securities account;
(i) a statement of commitment by the chief executive officer of the debtor to notify the financial service providers affected at the time of submission of the request for the opening of reorganisation proceedings on having the request filed, so as to enable the said financial service providers to obtain reliable information thereof by 15:00 hours of the previous working day relative to the publication of the temporary stay, and to refrain from initiating any payment transaction or credit transfer, that would be contradictory to the purpose of the stay, and from taking any measures by which to provide preferential treatment to any creditor;
(j) a data sheet containing the information prescribed by specific legislation for showing the debtor's financial standing, signed by the chief executive officer of the debtor.[486]

356. The request and its annexes are examined from an exclusively formal point of view; there is no hearing or court investigation. An appeal lies only against a dismissal order. If the request to open a reorganisation procedure is not summarily dismissed due to formal deficiencies, the debtor automatically enjoys a temporary moratorium/stay starting from the publication date of his request and the court order to this effect in the Company Journal. The court order must be issued within one working day after the receipt of the request.[487] The court must decide on the opening of a reorganisation procedure within five working days after the receipt of the request and must order the opening of the procedure or dismiss the request.[488] In either case, the temporary stay ends when the court order becomes final.[489] In fact, the court order does not necessarily become final five days after the receipt of the request if the court requires the submission of additional documents or there is an

486. BA Art. 8 (2).
487. BA Art. 9 (1).
488. BA Art. 9 (4).
489. BA Art. 9 (5).

appeal against the dismissal order. In a reorganisation procedure, there is no temporary administrator appointed in the interim period, thus the debtor unilaterally enjoys the benefits of the temporary stay without an effective representation of the creditors' interests.

357. On the debtor's request, if the request to open a reorganisation procedure is not summarily dismissed due to formal deficiencies, his request and the court order relating to the temporary stay is published in the Company Journal. Publication in the Company Journal shall take place in the form of an online entry on the official website of the Company Journal at 0:00 hours, updated on a daily basis.

358. If the court orders the opening of a reorganisation procedure the order is published in the Company Journal. Publication in the Company Journal shall take place in the form of an online entry on the official website of the Company Journal at 0:00 hours, updated on a daily basis. The court also orders the indication 'cs. a.' (under reorganisation) to be entered in the company register in the debtor's entry record.[490]

359. The debtor shall notify its creditors directly within five working days following the publication of the order the open reorganisation proceedings, and – furthermore – shall publish a notice in a daily newspaper of nation-wide circulation and also on its website (if available) advising the creditors to register their claims within the specified time limit and to make the payment charged for the registration of claims to the payment account of the administrator appointed by the court, and to attach the documents in proof of their claim, indicating that no claim will be registered in the event of their failure to do so in due time.[491]

360. In a reorganisation procedure, post-commencement claims must be registered with the administrator within eight days after they have become due. The administrator will register these claims together with and in the same ranking order as pre-commencement claims.[492]

B. Administrator

361. In a reorganisation procedure the role of the administrator is to monitor the debtor's business activities during the stay, with due regard to the creditors' interests and with the objective of facilitating the conclusion of a reorganisation agreement. The administrator reviews the financial position of the debtor and its books, accounts and assets, assists the debtor in enforcing its claims vis-à-vis third parties, and registers the creditors' claims. Following the commencement of reorganisation proceedings, the debtor may not undertake new obligations and make payments unless the administrator has previously approved them. In the absence of such prior

490. BA Art. 10 (1).
491. BA Art. 12 (1).
492. BA Art. 10 (2) f).

approval, the administrator may avoid such undertakings and payments.[493] During the stay, therefore, the rights and obligations of the debtor's management are not suspended, but they may only be exercised and performed in cooperation with the administrator.

C. Moratorium/Stay

362. Execution of monetary debt – as opposed to other obligations – is suspended during the moratorium/stay, and no execution may be ordered except for claims that are excluded from the stay.[494] Except for securities related to obligations excluded from the stay, securities may not be enforced during the stay.[495] Otherwise, the reorganisation procedure has no legal effect on the existence and scope of securities. Secured creditors form a distinct group of creditors, and a majority of the secured creditors must consent to the adoption of a reorganisation settlement.[496] There are a number of payment obligations that are excluded from the stay, *inter alia*:

- salaries and other payment obligations owed to employees of the debtor as well as taxes and other contributions related thereto;
- payment for public utilities (electricity, gas, etc.);
- fee and costs of the administrator;
- fee of financial accounts due to financial service providers;
- VAT, excise duties and similar tax obligations;
- return of mistakenly received funds;
- payment obligations assumed with the consent of the administrator with a view to continue the debtor's business.[497]

D. Costs

363. The costs of a reorganisation procedure are the fee and the expenses of the administrator. The administrator must keep a separate account of his expenses and must present it to the creditors, the debtor and the court. The fee and the justified expenses of the administrator shall be covered by the creditors' payments of the claim registration fees. If these payments do not cover the expenses and fees of the insolvency practitioner, the debtor is liable for the remainder.[498] The law sets a gradual regressive scale for the calculation of fees:

493. BA Art. 13 (3) c), e).
494. BA Art. 11 (2) c).
495. BA Art. 4/A (1) a); BA Art. 11 (2) d).
496. BA Art. 20 (1).
497. BA Art. 11 (1).
498. BA Art. 16 (2).

- if the debtor's assets are valued below HUF 100,000,000, the fee is 2% of the assets but not less than HUF 250,000;
- if the debtor's assets are valued between HUF 100,000,001 and 500,000,000, the fee is 2% of HUF 100,000,000, and 1.25% of the value over the threshold;
- if the debtor's assets are valued between HUF 500,000,001 and 1,000,000,000, the fee is 1.25% of HUF 500,000,000 and 0.75% of the value over the threshold;
- if the debtor's assets are valued over HUF 1,000,000,000, the fee is 0.75% of HUF 1,000,000,000, and 0.25% of the value over the threshold.[499]

364. There is a bonus up to 15% of the fee calculated above in case of a successful reorganisation agreement. The amount of the fee may be reduced by the court taking into account the length of the proceedings and the actual work done by the practitioner.[500]

E. *Reorganisation Settlement*

365. In a reorganisation procedure, the debtor must convene a general meeting of the creditors within sixty days of the commencement of the procedure with a view to adopt a reorganisation settlement.[501] If the draft reorganisation settlement is not adopted but the debtor agrees to revise the draft, further general meetings may be convened.[502]

366. The reorganisation plan is prepared by the debtor with the assistance of the administrator and – optionally – with the assistance of the majority shareholder (if any) and companies in the same company group (if applicable), the Works Council and company unions.[503] The debtor bears primary responsibility for the management and preparation of the negotiations under the monitoring of the administrator. Formally, creditors do not participate in the preparation of the draft reorganisation plan. The draft reorganisation plan must be made available to creditors at least five working days before the meeting and eight working days before a repeated meeting to negotiate a revised draft reorganisation agreement. Formally, creditors cannot propose an alternative rescue plan. They may propose the revision of the draft rescue plan submitted by the debtor (and they may do so in the form of presenting their own version) but if the debtor refuses the revision of the plan negotiations are closed. A reorganisation plan must be approved by the majority of votes in both secured and non-secured classes. (Cstv. 20. § (1)) Those who are eligible to vote but not present are counted as voting against. (Cstv. 18. § (5)).

367. The adopted reorganisation settlement must be confirmed by the court. The court verifies the legality of the settlement in general, with a special emphasis on

499. BA Art. 16 (3).
500. BA Art. 16 (4)–(5).
501. BA Art. 17 (1).
502. BA Art. 18 (3).
503. BA Art. 17 (3).

procedural and voting requirements, the formal requirements of the settlement, and non-discrimination of dissenting creditors. A confirmation order of a reorganisation settlement can be appealed. The appeal delays the implementation of a confirmed plan but the moratorium/stay is also maintained until the confirmation order becomes final. The deadlines are very short for both the appeal and the review (eight working days after notice of settlement and filing of appeal respectively).[504]

368. A confirmed reorganisation plan is binding on all registered creditors, including those who did not approve the plan (either because not present or voting against) and those with disputed claims. The reorganisation plan does not cover creditors who failed to register their claims in due time; they are barred from subsequently enforcing their claims except in a liquidation procedure initiated on the request from another party.[505]

F. End or Termination

369. In a reorganisation procedure the moratorium/stay ends on the second working day after the 120th day following the publication of the court order commencing the reorganisation procedure.[506] The moratorium may be extended until the 240th day after the publication of the order if a majority of creditors agree in all creditors' groups. The moratorium may be extended until the 365th day after the publication of the order if a two-thirds majority of creditors agree in all creditors' groups.[507]

370. A reorganisation procedure ends upon the confirmation of a reorganisation agreement by the court.[508] A reorganisation procedure is terminated by the court if there is no reorganisation agreement concluded or the reorganisation agreement violates legal provisions.[509] If a reorganisation procedure is terminated, it is ex officio converted into a liquidation procedure.[510]

III. Liquidation

A. Commencement and Legal Effects

371. Liquidation may be ordered by the court:

(a) on the request of:

504. BA Art. 21/C.
505. BA Art. 20 (2)–(3).
506. BA Art. 10 (4).
507. BA Art. 18 (2)–(3).
508. BA Art. 21/A (3).
509. BA Art. 21/B.
510. BA Art. 22 (1) a).

- the debtor;
- a creditor; or
- the administrator of a winding-up procedure if debts of the company winding up exceed its assets and its owners do not provide security to guarantee the timely and complete payment of outstanding debts.

(b) ex officio:
- if the reorganisation procedure of the debtor is terminated;
- on the initiative of the company registry court if the company registry court orders the removal of the firm from the company registry;
- on the initiative of the criminal court if the execution of financial sanctions against a legal person has been unsuccessful.

372. Liquidation may be requested by the debtor if it is unable or unwilling to initiate a reorganisation procedure. The request must contain the same elements as a request by the debtor to commence a reorganisation procedure.[511] If liquidation is requested by a creditor, the creditor must verify the title and expiry of its outstanding claim and justify why it considers the debtor insolvent.[512] The debtor may respond within eight days and may request a delay up to forty-five days (except if the liquidation procedure was preceded by a reorganisation procedure).[513]

373. In a liquidation procedure, there is a possibility to appoint a temporary administrator for the period between the filing of a request for a liquidation procedure and the actual opening of the procedure; however, the powers of an interim administrator are quite limited compared to those of a liquidator.[514]

374. By law at the commencement of the liquidation procedure all outstanding debts of the entity under liquidation become due and payable.[515] In addition, it is common contractual practice to include a clause enabling the parties to terminate the contract in case the other contracting party enters liquidation procedure.

B. Liquidator and Its Powers

375. In the course of liquidation proceedings, the debtor's external management is taken over by the insolvency practitioner, and the debtor's management and shareholders cease to have control over the assets of the debtor. These provisions relate to the external representation of the debtor and the disposal over its assets, and some internal management powers may remain with the owners and/or management. Accordingly, the insolvency practitioner may invoke all the company law

511. BA Art. 23 (1)–(2).
512. BA Art. 24.
513. BA Art. 26.
514. BA Art. 24/A.
515. BA Art. 35 (1).

rights of a shareholder if the debtor's assets include shares in a company. The debtor's management is required to extensively cooperate with the insolvency practitioner: must produce an inventory of assets and documents and a financial statement, and must hand over the assets and archives within thirty days of the commencement of the procedure.[516] The insolvency practitioner does not need prior authorisation to exercise his powers within the limits of everyday management activities. However, he must consult in advance with the creditors' committee if he intends to conclude contracts outside the scope of everyday management activities, to terminate existing contracts, or to write off assets. If he fails to do so, the creditors' committee or a creditor may initiate the dismissal of the insolvency practitioner.[517] If the insolvency practitioner intends to continue the business activities of the debtor during liquidation, he must acquire the assent of the creditors' committee.[518]

376. In liquidation procedures the insolvency practitioner – as a main rule – is authorised to terminate with immediate effect all contracts concluded by the debtor or is authorised to rescind from such contracts if none of the parties has rendered any services under the contract. All resulting claims must be notified by the other contracting party to the insolvency practitioner within forty days from the communication of the termination or rescission.[519] There are special legal provisions related to lease contracts concluded with natural persons for residential premises (with the exception of company housing and garage), employment contracts, vocational training contracts concluded with schools or students, non-economic loans, work contracts concluded by cooperatives with their members, and collective bargaining agreements. In these cases there is no right to terminate or rescind with immediate effect.[520]

377. Within ninety days of taking notice of the court order commencing the liquidation procedure but not later than one year after its publication the creditors or the insolvency practitioner on behalf of the debtor may avoid:

- all contracts and unilateral declarations made no earlier than five years before the filing of the request to start the liquidation procedure that resulted in a loss of assets on behalf of the debtor if the debtor's intention was to defraud the creditors and the other party was aware or should have been aware of this intention;
- all contracts and unilateral declarations made no earlier than two years before the filing of the request to start the liquidation procedure that resulted in a transfer of assets or assumption of obligations for no consideration or is manifestly unbalanced as to the value of services rendered to the benefit of a third party;
- all contracts and unilateral declarations made no earlier than ninety days before the filing of the request to start the liquidation procedure that creates preferential

516. BA Art. 34 (1)–(2).
517. BA Art. 39 (3), (5).
518. BA Art. 46 (3)–(4).
519. BA Art. 47 (1).
520. BA Art. 47 (3).

treatment for one of the creditors, e.g., modification of a contract to the benefit of a creditor or providing security for an unsecured obligation.[521]

378. Within the same deadline, the insolvency practitioner on behalf of the debtor may reclaim any services rendered by the debtor not earlier than sixty days before the filing of the request to start the liquidation procedure if it resulted in a preferential treatment of one of the creditors and the service rendered fell outside the scope of regular business activities (e.g., payment of a debt before it has become due).[522]

379. Upon successful avoidance, general provisions of CC on void and avoidable contracts[523] are applicable. The insolvency practitioner or the creditor may demand restitution in integrum and also the deletion of any registered rights or liens established on the thing subsequently to its transfer based on an avoided contract.[524]

380. Besides particular avoidance powers conferred upon the creditors and the insolvency practitioner by the BA, the CC also provides for a general *actio Pauliana.*[525] In this case, a contract frustrating the satisfaction of a creditor is ineffective vis-à-vis the creditor if the third party acted in bad faith or received services without consideration.

C. *Ranking of Claims*

381. The registered claims are verified by the liquidator within forty-five days after the registration deadline, following consultations with interested parties if necessary. Claims that are deemed disputable by the liquidator are referred to the court for review. Following court review, the interim liquidation balance sheet must be adjusted accordingly.[526]

382. Pre-commencement creditors are ranked for the purpose of a distribution of the debtor's assets as follows:

(a) liquidation costs (*see* below);
(b) pre-commencement secured claims up to the value of security;
(c) life-long regular payment obligations related to maintenance, indemnity, non-pecuniary damages, miners' benefits and pecuniary benefits due to members of agricultural cooperatives;

521. BA Art. 40 (1).
522. BA Art. 40 (2).
523. CC Art. 6:89, 6:108–6:115.
524. BA Art. 40 (1a).
525. CC Art. 6:120.
526. BA Art. 46 (6).

(d) claims registered by natural persons outside their scope of professional activities with the exception of bonds (e.g., warranty claims), claims of SMEs, claims of smallholder farmers, claims of the Financial Cooperatives' Capital Guarantee Fund based on succession of account holders;
(e) claims of social security funds, taxes and public debt (with the exception of those that are deemed liquidation costs), reclaimed national, EU or foreign financial assistance, public utility fees, condominium common charges, claims of the Financial Cooperatives' Capital Guarantee Fund not mentioned above;
(f) other non-specified claims;
(g) late payment interest, fines;
(h) shareholder, affiliated and management claims and claims of their close relatives, gratuities.[527]

383. Ordinary claims are classified as 'other non-specified claims' ((f) above), claims (a)–(e) are preferential, claims (g)–(h) are subordinated claims. If the assets do not cover all registered claims, priority is given to claims (a) and (b). If funds are still available afterwards, claims (c) followed by (d) must be covered proportionately. The same applies to claims (e)–(g), with the exception of claims by social security funds that have priority over other claims in the same ranking group.[528]

384. In a liquidation procedure, post-commencement claims that are not deemed liquidation costs must be registered with the liquidator within forty days after they have become due. The liquidator will register these claims together with and in the same ranking order as pre-commencement claims.[529]

D. Costs

385. The costs of a liquidation procedure are exhaustively enumerated in BA Article 57 (2) and include *inter alia*:

- salaries and other payments due to the employees of the debtor;
- costs of the termination of the debtor's business activities;
- costs of the sale of the debtor's assets;
- costs of court and administrative procedures that are borne by the debtor;
- costs of the storage of the debtor's archives;
- fee of the insolvency practitioner.

386. In the liquidation procedure the insolvency practitioner's fee is covered by payments from the creditors, with the possibility to top up insufficient funds from the debtor's assets with the court's permission. The State is the final guarantor of minimum fees not recoverable either from creditors or from debtors. The fee is 5% of the total amount of the proceeds from the assets sold in the course of liquidation

527. BA Art. 57 (1).
528. BA Art. 57 (4)–(6).
529. BA Art. 37 (2).

and the proceeds from claims received, but not less than HUF 300,000. If the debtor continues business operations during the insolvency procedure, 2% of the sales revenues can be taken into account as a fee. The court may depart from that rule in particularly complicated cases and may award a higher fee. In the case of a simplified liquidation, the fee is HUF 300,000 and 1% of the total amount of the proceeds from the assets sold in the course of liquidation and the proceeds from claims received. If an agreement is reached in the liquidation procedure, the fee is 5% of the value of the assets included within the agreement. If the value of assets exceeds HUF 1,000,000,000, the court may set a lower fee taking into account the actual work done by the insolvency practitioner.[530]

E. Liquidation Settlement

387. In a liquidation procedure, the liquidator must convene a general meeting of the creditors within seventy-five days of the commencement of the procedure with a view to establish a creditors' committee.[531] On the request of the debtor, the court also convenes a general meeting within sixty days of the receipt of the request with a view to adopt a liquidation settlement.[532]

388. The draft liquidation settlement including a plan to restore the solvency of the debtor is prepared by the debtor.[533] The liquidator also prepares a report for the negotiations summarising the financial situation of the debtor.[534] Formally, creditors do not participate in the preparation of the draft liquidation settlement. The meeting is convened by the court and all registered creditors are summoned to the meeting with a copy of the draft settlement. A liquidation settlement must be approved by at least half of the creditors' votes in all creditors' groups – excluding pre-commencement secured claims – representing at least two-thirds of all registered claims in value.[535]

389. A liquidation settlement must be confirmed by the court; the confirmation order may be appealed. A confirmed liquidation settlement is binding on all creditors with the exception of pre-commencement secured claims. Creditors who failed to register their claims in due time are barred from subsequently enforcing their claims.[536]

530. BA Art. 59 (1).
531. BA Art. 39 (1).
532. BA Art. 41 (5).
533. BA Art. 41 (4).
534. BA Art. 42.
535. BA Art. 44 (1).
536. BA Art. 41 (5).

F. End or Termination

390. A liquidation procedure is terminated if all admitted and non-disputed debts of the debtor are paid, and the debtor offers security to cover disputed debts and the fee of the insolvency practitioner.[537] A liquidation procedure ends upon the liquidation of the debtor and the distribution of its assets.[538]

G. Special Measures and Procedures

391. In order to protect environmental and natural resources, agricultural land or historical heritage, in a liquidation procedure the competent authorities may order the debtor to conduct a compulsory evaluation and to bear the costs of protective measures.[539]

392. If the assets of the debtor are presumably insufficient to cover liquidation costs, the insolvency practitioner initiates a simplified liquidation procedure that is basically a simple and accelerated distribution of the debtor's assets and outstanding claims – if any – between the creditors.[540]

393. There are separate legal provisions for liquidation procedures of companies deemed strategically important and designated as such by a Government decree. The procedure is not fundamentally different from the general rules, but in these cases State-owned non-profit IPCs are appointed, the procedure is accelerated, the rules on the sale of assets are more flexible (a non-public sale is also possible), and – especially in the case of public utility companies – the objective is to provide for the continuation of services by ceding the debtor's business to a similar service provider.[541]

§3. Personal Bankruptcy

I. Objectives and Scope

394. The objective of the debt settlement procedure for natural persons (hereinafter referred to as personal bankruptcy) is to settle outstanding debts of natural persons using their assets and income and restore their solvency.[542] Personal bankruptcy covers domestic natural persons (including private entrepreneurs). A natural

537. BA Art. 45/A (1).
538. BA Art. 60 (1).
539. BA Art. 48 (4)–(5).
540. BA Art. 63/B.
541. BA Arts 65–70.
542. For a detailed description of personal bankruptcy *see*: L. Juhász, *A magyar magáncsőd kézikönyve (A Handbook of Personal Bankruptcy in Hungary)*, HVG Orac: Budapest, 2017, 536 p.

person is deemed domestic if it fulfils the criteria set for persons with domestic domicile in Act No. CXVII of 1995 (Article 3 point 2) on personal income tax. That includes:

- Hungarian citizens (except persons with multiple citizenships without a domestic residence);
- natural persons exercising their right of free movement and residence within the EU for at least 183 days a year in Hungary;
- natural persons with a residence permit or stateless natural persons;
- natural persons whose only registered residence is in Hungary; natural persons with their centre of main interests in Hungary if their registered residence is not or not only in Hungary; and
- natural persons with a habitual residence in Hungary if their registered residence is not or not only in Hungary and their centre of main interest cannot be ascertained.

395. Personal bankruptcy is not designed to tackle minor outstanding debts or provide relief for debtors without sufficient income or assets to realistically engage in a restructuring of debts. Therefore the legislator set a number of concurrent eligibility criteria for the debtor:

- the overall overdue and actionable debt shall be between HUF 2 million and HUF 60 million including interest and accessories;
- the overall overdue debt shall exceed the relevant assets of the debtor but shall not exceed 200% of the relevant assets; for the latter calculation relevant assets also include the debtor's expected income for the next five years;
- at least 80% of the overdue debt is not contested;
- there is at least one payment obligation that is overdue for at least ninety days and is over HUF 500,000 in value;
- there is at least one payment obligation arising from a consumer credit or a business loan related to the activities of a private entrepreneur;
- there are no more than five payment obligations due to close relatives of the debtor, business entities where the debtor has been executive officer or owner over 5% of the shares or to entities and persons that share payment obligations with the debtor;
- none of the payment obligations results from court decisions rendered because the debtor failed to honour his unlimited liability to creditors following the winding up of a company, abused rules on limited liability of members or as chief executive, his liability was established for acting against the interest of creditors of a dissolved company;[543]
- the debtor may not initiate personal bankruptcy if he has already participated in such procedure in the past ten years.[544]

543. DSNP Art. 7 (1).
544. DSNP Art. 8.

II. Commencement

A. *Out-of-Court Phase*

396. The legislator's intention is to keep the procedure out of courts as much as possible.[545] Therefore an out-of-court procedure is envisaged under the coordination of the main creditor. The procedure is commenced on the application of the debtor submitted in writing to the Family Insolvency Service[546] or the main creditor. The main creditor is a credit institution that has a mortgage on the debtor's real estate used for residential purposes and its related rights are registered first in order of priority.[547] The main creditor is under an obligation to coordinate the out-of-court procedure if the debtor's outstanding debt is owed exclusively to the main creditor or to creditors connected to the main creditor and it is not under an insolvency procedure.[548] If there is no main creditor or the main creditor is not under an obligation to coordinate the out-of-court procedure and it does not volunteer to do so, the application is forwarded to the court having jurisdiction according to the residence of the debtor and the out-of-court procedure is transformed into an in-court procedure.

397. The eligibility of the debtor is verified by the Family Insolvency Service and an official survey of the debtor's financial situation and living conditions is also conducted. At the commencement of the procedure the debtor is required to pay the main creditor a lump sum of HUF 30,000 for administrative expenses and a minimum monthly instalment until the sum of monthly instalments is otherwise decided in an agreement with the creditors or by the court.[549] The Family Insolvency Service issues a public notice, registers the procedure in the Debt Settlement Registry and initiates the registration of the procedure in the real estate registry if the debtor owns such property.

398. The main creditor establishes a list including all involved parties with names, contact details and claims. The main creditor – with the debtor's assistance – prepares a draft agreement with the creditors that is communicated to all involved parties. The parties may comment within fifteen days and the draft agreement may be revised based on these comments. The parties may formally endorse the revised draft agreement within another fifteen days. The agreement is accepted if all involved parties agree. The successful agreement is registered in the Debt Settlement Registry.

---

545. DSNP Arts 17–34.
546. Since 1 Jan. 2017, the central functions of the Family Insolvency Service are exercised by the Ministry of Justice; the local functions are exercised by district government offices located at the seats of each county. *See* Government Decree No. 362/2016. (XI.29.) on certain functions and competences related to judicial services.
547. DSNP Art. 5 point 24.
548. DSNP Art. 20 (3).
549. The minimum monthly instalment is one-twelfth of 7.8% of the secured debt but not more the one-twelfth of 7.8% of the security's market value. DSNP Art. 21 (1).

399. If no agreement is reached after 90 days following the public notice – 120 days if there are creditors involved other than the main creditor and connected entities – or the debtor has failed to disclose overdue debt during the procedure, or the debtor has not complied with his obligations under the agreement for thirty days after notice, the out-of-court procedure is deemed unsuccessful. In this case the out-of-court procedure is transformed into an in-court procedure.

B. In-court Phase

400. The in-court phase of personal bankruptcy is under the supervision of the district court having jurisdiction according to the debtor's residence.[550] The court is assisted by a family administrator appointed by the Family Insolvency Service. The family administrator is an employee of the Family Insolvency Service to whom qualification and incompatibility rules apply.

401. The family administrator issues a new public notice on the website of the Family Insolvency Service calling on all creditors with a claim that is already due or will be due in the next five years and exceeds HUF 50,000 to register in writing within thirty days by the administrator. Within thirty days after the deadline for registering the claims the administrator ranks the claims in the following order:

- high priority claims: secured claims and advanced costs of singular execution procedures commenced before the bankruptcy procedure and subsequently suspended;
- privileged claims: maintenance obligations, damages (also awarded in the form of an annuity) and compensations, common costs of apartment houses, public interest claims (public utility claims, tax or other public claims, student loans, etc.);
- non-specific claims;
- low priority claims: payment obligations due to close relatives of the debtor, business entities where the debtor has been executive officer or owner over 5% of the shares or to entities and persons that share payment obligations with the debtor.

402. The creditors' ranking is relevant for the weighting of votes during the approval of the agreement with the debtor. A registered claim in the value of HUF 20,000 is accorded forty votes if it is ranked as a high priority claim, twenty votes as a privileged claim, eighteen votes as a non-specific claim and one vote as a low priority claim.

403. The administrator and the debtor jointly prepare a draft programme to restore the debtor's solvency and settle outstanding debts. The draft is circulated among creditors who have an opportunity to propose amendments and initiate a formal round of negotiations. A formal round of negotiations is held if a majority of creditors so require. In the absence of a formal round of negotiations the draft or

550. DSNP Arts 35–68.

revised draft is directly submitted to approval by the debtor and the creditors. The draft is accepted if it is endorsed by the debtor, the main creditor, a majority of high priority claims and a combined majority of all other claims. The administrator verifies the legality of the vote and in case of compliance submits the adopted agreement for confirmation to the court. In case of non-compliance or lack of an agreement the administrator convenes a formal round of negotiations.

404. A formal round of negotiations is convened and chaired by the administrator. During the negotiations several rounds may be convened if necessary. The draft programme is presented by the administrator and may be revised if so requested by the creditors. The draft programme is adopted in formal negotiations if it is not rejected by the debtor, the main creditor and a combined majority of all other creditors. Voting is open (not secret). If an agreement is reached, it is submitted by the administrator to the court for confirmation. If no agreement is reached within 150 days, the process is closed. If an agreement is reached but the procedure was flawed the court orders a repeated procedure to be completed within forty-five days. The agreement or the unsuccessful closure of procedure is registered in the Debt Settlement Registry. If the procedure is closed unsuccessfully a debt reimbursement procedure takes place (*see* below).

405. The agreement may include release from certain debts, the restructuring of debts, modification of deadlines or payment conditions, change in the currency of the debt. The agreement may also include the sale of certain assets of the debtor by the administrator and the division of the proceedings among the creditors. If the debtor acquires an unexpected income over the value of HUF 200,000 after the conclusion of the agreement (collection of debt, prize, inheritance, etc.), it shall be divided proportionately among the creditors. The debtor shall refrain from all future transactions that may endanger his payment obligations under the agreement. The debtor shall submit a written report to the administrator in every six months on the implementation of the agreement and all circumstances that may be relevant for the purposes of the agreement. If the debtor fails to honour payment obligations under the agreement after notice from the creditor the procedure is transformed into a debt reimbursement procedure (*see* below).

406. The agreement may be modified on the request of the creditors if the debtor acquires an unexpected income over the value of HUF 200,000 after the conclusion of the agreement, and the income was not divided proportionately among the creditors, or if the debtor acquires an unexpected income over the value of HUF 500,000 that enables an early repayment of some of the debts. The debtor may also request the modification of the agreement if due to unexpected circumstances beyond his fault (e.g., serious illness, unemployment, and natural disaster) make it impossible to honour the terms of the agreement. The debtor may request such modification only twice. The modification is negotiated and voted according to the same rules as the agreement itself. If the modification is not adopted a debt reimbursement procedure takes place (*see* below). The administrator submits the adopted modification to the court for confirmation.

*C. Debt Reimbursement Procedure (*Adósságtörlesztési Eljárás*)*

407. The debt reimbursement procedure aims at the division of the debtor's asset and the reimbursement of his debts based on a reimbursement plan taking into account the legitimate interests of the debtor and the creditors as well as the living conditions of the debtor.[551] The draft plan is prepared by the administrator and confirmed by the court. The plan entails the sale of all non-essential assets of the debtor by the debtor (below the value of HUF 300,000) or by the administrator (over the value of HUF 300,000). The debtor may dispose of a sum equal to the monthly minimum old-age pension every month to cover basic living expenses, the rest of his income and liquid assets are placed on a separate account under the supervision of the administrator. The plan determines monthly instalments to be paid from this account to the benefit of creditors.

408. This period of financial supervision lasts for five years and may be prolonged by another two years if minimum reimbursement requirements (5% for low priority claims; 38% for non-specific claims; for privileged claims 120% of the reimbursement rate for non-specific claims; for high priority claims the market value of the security) are not met during five years. If the debtor fulfils his obligations during the supervision period he is released from further obligations after the expiry of the period. If the debtor violates the terms of the reimbursement plan the reimbursement procedure is terminated and all outstanding debt will be enforced according to the general rules.

409. The outline of personal bankruptcy procedure is summarised in the chart below:

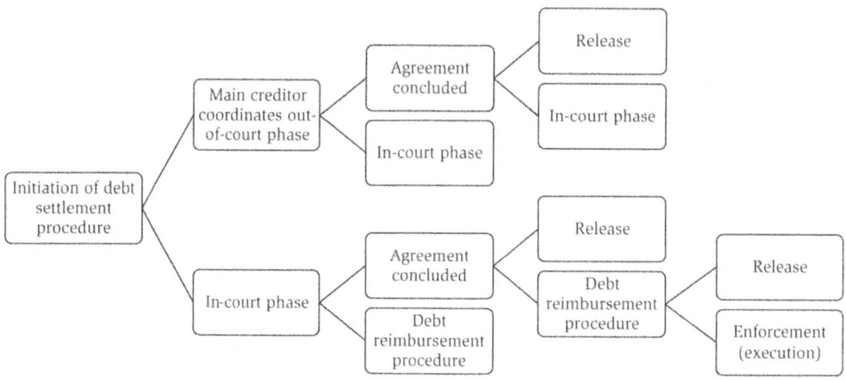

551. DSNP Arts 69–88.

III. Legal Effects

A. *Moratorium/Stay*

1. Out-of-Court Procedure

410. From the commencement creditors may enforce their claims only in the framework of the procedure, loans and basic public utility contracts may not be cancelled and ongoing enforcement (singular execution) of outstanding claims is suspended.[552]

2. In-court Procedure

411. From the commencement adverse legal effects for non-payment of obligations shall apply only to payments required under law or court orders. Gratuitous payment obligations may not be performed by the debtor and such obligations may not be enforced. Creditors may enforce their claims only in the framework of the procedure, loans and basic public utility contracts may not be cancelled and ongoing enforcement (singular execution) of outstanding claims is suspended. Securities (including options) may not be enforced, and outstanding claims may not be set off.[553]

B. *Supervision of the Debtor's Economic Activities*

1. Out-of-Court Procedure

412. From the commencement the debtor may undertake obligations only to the extent of day-to-day regular transactions and may not enter into gratuitous or new loan or credit arrangements. The debtor may not sell assets involved in the bankruptcy procedure, and may not assign his claims to third persons.[554]

2. In-court Procedure

413. The debtor may undertake new obligations only with the administrator's consent. The debtor shall open two bank accounts: one for the purposes of debt reimbursement and one for day-to-day regular transactions. The former is at the disposal of the administrator, the latter is at the disposal of the debtor but he may use

552. DSNP Arts 26 (3), 28 (1).
553. DSNP Arts 41–44.
554. DSNP Art. 26.

only a sum equivalent to 150% of the minimum old-age pension for monthly personal expenses. The debtor submits a report on such expenses to the administrator every two months.[555]

§4. International Insolvency Proceedings

414. As regards insolvency proceedings commenced after 26 June 2017 for those general business entities and associations whose centre of main interests (COMI) is located in the EU, rules on jurisdiction, applicable law, recognition and enforcement of decisions taken by EU Member States' authorities, as well as international procedural cooperation are provided by the Insolvency Regulation (recast).[556] The scope of the insolvency regulation does not extend to credit institutions, insurance undertakings, investment firms and collective investment undertakings. The private international law of insolvency proceedings for credit institutions is regulated by Act No. CCXXXVII of 2013 on credit institutions and financial service providers and Act No. XXXVII of 2014 on the development of institutions strengthening the security of certain actors in the financial system that implements Directive 2014/59/EU establishing a framework for the recovery and resolution of credit institutions and investment firms.[557] As regards insurance undertakings, similar provisions are included in Act No. LXXXVIII of 2014 on insurance that implements the Solvency II Directive.[558] No specific private international law rules are provided by domestic law for insolvency procedures against investment firms and collective investment undertakings. Hungary has decided not to include insolvency proceedings other than the reorganisation and liquidation procedures regulated by BA in the annexes of the Insolvency Regulation; therefore, its provisions are not applicable to any other such procedures, including the personal bankruptcy procedure that is available only for domestic natural persons.

415. There are not any bilateral or multilateral international agreements concluded by the EU or Hungary related to the private international law of insolvency proceedings.

416. Act XXVIII of 2017 on private international law (PIL) provides for the jurisdiction of Hungarian courts as regards insolvency and related procedures

555. DSNP Art. 45.

556. Regulation 2015/848/EU of the European Parliament and of the Council of 20 May 2015 on insolvency proceedings (recast); for proceedings commenced before 26 Jun. 2017 Regulation 1346/2000/EC of the Council is still applicable.

557. Directive 2014/59/EU of the European Parliament and of the Council of 15 May 2014 establishing a framework for the recovery and resolution of credit institutions and investment firms and amending Council Directive 82/891/EEC, and Directives 2001/24/EC, 2002/47/EC, 2004/25/EC, 2005/56/EC, 2007/36/EC, 2011/35/EU, 2012/30/EU and 2013/36/EU, and Regulations (EU) No. 1093/2010 and (EU) No. 648/2012, of the European Parliament and of the Council.

558. Directive 2009/138/EC of the European Parliament and of the Council of 25 Nov. 2009 on the taking up and pursuit of the business of Insurance and Reinsurance (Solvency II).

against companies with a registered seat in Hungary or companies that conduct non-temporary economic activities in the country.[559] Decisions by foreign authorities may be recognised in Hungary if there is reciprocity between the countries involved. Recognition of a foreign decision does not exclude the commencement of a secondary insolvency procedure in Hungary.[560] It must be recalled that provisions of PIL apply only to cases not covered by the Insolvency Regulation of special legislation (e.g., on credit or insurance institutions).

417. BA covers entities with a COMI within the EU. The only exception is provided by Act No. CXXXII of 1997 on Hungarian branch offices and commercial representative offices of foreign-registered companies that allows for liquidation procedures against Hungarian branches of companies with a COMI outside the EU as well as the recognition of such proceedings against a non-EU company with a registered office in Hungary.

418. Hungary has not yet incorporated the 1997 UNCITRAL Model Law on Cross-Border Insolvency into BA and cross-border insolvency proceedings are only regulated in detail since October 2017,[561] unpredictable and sometimes incoherent court rulings still remain.[562]

559. PIL Art. 100.
560. PIL Art. 114.
561. BA Arts 6/B-6/Q.
562. For a detailed analysis of cross-border insolvency procedures in Hungary *see*: A. Csőke, *A határokon átnyúló fizetésképtelenségi eljárások (Cross-border Insolvency Procedures)*, HVG Orac: Budapest, 2016, 604 p.

Chapter 7. Negotiable Instruments

§1. Regulation, Notion and Basic Characteristics

419. Hungarian legal terminology uses the expression *értékpapír* (a mirror translation from the German *Wertpapier*) for negotiable instruments. The basic definition for negotiable instruments is included in the new CC that entered into force on 15 March 2014. However, according to Article 56 of Act No. CLXXVII of 2013 on transitional measures related to the entry into force of the Civil Code, negotiable instruments issued before that date still fall under the scope of the regulations previously in force.

420. The legislation currently in force defines negotiable instruments as unilateral legal declarations that embody in material or dematerialised form the rights contained therein with the effect that the exercise or disposal of those rights is legally possible only through and in possession of the instrument.[563] The CC determines the minimum formal requirements for a negotiable instrument as follows:

- name and address of the issuer;
- an indication that the declaration is intended as a negotiable instrument;
- the right embodied in the instrument;
- serial number, code[564] and the number of instruments issued in the series (for instruments issued in a series);
- place and date of issue;
- signature of the issuer (for instruments in material form).[565]

421. Besides the minimum formal requirements separate regulations may provide for additional requirements for specific types of negotiable instruments,[566] and may limit or prohibit the issue of certain instruments.[567] The old CC in force before 15 March 2014 was more restrictive as regards the concept of negotiable instruments. The old CC required specific legal authorisation and recognition for a unilateral legal declaration to qualify as a negotiable instrument and explicitly provided for the types of rights and obligations that may be embodied in a negotiable instrument.[568]

---

563. CC Art. 6:565 (1).
564. International Securities Identification Number, for the relevant Hungarian regulation *see* Decree No. 20/2014. (VI.3.) of the Hungarian National Bank on ISIN.
565. CC Art. 6:565 (3).
566. CC Art. 6:565 (2). A number of such rules are stipulated by Act No. CXX of 2001 on capital markets (CM).
567. For Example, with the exception of companies limited by shares, no other association may issue instruments embodying rights related to membership (ownership), CC Art. 3:11. Before 1 Jul. 2006, cooperatives could also issue business shares but these had to be cancelled or transformed into non-transferable investor share units by 30 Jun. 2007.
568. Old CC Art. 338/A (1)–(2), 338/D.

422. The CC stipulates some general provisions on negotiable instruments that are to a large extent modelled on the rules applicable for bills of exchange. Negotiable instruments may be issued in material or dematerialised form. Dematerialised instruments are computer data (signal) created, stored and transferred via electronic securities accounts. Since 1 January 2003, public issue of negotiable instruments (with the exception of instruments issued by the State) is allowed only in a dematerialised form, and all such circulating instruments had to be dematerialised by 31 December 2004. Shares of publicly listed stock companies (including temporary or privately issued shares) may be issued only in a dematerialised form.[569] Negotiable instruments in a material form may be issued in a series or (with the exception of instruments in a dematerialised form) individually. Negotiable instruments may be issued to bearer or may have a specified beneficiary; however, dematerialised instruments and instruments issued in a series must always have a specified beneficiary.[570] In the case of an instrument issued to bearer the possessor of the instrument is regarded as the beneficiary; the same applies to an instrument with a blank endorsement. If an instrument is issued to a specified beneficiary, the beneficiary is the person so specified by the issuer or the person at the end of an uninterrupted series of endorsements. As regards dematerialised instruments, the presumed beneficiary is the beneficiary of the securities account where the instrument is registered.[571]

423. Against a holder in good faith, the issuer or drawer of a negotiable instrument may only have recourse to such legal objections or defences that are based on the content of the instrument itself. Accordingly, the issuer may not raise any objections based on the legal relationship between him and a previous holder of the instrument.[572]

424. There are no special provisions on the issue of individual instruments (e.g., promissory notes, bills of exchange, cheques or warehouse certificates). On the other hand, the issue – public or private – of instruments in a series is strictly regulated by Act No CXX of 2001 on capital markets (CM). Instruments in a material form are printed and may be overprinted. Printing may be done by specially authorised printers in accordance with formal and procedural requirements.[573] Dematerialised instruments are produced by opening a central securities account at the central securities depository (CSD),[574] crediting the account with the instruments

569. CC Art. 3:214; CM Art. 6 (3).
570. CC Art. 6:565 (4)–(5); CM Art. 6 (2).
571. CC Art. 6:566 (3)–(6).
572. CC Art. 6:567.
573. Government Decree No. 98/1995. (VIII.24.) on security provisions related to the production, handling and physical destruction of certain negotiable instruments.
574. Since 1994 KELER Central Depository Ltd. is designated to undertake central securities depository activities in Hungary. KELER was founded in 1993 and is now owned by the Hungarian National Bank and the Budapest Stock Exchange.

created and drawing up a printed certificate of issue for the whole series.[575] Instruments issued in a series in a material form may be later dematerialised. Hungarian regulations do not support the re-materialisation of dematerialised instruments, with the exception of dematerialised shares if a public company limited by shares is transformed into a private company or a private company limited by shares decides to switch from dematerialised shares to material ones.[576]

425. Negotiable instruments are by definition transferable even if the instrument is not explicitly drawn to order. Instruments issued to bearer may be transferred by a simple transfer of possession (delivery) based on a valid legal cause. For the transfer of instruments issued to a specified beneficiary an endorsement is also required. The endorsement is a written declaration by the transferor placed on the instrument or on a slip affixed thereto (allonge) expressing the intention of the transferor to transfer the instrument with or without naming the new beneficiary (in the latter case the endorsement is blank). Dematerialised instruments may be transferred by charging and crediting the appropriate securities accounts based on a valid legal cause. The transfer of an instrument transfers all rights embodied therein regardless of the fact whether the transferor was actually entitled to those rights. As an exception, the issuer of an instrument issued in a material form to a specific beneficiary may exclude the transfer of the instrument ('not to order') if so authorised by law; in this case the transfer has the legal effects of an ordinary assignment.[577] Even though in principle a valid legal cause is required for the transfer of instruments, the absence or invalidity of any previous underlying transaction does not affect a bona fides possessor's rights attached to the instrument.[578]

426. The beneficiary of a negotiable instrument may also change through inheritance, succession or the division of matrimonial property. In the case of an instrument drawn to bearer these changes do not require specific procedures. As regards instruments issued to a specific beneficiary the new beneficiary must verify his title. In case of printed shares the verification of title is registered on the back of the instrument and forms part of the series of endorsements. In case of dematerialised shares the securities account of the successor is credited and the account of the predecessor is charged (i.e., the account itself is not the object of succession).[579]

427. As regards maturity, negotiable instruments may be classified into four categories:

(1) short-term instruments (not more than one year): e.g., cheques, promissory notes and bills of exchange, commercial orders, treasury bills, warehouse certificates;

575. Government Decree No. 284/2001. (XII.26.) on security provisions related to the production and transfer of dematerialised instruments, and provisions on opening and management of securities accounts., central securities accounts and client accounts.
576. CM Art. 6 (5).
577. CC Art. 6:569.
578. CC Art. 6:566 (2).
579. CC Art. 3:221.

(2) medium-term instruments (one to five years): e.g., bonds, certificates of deposit;
(3) long-term instruments (over five years): e.g., bonds, mortgage bonds;
(4) without maturity: shares, asset certificates, convertible and converting bonds.

428. A negotiable instrument may be annulled if it becomes unidentifiable, is lost, destroyed or damaged to an extent that its content is no longer intelligible. The annulment procedure may be initiated by the last possessor of the instrument or by anyone who has rights or obligations under the instrument. The procedure is conducted by a notary public and starts with a public call for the presentation of the instrument in question or the provision of information as to its whereabouts. If the instrument is not presented or reliable information is not provided within six months (in the case of bills of exchange or cheques the deadline is one month) the notary public annuls the instrument. After annulment the legal effects of a negotiable instrument are no longer attached to the document even if it is subsequently recovered. Accordingly, rights attached to an annulled instrument may only be enforced through ordinary legal remedies available for the rights concerned.[580] The annulment procedure must be distinguished from the procedure of physical destruction of instruments that applies to expired, exhausted or replaced instruments. The process of physical destruction is also overseen by a notary public and may commence only after at least six months of expiry.[581]

§2. An Overview of Specific Negotiable Instruments

429. Even though the CC now does not require a specific legal basis for the recognition of negotiable instruments, in practice all negotiable instruments are regulated as to content, formalities and issuer. The table below provides an overview of the regulatory framework:

Instrument	*Legal Base*	*Nature of Rights or Legal Relationship Represented*	*Issuer*
Commercial order	Act No. XXXVII of 1875 on commerce, Articles 291–298	right to payment, delivery of instruments or fungible goods	not specified
Promissory note/ Bill of exchange	Geneva Convention of 1930[582]	right to payment	not specified

580. CC Art. 6:571; Arts 28–36 of Act No. XLV of 2008 on certain non-contentious proceedings conducted by notaries public.
581. Government Decree No. 98/1995. (VIII.24.) on security provisions related to the production, handling and physical destruction of certain negotiable instruments.

Instrument	*Legal Base*	*Nature of Rights or Legal Relationship Represented*	*Issuer*
Cheque	Geneva Convention of 1931[583]	right to payment	not specified
Bond	CM Article 12/B	right to payment (debt)	State (including foreign States), Hungarian National Bank, municipalities, international organisations, foreign organisations (if so authorised by their own legal system), economic associations with legal personality, branches of foreign economic associations, other entities authorised by special legislation
Treasury bill	Government Decree No. 286/ 2001. (XII.26.) on treasury bills	right to payment (debt)	State of Hungary

582. Convention Providing a Uniform Law for Bills of Exchange and Promissory Notes. Promulgated in Hungary by Decree-Act No. 1 of 1965; additional and implementing measures in Decree No. 1/1965. (I.24.) by the Minister of Justice.
583. Convention Providing a Uniform Law for Cheques. Promulgated in Hungary by Decree-Act No. 2 of 1965; additional and implementing measures in Decree No. 2/1965. (I.24.) by the Minister of Justice.

Instrument	*Legal Base*	*Nature of Rights or Legal Relationship Represented*	*Issuer*
Certificate of deposit	Government Decree No. 287/ 2001. (XII.26.) on certificates of deposit	right to payment (debt)	Hungarian National Bank, financial institutions, branches of foreign financial institutions
Mortgage bond	Act No. XXX of 1997 on mortgage banks and mortgage bonds	right to payment (debt)	mortgage banks
Investment certificate	Act No. XVI of 2014 on collective investment forms and their management	monetary claim and other rights established by the investment fund	investment funds
Share	CC Article 3:213	membership rights in the company	companies limited by shares
Warehouse certificate	Act No. XLVIII of 1996 on warehousing	property and related rights in the goods stored	warehouses
Bill of lading (maritime)	Brussels Convention of 1924[584]	right to dispose of the goods carried	carrier, master or agent of carrier
Bill of lading (inland waterway)	Budapest Convention of 2001[585]	right to dispose of the goods carried	carrier
Compensation ticket	Act No. XXV of 1991 on compensation tickets	compensation claim against the State of Hungary	State of Hungary

584. International Convention for the Unification of Certain Rules of Law Related to Bills of Lading. Promulgated in Hungary by Act No. VI of 1931. Hungary is also party to the 1978 UN Convention on the Carriage of Goods by Sea (Hamburg Convention) but it has not been promulgated yet.
585. Budapest Convention on the Contract for the Carriage of Goods by Inland Waterway (CMNI). Promulgated in Hungary by Act No. CXLI of 2005.

Instrument	*Legal Base*	*Nature of Rights or Legal Relationship Represented*	*Issuer*
Secondary instrument (depository receipt)	CM Article 24	right to dispose of and exercise the rights related to the primary instruments deposited	CSD, authorised investment service provider
Asset certificate	Council of Ministers Decree No. 94/1988 (XII.22) on asset certificates	right to dividend (and to the principal in case of winding up)	economic associations (until 15 March 1993)

§3. Selected Specific Negotiable Instruments

I. Promissory Notes and Bills of Exchange

430. Promissory notes (*saját váltó*) and bills of exchange (*idegen váltó*) were widely used in Hungary before the mid-1940s both in domestic and international transactions but almost completely disappeared by the 1950s. They reappeared first in the second half of the 1960s but did not gain real significance again until the second half of the 1980s when economic actors started using them in the absence of other recognised and regulated negotiable instruments. Promissory notes and bills of exchange, however, never managed to regain their previous popularity due to most commercial banks' rather cautious approach to discounting them.

431. A bill of exchange contains:

- the term 'bill of exchange' inserted in the body of the instrument and expressed in the language employed in drawing up the instrument;
- an unconditional order to pay a determinate sum of money;
- the name of the person who is to pay (drawee);
- a statement of the time of payment;
- a statement of the place where payment is to be made;
- the name of the. person to whom or to whose order payment is to be made;
- statement of the date and of the place where the bill is issued;
- the signature of the person who issues the bill (drawer).

432. An instrument in which any of the requirements mentioned in the preceding article is wanting is invalid as a bill of exchange, except in certain specified cases.

433. When a bill of exchange is payable at sight, or at a fixed period after sight, the drawer may stipulate that the sum payable shall bear interest. In the case of any other bill of exchange, this stipulation is deemed not to be written. The rate of interest must be specified in the bill.

434. The drawer guarantees both acceptance and payment. He may release himself from guaranteeing acceptance; every stipulation by which he releases himself from the guarantee of payment is deemed not to be written.

435. Every bill of exchange, even if not expressly drawn to order, may be transferred by means of endorsement. When the drawer has inserted in a bill of exchange the words 'not to order' (*nem rendeletre*) or an equivalent expression, the instrument can only be transferred according to the form, and with the effects of an ordinary assignment. An endorsement must be unconditional. A partial endorsement is null and void. An endorsement must be written on the bill of exchange or on a slip affixed thereto and must be signed by the endorser. The endorsement may leave the beneficiary unspecified or may consist simply of the signature of the endorser (endorsement in blank). An endorsement transfers all the rights arising out of a bill of exchange. In the absence of any contrary stipulation, the endorser guarantees acceptance and payment but may prohibit any further endorsement.

436. Until maturity, a bill of exchange may be presented to the drawee for acceptance at his domicile, either by the holder or by a person who is merely in possession of the bill. An acceptance is written on the bill of exchange. It is expressed by the word 'accepted' (*elfogadom*) or any other equivalent term. It is signed by the drawee. The simple signature of the drawee on the face of the bill constitutes an acceptance. An acceptance is unconditional, but the drawee may restrict it to part of the sum payable. By accepting, the drawee undertakes to pay the bill of exchange at its maturity. In default of payment, the holder has a direct action on the bill of exchange against the acceptor.

437. Payment of a bill of exchange may be guaranteed by an 'aval' (*váltókezesség*) as to the whole or part of its amount.

438. It is expressed by the words 'good as aval' (*kezességet vállalok*) or by any other equivalent formula. It is signed by the giver of the 'aval'. It is deemed to be constituted by the mere signature of the giver of the 'aval' placed on the face of the bill, except in the case of the signature of the drawee or of the drawer. An 'aval' must specify for whose account it is given. In default of this, it is deemed to be given for the drawer. The giver of an 'aval' is bound in the same manner as the person for whom he has become guarantor.

439. A bill of exchange may be drawn payable at sight, at a fixed period after sight, at a fixed period after date or at a fixed date. Bills of exchange at other maturities or payable by instalments are null and void. A bill of exchange at sight is payable on presentment within a year of its date.

440. At maturity the holder may exercise his right of recourse against the endorsers, the drawer and the other parties liable if payment has not been made. The holder may exercise his right of recourse even before maturity if there has been total or partial refusal to accept or in the event of the bankruptcy of the drawee, whether he has accepted or not, or in the event of the bankruptcy of the drawer of a non-acceptable bill. Default of acceptance or of payment must be evidenced by an authentic act (protest, *óvás*). Protest for non-acceptance dispenses with presentment for payment and protest for non-payment.

441. All drawers, acceptors, endorsers or guarantors by 'aval' of a bill of exchange are jointly and severally liable to the holder. The holder has the right of proceeding against all these persons individually or collectively without being required to observe the order in which they have become bound. The same right is possessed by any person signing the bill who has taken it up and paid it. Proceedings against one of the parties liable do not prevent proceedings against the others, even though they may be subsequent to the party first proceeded against.

442. The holder may recover from the person against whom he exercises his right of recourse:

- the amount of the unaccepted or unpaid bill of exchange with interest, if interest has been stipulated for;
- interest at the rate of 6% from the date of maturity;
- the expenses of protest and of the notices given as well as other expenses;
- commission at the rate of 3%.

443. If the right of recourse is exercised before maturity, the amount of the bill shall be subject to a discount.

444. Actions by endorsers against each other and against the drawer are barred after six months, reckoned from the day when the endorser took up and paid the bill or from the day when he himself was sued. The CP provides for special deadlines and shortened periods for the disposal of claims arising from bills of exchange.[586]

445. Rules related to bills of exchange are applicable to promissory notes as well with the appropriate modifications reflecting the nature of the instrument.

II. Cheques

446. A valid cheque contains the term 'cheque' (*csekk*) inserted in the body of the instrument, an unconditional order to pay a determinate sum of money, the name of the person who is to pay (drawee), a statement of the place where payment is to be made, a statement of the date when and the place where the cheque is drawn, and the signature of the person who draws the cheque (drawer).

586. CP Arts 125 (2), (4); 217 (4), 234 (1).

447. A cheque must be drawn on a banker holding funds at the disposal of the drawer and in conformity with an agreement, express or implied, whereby the drawer is entitled to dispose of those funds by cheque. Nevertheless, if these provisions are not complied with, the instrument is still valid as a cheque. A cheque may be made payable to a specified person with or without the express clause 'to order' ('*rendeletére*'), or 'not to order' ('*nem rendeletre*') or to bearer. Any stipulation concerning interest which may be embodied in the cheque shall be disregarded.

448. A cheque made payable to a specified person may be transferred by means of endorsement. A cheque made payable to a specified person, in which the words 'not to order' or any equivalent expression have been inserted, can only be transferred according to the form and with the effects of an ordinary assignment. An endorsement must be unconditional. A partial endorsement is null and void. An endorsement must be written on the cheque or on a slip affixed thereto, and signed by the endorser. The endorsement may leave the beneficiary unspecified or may consist simply of the signature of the endorser (endorsement in blank). An endorsement transfers all the rights arising out of a cheque. If the endorsement is in blank, the holder may fill up the blank either with his own name or with the name of some other person; re-endorse the cheque in blank or to some other person or transfer the cheque to a third person without filling up the blank and without endorsing it. The endorser may prohibit further endorsement.

449. The drawer and the endorser guarantee payment. Payment of a cheque may also be guaranteed by an 'aval' (*csekk-kezesség*) as to the whole or part of its amount. It is expressed by the words 'good as aval' ('*kezességet vállalok*'), or by any other equivalent formula. It is signed by the giver of the 'aval'. It is deemed to be constituted by the mere signature of the giver of the 'aval', placed on the face of the cheque, except in the case of the signature of the drawer. An 'aval' must specify for whose account it is given. In default of this, it is deemed to be given for the drawer. The giver of an 'aval' is bound in the same manner as the person for whom he has become guarantor.

450. A cheque is payable at sight. A cheque payable in the country in which it was issued must be presented for payment within eight days. A cheque issued in a country other than that in which it is payable must be presented within a period of twenty days or of seventy days, according as to whether the place of issue and the place of payment are situated respectively in the same continent or in different continents.

451. The countermand of a cheque only takes effect after the expiration of the limit of time for presentment. If a cheque has not been countermanded, the drawee may pay it even after the expiration of the time limit. Neither the death of the drawer nor his incapacity taking place after the issue of the cheque shall have any effect as regards the cheque.

452. The holder may exercise his right of recourse against the endorsers, the drawer and the other parties liable if the cheque on presentment in due time is not paid, and if the refusal to pay is evidenced by a formal instrument (protest, *óvás*), by a declaration dated and written by the drawee on the cheque and specifying the day of presentment, or by a dated declaration made by a clearinghouse, stating that the cheque has been delivered in due time and has not been paid. The protest or equivalent declaration must be made before the expiration of the limit of time for presentment. In Hungary, protest is taken up by a notary public.

453. All the persons liable on a cheque are jointly and severally bound to the holder. The holder has the right to proceed against all these persons individually or collectively without being compelled to observe the order in which they have become bound. The same right is possessed by any person signing the cheque who has taken it up and paid it. Proceedings against one of the parties liable do not prevent proceedings against the others, even though such other parties may be subsequent to the party first proceeded against.

454. The holder may claim from the party against whom he exercises his right of recourse:

- the unpaid amount of the cheque;
- interest at the rate of 6% as from the date of presentment;
- the expenses of the protest or equivalent declaration, and of the notices given as well as other expenses;
- cheque commission at the rate of 3%.

455. Actions of recourse by the holder against the endorsers, the drawer and the other parties liable are barred after six months as from the expiration of the limit of time fixed for presentment. Actions of recourse by the different parties liable for the payment of a cheque against other such parties are barred after six months as from the day on which the party liable has paid the cheque or the day on which he was sued thereon.

456. In Hungary, documents used for postal cash transfer (‘*készpénzátutalási megbízás*’) or postal invoice settlement (‘*postai számlabefizetési megbízás*’) are also commonly referred to as cheques. These documents, however, are not cheques, and they are not under the scope of regulations applicable for cheques.

III. Shares

457. For shares (*részvény*) *see* paragraphs 76–180 in §2 (Partnerships and Corporations) of Chapter 2 (The economic operators).

IV. Warehouse Certificates

458. Warehouse certificates (*közraktári jegy*) are negotiable instruments drawn to order by a warehouse certifying the receipt of goods (chattel excluding cash or negotiable instruments) under a warehousing contract and representing ownership and related rights attached to the goods stored. Warehouse certificates are individual instruments produced in a material form by removing a coupon from the warehouse inventory. The coupon consists of two parts: a *cedule* (*árujegy*) and a warrant (*zálogjegy*) which are identical in content and may be separated. The certificate contains:

- the terms 'warehouse certificate', '*cedule*' and 'warrant';
- the business name of the warehouse;
- the serial number of the inventory;
- the name and seat (address) of the depositor;
- the identification, quality, quantity and value of goods deposited;
- the fee of warehousing and other related services;
- the period of warehousing with a specific expiry date;
- the place of storage;
- the place of issue and signature by a representative of the warehouse.

459. A warehousing contract may only be concluded for a definite period and for a maximum of one year. After the expiry of the contract the parties may conclude a new contract by cancelling the warehouse certificate and issuing a new one. A warehouse certificate based on a void warehousing contract is also void. However, the invalidity of a warehousing contract cannot be held against the holder of a warehouse certificate in good faith. In such a case, the warehouse shall call on the depositor to collect the goods within thirty days.

460. The goods deposited may only be reclaimed by a holder of both the *cedule* and the warrant. The warrant may be transferred by endorsement with or without the *cedule*. The joint endorsement of the *cedule* and the warrant transfers the unburdened right to dispose of the goods. A separate endorsement of the warrant makes the goods stored eligible as collateral for loans. In this case the first endorsement on the back shall contain:

- the name, seat and account number of the creditor;
- the payment obligation at expiry including interest (payment obligation cannot exceed the value indicated on the warehouse certificate);
- the deadline for payment (maturity date) which is not later than one year after the expiry of the warehouse certificate;[587]
- the name and address of the first endorser (debtor).

587. Authorised warehouses may also offer loans themselves against the deposited goods as collateral. In such cases the amount of the loan cannot exceed two-third of the value indicated on the warehouse certificate and the maturity date cannot be later than the expiry of the warehouse certificate.

461. The content of the first endorsement of the warrant must also be reproduced in the inventory and on the *cedule*.

462. The refusal to pay the debt in due time must be evidenced by a protest (*óvás*) at a notary public or by a declaration of the first endorser. Protest is a precondition of the recourse against previous endorsers if the holder of the warrant still has outstanding claims after the forced sale of the goods deposited. Previous endorsers are jointly and severally liable. Protest, however, is not a precondition of the forced sale of the goods deposited. The forced sale of the goods may be requested by the holder of the warrant after three days of maturity. Forced sale is conducted through the BSE or by auction.

463. The *cedule* may also be endorsed separately. In this case the *cedule* in itself represents a right to dispose of the goods burdened with the rights of the holder of the warrant. The holder of the *cedule* is not entitled to reclaim the goods without holding the warrant as well. If the holder of the warrant cannot be located or there is a disagreement as to the conditions of payment the holder of the *cedule* may reclaim the goods by depositing the payment and the warehouse fee at the warehouse.

464. Actions of recourse by the holder of the warrant against the endorsers are barred after one year as from the date of protest. Actions of recourse by the endorser against previous endorsers are barred after six months as from the day on which the party liable has paid the holder of the warrant. Claims arising out of warehouse certificates are disposed of according to the CP under the rules applicable for bills of exchange.

465. Warehouses are liable for all damages in the goods deposited except for force majeure and for reasons attributable to the depositor. Warehouses are not required to verify ownership and identity of the depositor. Warehouses have a lien on the goods stored covering the warehouse fee. Warehouses are supervised by the Warehousing Department of the Hungarian Trade Licensing Office.

V. Bonds

466. Bonds (*kötvény*) were reintroduced into the Hungarian legal system in 1982. The definition and basic characteristics of the instrument are now included in CM, further detailed regulations can be found in a separate government decree.[588] Under the current regulations, bonds can only be issued to a specific beneficiary (not to bearer) by a debtor who undertakes to pay the value indicated on the instrument together with interest and accessories at a time and in a way indicated on the bond. Since 2013, bonds can be issued with or without maturity; the latter option is applicable in the case of convertible or converting bonds (*see* below). Bonds usually bear

588. Government Decree No. 285/2001. (XII.26.) on bonds.

interest that can be fixed or variable; but the debtor may undertake to provide other benefits beside or instead of interest (e.g., dividend, option to underwrite shares).

467. The bond must contain:

- a reference to the authorisation to issue;
- the identification of the bond and the objectives of the issue;
- the face value, code and serial number of the bond;
- the name of the issuer;
- the name and details of the beneficiary;
- restrictions on endorsement (if applicable);
- maturity of the bond (if applicable), time and conditions of interest payment and reimbursement;
- guarantees and security (if applicable);
- place and date of issue;
- signature of issuer.

468. Bonds are negotiable by endorsement however the transfer of bonds may be limited or excluded by the issuer or by law. An endorsement must be unconditional. A partial endorsement is null and void. The debt of the issuer represented by the bond is not secured unless explicitly provided otherwise; in case of default the creditor must seek legal remedy at courts of justice. In an insolvency proceeding, these claims are not privileged claims even if the beneficiary is a private individual. There is no limitation period for claims based on bonds.

469. The CC provides for special bonds that may be issued by companies limited by shares. Convertible bonds may be converted into shares upon request by the creditor or a decision by the board of directors of the company. Converting bonds are automatically converted into shares if predetermined conditions for conversion are met.[589] The issue of convertible or converting bonds is practically a conditional increase of the company's capital and is limited in value to 50% of its capital. Bonds providing an option for the creditor to underwrite shares of the company may also be issued.[590] The option may be exercised if the company decides to increase its capital by issuing shares; in this case beneficiaries of optional bonds have priority. Unlike convertible or converting bonds, optional bonds themselves are not converted into shares, they remain bonds until maturity.

VI. Treasury Bills

470. Treasury bills (*kincstárjegy*) are special bonds issued by the State with a maturity period not exceeding one year. A treasury bill may be interest bearing on

589. CC Art. 3:303–3:305.
590. CC Art. 3:297.

a non-interest bearing instrument. In the latter case the nominal value of the treasury bill is paid upon maturity. In other aspects the regulations applicable to bonds apply to treasury bills as well.

VII. Mortgage Bonds

471. Mortgage bonds (*jelzáloglevél*) may be issued by mortgage banks[591] in order to finance mortgage loans. In most aspects the regulations applicable to bonds apply to mortgage bonds as well. Mortgage bonds purchased by the issuing mortgage bank may not be reissued and must be cancelled. In case of insolvency of the mortgage bank special rules apply in order to provide legal protection for mortgage bond creditors and ensure the continuity of outstanding mortgage loans:

- payment obligations under mortgage bonds do not become due at the commencement of the insolvency proceedings;
- payment obligations under mortgage bonds are honoured independently of the insolvency proceedings and according to the terms of the mortgage bond;
- the collateral provided for mortgage bonds is not considered as part of the mortgage bank's assets for the purposes of the insolvency proceedings and may only be used to honour obligations under mortgage bonds.

VIII. Certificates of Deposit

472. Certificates of deposit (*letéti jegy*) are issued to specific beneficiaries and represent a right to payment of the nominal value of the instrument and interest at a time and in a way indicated on the certificate. The maturity period of the instrument may not exceed three years. The certificate contains:

- the name of the issuer;
- value, code and serial number of the instrument;
- name and details of the beneficiary;
- interest, payment and reimbursement conditions;
- place and date of issue;
- signature of the issuer.

473. Certificates of deposit are negotiable by endorsement. An endorsement must be unconditional. A partial endorsement is null and void. The limitation period for claims based on certificates of deposit is ten years from maturity.

591. Mortgage banks (*jelzálog-hitelintézet*) are financial institutions specialised in offering loans secured by mortgage established on real estate properties. Besides mortgage bonds, mortgage banks may finance loans by bonds or certificates of deposit as well but may not accept bank deposits and may offer only a limited variety of financial services.

IX. Compensation Tickets

474. Compensation tickets (*kárpótlási jegy*) are negotiable instruments issued to bearer by the State representing compensation claims against the State for wrongs committed under certain specified legislative and executive acts in the period starting from 1 May 1939. Compensation tickets bore interest in the period between 10 August 1991 and 31 December 1994 at the rate of 75% of the central bank's basic interest rate. The bearer was, however, not entitled to the payment of the interest; it was added to the face value of the compensation ticket.

475. Compensation tickets could be used for acquisition of:

- state property through privatisation;
- agricultural land (until 2016);[592]
- housing units ceded by the State to municipalities; and
- life annuity against the value of compensation tickets.

476. The State has issued compensation tickets in the value of over HUF 160 billion. There are still outstanding unused or unclaimed compensation tickets in the value of around HUF 2.9 billion. However, the market for compensation tickets is practically defunct because the State has not offered any property for sale in exchange for compensation tickets for more than a decade.

592. This possibility was cancelled by Act No. CII of 2016 as of 20 Oct. 2016.

Chapter 8. Stock and Commodity Exchanges

§1. History

477. The first stock exchange in Budapest started its activities in 1864 trading only in negotiable instruments.[593] Four years later it acquired the Grain Hall – the centre of grain exchange at the time – and continued its business under the name of Budapest Commodity and Stock Exchange (BCSE). Trade in negotiable instruments didn't really thrive until 1872 and has been seriously affected by the panic of 1873 and has not recovered for more than a decade. Between 1890 and 1914 BCSE experienced its golden age: it was Europe's leading grain exchange and conducted over 1 million transactions annually in 500 listed negotiable instruments.

478. The outbreak of World War I resulted in the closure of BCSE; this, however, could not stop trading itself. BCSE experienced difficult times after reopening due to hyperinflation that was ended by the introduction of the new currency (*pengő*) in 1925 and later by the collapse of the banking system in Europe in 1931. BCSE recovered only by 1934 and peaked in 1936. It continued trading until December 1944 when the siege of Budapest began. BCSE officially reopened in August 1946 after the introduction of yet another new currency (*forint*, HUF) but listed prices kept dramatically falling because bonds issued in the old currency were not honoured and listed companies didn't pay any dividends due to wartime losses. BCSE was finally closed in 1948 after a sweeping wave of nationalisation and its assets were taken over by the Hungarian State.

479. The BSE was reorganised in 1990 and started trading in a single listed share. In the following years, it played an important role in the privatisation of a number of leading State-owned enterprises. BSE started trading in derivatives in 1995 and switched to completely electronic trading in 1999. The Budapest Commodity Exchange (BCE) was reorganised in 1989 and by 1995 it has grown into one of the top forty global commodity exchanges. In 2005, its markets were integrated into BSE and BCE ceased its activities the following year.

480. BSE is currently operating as a private company limited by shares. Since 2015, its majority and controlling shareholder has been the Hungarian National Bank (81.35% – as of 30 November 2017) with KBC Securities (Hungarian branch) being the biggest minority stakeholder with 5.2% of the shares.

§2. Performance of BSE

481. BSE measures stock market trends using three indexes: BUX, BUMIX and CETOP20. BUX measures the performance of the equities prime market's twelve

593. T. Korányi G. & N. Szeles, *Tőzsde születik 1864–1990 (Birth of an Exchange 1864 – 1990)*, BÉT: Budapest, 2007.

to twenty-five largest Hungarian companies in terms of order book volume and market capitalization. BUMIX is a stock market index composed of twelve to twenty-five small and medium-sized companies listed on BSE. CETOP20 is a stock market index which reflects the performance of the companies with the biggest market value and turnover in the Central European region.

482. The following chart shows BUX maximum and minimum values in the years 2013–2018:[594]

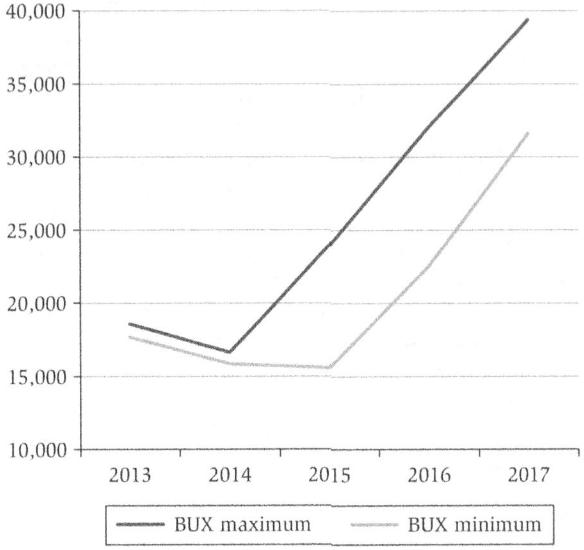

§3. REGULATION OF EXCHANGE MARKET OPERATIONS

483. Exchange market operations are activities involving the buying and selling of standardised exchange market instruments in an organised fashion. Exchange market operations may only be conducted via exchanges. On the other hand, exchanges may only engage in exchange market operations and closely related activities (e.g., educational, publication, data provision and information technology services).[595]

484. According to Act CXI of 1996 on the issue of securities, investment services and the stock exchange (Securities Act, SA) and the Capital Market Act (CM) a stock exchange may be established in the form of a company limited by shares holding dematerialized shares only with the participation of at least fifteen founding

594. *Source of data*: www.bet.hu.
595. CM Arts 297–298.

members or as a branch of a foreign exchange. The subscribed capital of the company must be at least HUF 150 million for an exchange trading in commodities, foreign currencies and forward interest-rate agreements only and at least HUF 500 million for an exchange trading in other instruments as well.[596]

485. The establishment of an exchange requires the prior authorization (license to establish) of the regulatory authority, i.e., the Hungarian National Bank. The commencement of activities by the exchange requires further authorization (licence to operate) from the regulatory authority. Such authorization may be granted if:

- non-discriminative (neutral) access is provided to the trading system;
- personal, material and security requirements for the exchange activities are provided;
- financial settlement of transactions is provided through an agreement with a clearinghouse or a central counterparty (CCP);
- the exchange has a business plan for a period of at least three years that substantiates its stable and reliable operation;
- the exchange has adopted and obtained approval for the required internal regulations;
- the exchange has a liability insurance coverage in the value of at least HUF 100 million per claim and HUF 150 million per annum.[597]

486. There is no legal limitation as to the share of a member in the subscribed capital of the exchange. However, prior authorization by the regulatory authority is required if a member's share reaches the threshold of 33%, 50%, 66%, 75% or 100%. The authority may refuse to give its assent if:

- the member's activity or influence endangers the independent, reliable and prudent exercise of ownership rights; or
- the member's activities, business relations or ownership structure obstructs regulatory oversight.[598]

487. Detailed rules of incompatibility apply as to employment and investment by the exchange. An employee of the exchange:

- may not hold an executive or administrative position at a member of the exchange or an exchange trader;
- may not hold direct or indirect shares in an exchange trader;
- may not hold an executive or administrative position at the issuer of a security listed at the exchange.[599]

596. CM Art. 299, SA Art. 175.
597. CM Art. 303.
598. CM Arts 307–310.
599. CM Art. 311.

488. The exchange may not invest in any of the exchange instruments listed by the exchange except for government papers and shares in clearing houses or CCPs. The exchange may not invest in a security issued by its members having at least 33% of the shares in the exchange.[600]

489. Even though the number of traders may not be limited, trading on the exchange is reserved for exchange traders who:

- are licensed by the regulatory authority for the trade of one or more instruments;
- conclude a contract with the exchange undertaking to comply with the internal regulations of the exchange;
- conclude an agreement with a clearinghouse or CCP for the settlement of transactions.[601]

490. An exchange transaction is a contract concluded by an exchange trader on the exchange market for the instruments and in the manner provided for by the internal regulations of the exchange. An exchange transaction may be:

- a spot transaction: an exchange transaction without specified modalities and date of settlement;
- a futures (forward) transaction: an exchange transaction that stipulates delivery at a specified future date;
- an option transaction: an exchange transaction where a person may exercise the unilateral right to sell (put option) or buy (call option) an instrument at the price and in the period (max. five years) agreed in exchange for an option premium;
- or the combination of the above.[602]

491. An exchange transaction is concluded if all the relevant data and information are recorded according to the internal regulations of the exchange and – in case of futures and option transactions – is registered and confirmed by the clearinghouse.[603]

492. Trade of a specific instrument may be suspended by the representative of the exchange for a maximum of ten trading days if orderly, transparent and fair trading cannot be guaranteed, there is a possibility that the issuer violates rules on information and disclosure or settlement of the transactions is not guaranteed. Prior authorisation of the regulatory authority is required for a suspension of over three trading days.

493. Trade of specific types of instruments or all trading activities may be suspended by the representative of the exchange for a maximum of one trading day

600. CM Art. 330.
601. CM Art. 312.
602. CM Arts 320–322.
603. CM Art. 319 (3).

with immediate notice to the regulatory authority if trade would endanger the legitimate interest of investors, market balance or the operation of the exchange. A suspension of thirty trading days may be ordered in similar cases by the Board of the exchange or the regulatory authority. A suspension of all trading activities for over ten trading days may be ordered with the approval of the Minister for National Economy only.[604]

494. Operations of the exchange are public and the exchange must allow reasonable access to data in order to keep exchange traders and investors informed. The exchange may adopt internal rules on delayed access to information in certain cases. The exchange may charge a fee for the provision of information on transactions within twenty minutes.[605]

§4. CSD and CCP

495. The rules on CSDs and CCPs are provided by the relevant EU regulations.[606] A CSD is a legal person that operates a securities settlement system. A CCP is a legal person that interposes itself between the counterparties to the contracts traded on one or more financial markets, becoming the buyer to every seller and the seller to every buyer.

496. In Hungary, CSD and CCPs are licensed by the Hungarian National Bank. These functions are performed by KELER CSD Zrt. and KELER CCP Zrt. respectively.

604. CM Arts 325–329.
605. CM Art. 331.
606. Regulation 909/2014/EU of the European Parliament and of the Council of 23 Jul. 2014. on improving securities settlement in the European Union and on central securities depositories and amending Directives 98/26/EC and 2014/65/EU and Regulation (EU) No. 236/2012; Regulation 648/2012/EU of the European Parliament and of the Council of 4 Jul. 2012. On OTC derivatives, central counterparties and trade repositories.

Chapter 9. Commercial Contracts

§1. General Principles of Contract Law

497. In the academic legal literature there are two approaches regarding the *usage of the general principles of private law*:

- the general principles are conductive to the interpretation of regulation of private law for the judges;
- the general principles may fill the gaps of legislation (subsidiary and directly applicable) and can help to decide upon legal disputes.[607]

498. There are *leading motives* in the Hungarian private law: rationality, reasonability, justice, legal certainty and equity;[608] these – as legal values – conduct the judges at sentencing.

499. The Hungarian Code Civil governs the property and personal relations of persons under the principle of interdependence and the principle of equality. The provisions of the Hungarian Civil Code shall be interpreted in accordance with the constitutional order of Hungary and the legislation relating to civil law shall be explained in accordance with the provisions of the Hungarian Civil Code.[609]

500. Principle of good faith and fair dealing (Treu und Glauben): In exercising rights and in fulfilling obligations the requirements of good faith and fair dealing shall be observed. The requirements of good faith and fair dealing shall be considered breached when a party's exercise of rights is contradictory to his previous actions which the other party had reason to rely on.[610]

501. Principle of reasonable conduct: Unless otherwise provided for by the Hungarian Civil Code, in civil law any reference to what can be expected of or by a person, or in a particular situation, is a reference to what can reasonably be expected. A person may not rely, in support of his claim, on an unlawful act he has committed ('attributability'). A person who himself engaged in an unlawful act may also rely on the wrongful act committed by others.[611]

502. Prohibition of abuse of rights: Abuse of rights is prohibited by law; where the abuse of a right is manifested in the repudiation of a statement required by law and this conduct does injury to an overriding public interest or a private interest in

607. Á. Boóc, *General Principles of the Hungarian Private Law,* In: Business Law in Hungary, ed. I. Sándor, Budapest: Patrocinium, 2016, 115.
608. Boóc, *supra* n. 607, 116–117.
609. Section 1:1 and 1:2 CC.
610. Section 1:3 CC.; BH 1995. 216.
611. Section 1:4 CC.; BH 2000. 114.

cases of exceptional circumstances, the court is entitled to substitute its judgment for the party's legal statement, provided there is no other way of averting the injury.[612]

503. Freedom of contract: The parties are free to conclude a contract, to choose the other party and to determine the contents of the contract. The parties may depart from the provisions relating to their rights and obligations with mutual consent, unless prohibited by the Hungarian Civil Code.[613]

504. Presumption of reciprocity: Unless the contract or the applicable circumstances expressly indicate otherwise, a consideration is due for services set forth in the contract.[614]

505. Duty to cooperate and communicate information: The parties shall be required to cooperate during preliminary negotiations, at the time of the conclusion and termination, and during the life of the contract, and shall be duty bound to communicate information to each other on circumstances relevant to the contract. The party may not allege the infringement of the duty to provide information with respect to rights, facts and circumstances of which he was aware, or should have known from a public register or any other source. If the contract is concluded, the party who breaches the obligations for cooperation and communication shall be subject to liability for damages for loss caused by non-performance of an obligation to the other party. If conclusion of the contract fails, the parties shall not be liable for payment of compensation. If the contract is not concluded, the party who breaches the obligation for cooperation and communication during preliminary negotiations shall be subject to liability for damages in accordance with the general provisions of non-contractual liability.[615]

506. Interpretation of contracts: The contract terms and statements are to be interpreted in accordance with the contract as a whole. If the meaning of a standard contract term or the contents of the contract term which has not been individually negotiated cannot be clearly established by the application of the aforementioned principle for the interpretation of the legal statement, the interpretation that is more favourable to the party entering into a contract with the person imposing such contract term shall prevail. In connection with a contract that involves a consumer and a business party, this provision shall also apply to the interpretation of any contract term; this provision shall not apply to actions brought in the public interest.[616]

612. Section 1:5 CC.; EBH 1999. 92.
613. Section 6:59 CC.
614. Section 6:61 CC.
615. Section 6:62 CC.
616. Section 6:86 CC.; BH 1996. 485.

§2. Sale of Goods

507. The title-transfer contracts of Hungarian Civil Code are the sales contract, the exchange contract and the contract of gift. The sales contract is one of the most in use type of contract in everyday life.

508. *Sales contract* means any contract under which the seller undertakes to transfer the ownership of a thing to the buyer, and the buyer undertakes to pay the price thereof, and to take possession of the thing.[617]

509. If the object of the sales contract is a *real estate property*, in addition to transferring ownership the seller shall also transfer possession of the thing and the contract shall be executed in writing.[618]

510. The provisions relating to the sale of things shall also apply to contracts for commitments for the transfer for valuable consideration of a *right or claim*.[619]

511. The seller shall be entitled to *retain title of ownership* until the purchase price is paid in full. The agreement on the retention of title shall be executed in writing. In the case of retention of title relating to real estate property, the seller shall have it recorded in the real estate register in the form of an entry showing the fact of retention of title and the name of the buyer. In the case of retention of title relating to movable property, the seller shall have it registered in the collateral register showing the fact of retention of title and the name of the buyer, or in the relevant registry if ownership of the movable property is recorded in a public register and if hypothecation of the thing is to be registered in the proper registry by law. In the absence of registration:

- where ownership of a movable property is acquired from the buyer for consideration in good faith, the transferee shall acquire ownership by way of transfer;
- the lien established by the buyer on the movable property for a third party shall come into existence even if the buyer has no right of disposition.[620]

512. If the seller *transfers possession of the real estate property* which is the subject of the sale to the buyer *before the registration of ownership in the real estate register*, the buyer shall, as of the date of taking possession, collect the proceeds of the thing, and shall, furthermore, be liable for its encumbrances and for the damages for which no indemnification can be demanded from anyone.[621]

513. The seller shall bear all of the *costs* related to the transfer of possession and the correction of the status recorded in the real estate register. The costs of taking

617. Section 6:215 (1).
618. Section 6:215 (2).
619. Section 6:215 (3).
620. Section 6:216 CC.
621. Section 6:217 CC.

possession of the thing and the costs of registering the change in ownership in the real estate register shall be covered by the buyer.[622]

514. The *types of sales contract* are the forward transaction for the sale of things defined by type and quantity, the sales contract for the supply of own produced agricultural goods and the sales contract for the supply of agricultural goods produced with the buyer's involvement.

515. *Forward transactions for the sale of things defined by type and quantity*: If the seller undertakes an obligation for the supply in the future of things defined by type and quantity, and the parties stipulate the range of discrepancy as to quantity by which the seller may deviate from the quantity fixed in the contract to either direction, the buyer shall pay the purchase price for the quantity actually supplied. If the seller supplies below the minimum prescribed quantity, the consequences for such non-performance shall be determined in due account of the contracted quantity. If the seller undertakes an obligation for the supply of things defined by type and quantity in the future, the buyer shall have the right to withdraw from the contract until such time as the seller's offer for the delivery of supplies; if the seller is to perform the contract in segments, and already offered to deliver a part of the services contracted, the buyer shall have the right to withdraw from the contract with respect to the part not yet offered. The buyer shall be held liable for damages caused to the seller through exercising the right of withdrawal or the right to terminate.[623]

516. *Sales contracts for the supply of own produced agricultural goods*: If the seller undertakes an obligation for the supply of agricultural goods and/or produce of his own production or livestock that he himself has raised at a future date, he shall be entitled to perform 10% below the quantity stipulated in the contract. The seller shall also be entitled to effect performance of the contract before the stipulated delivery date, provided that the buyer is notified in advance of commencement of performance while ample time is provided to him to make the necessary preparations.[624]

517. *Sales contracts for the supply of agricultural goods produced with the buyer's involvement*: If the seller undertakes an obligation for the supply of agricultural goods and/or produce of his own production or livestock that he himself has raised at a future date, and based on the parties' agreement the buyer is required to provide assistance to facilitate performance, and to provide information to the seller in that context, the seller shall cooperate in the provision of such service by following the instructions communicated. The seller shall pay the contracted price for the buyer's service provided to facilitate performance, and shall repay the part of any production advance received from the buyer that is not covered by the purchase price even if the production result is insufficient to cover such payments.[625]

622. Section 6:218 CC.
623. Section 6:231 CC.
624. Section 6:232 CC.
625. Section 6:233 CC.

518. The *special modes of sale* are the right of pre-emption, the repurchase right, the purchase option and right to sell, the hire purchase, the purchase upon delivery subject to inspection, the purchase upon delivery subject to testing and the purchase by sample.

519. Right of pre-emption: If an owner grants a right of pre-emption to a specific thing in an agreement and wishes to sell the thing by accepting the offer of a third party, the person who has the right of pre-emption shall be entitled to buy the thing under the conditions fixed in the offer, preceding the third party. If the owner grants consecutive rights of pre-emption to more than one person for the same thing, these persons shall be able to exercise their rights in the sequence in which their rights of pre-emption were established.[626]

520. Repurchase right: If at the time of conclusion of the sales contract the buyer grants the option for the seller to repurchase the thing sold by agreement of the parties, the seller may purchase the thing by way of a statement made to the buyer. The parties shall fix the repurchase price in the agreement on granting the repurchase option. Failing this, the holder of the option shall be able to repurchase the thing at the market value prevailing at the time of exercising the option to repurchase.[627]

521. Purchase option and right to sell: If the owner establishes the right to purchase a specific thing under contract, the holder of such option shall be entitled to buy the thing with a unilateral statement, at the price fixed in the contract. If the owner acquires the right to sell a specific thing under contract, he shall be entitled to sell the thing with a unilateral statement to the obligor of the option to sell, at the price fixed in the contract.[628]

522. Contracts relating to pre-emption rights, repurchase rights, purchase options and sell options shall be executed in writing. If a right of pre-emption, repurchase right, purchase option or sell option established on a real estate property under contract is recorded in the real estate register, and a right of pre-emption, repurchase right, purchase option or sell option established on a movable property shown in a public register is registered in the public register, it shall affect everybody who acquires any right on such a thing following such registration. The provisions on the right of pre-emption, repurchase right, purchase option or sell option shall also apply to statutory rights of pre-emption, repurchase rights, purchase options or sell options. Statutory rights of pre-emption, repurchase rights, purchase options or sell options shall precede contractual rights of pre-emption, repurchase rights, purchase options or sell options. The obligor of repurchase right, right to purchase or right to sell shall refrain from all such conducts as to hinder or prevent the

626. Section 6:221 CC.
627. Section 6:224 CC.
628. Section 6:225 CC.

exercise of the repurchase right, right to purchase or right to sell. The repurchase right, right to purchase or right to sell shall cease if the thing is destroyed due to reasons beyond the obligor's control.[629]

523. *Hire purchase*: Based on the parties' agreement, the buyer shall be entitled to pay the purchase price in several instalments at specific dates, where possession of the thing is transferred to the buyer before the purchase price is paid in full, the seller shall have the option to either withdraw from the contract or to terminate the payment facilities granted in the event of the buyer's failure to make the instalment payments when due. The seller shall be entitled to exercise this right the first time an instalment payment is defaulted only if the buyer has been informed thereof in advance and sufficient time has been allowed for performance. If the seller withdraws from the contract, the buyer shall pay a charge for use of the thing transferred to his possession under the contract, and shall be liable to pay compensation for any loss in value that exceeds depreciation implied by the proper use of the thing.[630]

524. *Purchase upon delivery subject to inspection*: If the consumer is not able to inspect the subject matter of the contract before concluding the contract, and the buyer has the right by agreement of the parties to declare his intention whether or not to conclude the contract after visual inspection of the thing, the seller shall provide the inspection of the thing. In that case, the effect of the contract shall be conditional upon the buyer's statement. No explanation shall be required from the buyer regarding such statements. If the seller allowed the inspection of the thing, he may set an appropriate deadline for the buyer to declare his intention. If the buyer fails to meet the deadline fixed in the contract or stipulated by the seller for making the statement, the contract shall not enter into effect. The seller is not liable for any lack of conformity if able to verify that the buyer has detected, or should have detected, the defect upon the inspection.[631]

525. *Purchase upon delivery subject to testing*: If the sales contract contains a clause allowing the buyer to test the subject matter of the contract before concluding the contract, and to declare his intention whether or not to conclude the contract after testing, the effect of the contract shall be conditional upon the buyer's statement. No explanation shall be required from the buyer regarding such statements. If the buyer fails to make the statement within the time limit usually deemed necessary for testing the thing or within the deadline set by the seller, the contract shall remain in effect. The seller is not liable for any lack of conformity if able to verify that the buyer has detected, or should have detected, the defect during testing.[632]

526. *Purchase by sample*: If the parties decide to define a certain characteristic of the subject matter of the contract by reference to a sample, the seller shall supply

629. Section 6:226 CC.
630. Section 6:227 CC.
631. Section 6:228 CC.
632. Section 6:229 CC.

a thing corresponding to the cited properties of the sample. The seller shall be liable for any latent defect in a thing if the defect also existed in the sample. If the buyer fails to present the sample, the burden of proof to verify the characteristic the sample has had shall lie with the buyer.[633]

527. Exchange contracts: If the contracting parties undertake reciprocal transfer of the ownership of things, other rights and receivables, the provisions pertaining to sales shall be duly applied. In such cases each party shall be deemed as the seller in respect of his own service and the buyer in respect of the other party's service.[634]

§3. Commercial Services

I. Distribution

528. According to the definition of the *case law* the distributor is a reseller that in return for the discount given to him/it (*rabatt*) distributes a product (mainly from his own depository) bought in his own name and for his own account (benefit) based on a framework establishing a permanent legal relation, referring to a defined area (in geographical sense or from the aspect of the product and the user).[635,636]

529. According to this definition the *distribution contract covers* a system of purchases in which both the elements of transport (both from the producer's and the distributor's side) and commission (especially in connection with organizing the marketing). The elements of agency cannot be found, the elements of undertakings can be found accidentally. The consignment character is not relevant either according to the Tribunal of Szeged: it is not consignment between the foreign producer and the national distributor, if the distributor buys a product by contract and then he/it resells the product registered as his own stock to other resellers/users and the difference in the two prices covers his profit.[637]

530. To nominate the contractual *parties* there are more options: commissioner – commissioned, producer-transporter, seller-buyer, transporter – reseller (the second element in each pair refers to the distributor); these different names do not result in the application of other rules.

531. When creating the *content* of the distribution contract, the members aren't bound to the formal characteristics laid down by legal norms: the agreement can be made in words, written form or by conduct; but the written form is widely-spread. In this case the parties didn't dispute the existence of the contract but the orders and the account were also in written form which led the court declare the establishment

633. Section 6:230 CC.
634. Section 6.234 CC.
635. With application: T. Papp, *Opuscula civilia, Magánjogi látlelet, Report on Hungarian Private Law, Befundbericht über das ungarische Privatrecht*, Szeged: Lectum Kiadó, 2013, 75–78.
636. Vb/01103.
637. BDT 2008. 69.

of a framework of transport.[638] In another case the plaintiff could not prove the establishment of the distribution agreement with orders but as evidence he attached the accounts and the letter of carriage. According to the Budapest Capital Regional Court of Appeal there was no documental evidence for the existence for the framework that created the legal basis for the long-term business relationship and for the consent in the important elements of the distribution and transportation contract (e.g., product, quantity, price, date of performance) the delivery could have based on individual sales.[639]

532. The determination of the aim (*direct object* of the) distribution contract is an essential part of the contract, based on this the contract is established in order to buy and resell a product so to distribute. The action of the distributor is a kind of direct marketing method which efficiency is increased by the discount appearing after performance.[640] The aim of the contract can only be achieved if the distributor settles the price of the product towards the commissioner according to the payment conditions settled in the contract: in the case the dealer, during the resale, imputed the price paid by the buyer for the car in the amount of the rental he owed to the buyer and by this financial compensation he considered the cars to be paid. The Budapest Capital Regional Court of Appeal held that the transporter (commissioner) had the property right until he got the price so the contract between the dealer and the seller is void.[641]

533. The determination of the indirect object of the distribution contract can happen with exact description based on catalogue or in general: by transferring to the spectrum of products or by using the expression widely accepted in that economic branch.

534. In the procedures aiming to declare the *invalidity* of the contract we can find both reasons of which result in that the contract will be void or voidable:

- the plaintiffs asked the court to declare that the merchandise contracts are void because they are contrary to good morals (because of adverse contractual conditions, e.g., instruction of the obligation of their own investment that joins the credits with long expiry, the uncertainty because of the option of prolonging the contract annually, the restriction of resignation), the court held that the contract could not be contrary to good morals as the violation of the business fair play and restriction of the economic freedom weren't proven;[642]
- the merchandiser referred to unfair general contractual conditions in connection with the definition of the right to resignation but he missed the deadline so the court could not discuss the case.[643]

---

638. 1-H-GJ-2007-144.
639. FIT-H-GJ-2008-79.
640. 1/1-H-GJ-2006-27.
641. FIT-H-GJ-2008-155.
642. 1-H-GJ-2006-17.
643. FIT-H-GJ-2009-16.

535. The *element of the content* of the distribution contract is to define the *right to distribute*,[644] it has dual references: on the one hand the definition of the distributing area belongs here, on the other hand the rules of restriction of the competition in connection with distribution. The definition of the *distributing area* can occur traditionally so by geographic limits but it can be defined by the circle of products or users or these can mix too. A prohibition of re-export can refer to the area which does not let the distributor distribute outside this area. The contract not only can restrict the area but it can restrict the activity of the distributor too: he cannot distribute the products of the rivals of the commissioner. In general the commissioners balance these prohibitions by providing *exclusive distribution rights* for the distributor on the market.

536. If the distributor *breaches* the prohibitions the commissioner can terminate the contract immediately. In a relevant court case the distributor sold cosmetics and he also sold medical bio lamps of another company for his for fiends; with respect to this (that the distributor acted for different aim and product) the producer ended the contract immediately referring to infringement. In order to define the distribution right the distributor may be entitled to build a marketing network, contract with sub distributors for the more efficient sale of the product.[645]

537. In the distribution contract the *price* of the product paid by the distributor is also given (often the price of the distribution/resale is defined too which is also doubtful from the aspect of competition law). This often happens in general: by taking into accounts the inflation or the variation of the prices in the world or the prices at the stock exchange. The 'm.f.c.' price-t (most favoured customer price) is used too: the distributor should pay the price paid by the consumer who had the greatest discount. If the distributor is late with paying, he does not settle the price of the products given to him, the producer can terminate the agreement immediately because of breach.[646]

538. In connection with the product not only the marketing are and the price is given but in the contract a *regular minimum of ordering-registration* is stipulated; this contractual condition means an obligation to both parties in connection with its delivery (submission) and resale. The commissioner checks the adherence of the limit of orders (and sale); thus he can observe – because of the instructions of the contract – that at an exact moment how many unpaid products the distributor can dispose of all together (including expired and unexpired claims). The delay and exceed of the limit also means breach of the contract and result in immediate termination of the contract.[647]

539. The detailed and exact description of the *cooperational obligation of the parties* is an important part of the contract. These are:

644. FIT 13.Gf.40.534/2010/4.
645. 1/1-H-GJ-2006-27.
646. GYIT-H-GJ-2008-15.
647. 8-H-GJ-2007-13.

(a) mutual obligation to give information
  - from the producer's aspect about the characteristics, timing of the delivery, promoting the goods, etc.;
  - from the distributor's aspect about the circumstances of the marketing (demands, local standards), the violation of the rights of the producer referring to the product by third person, etc.;(e.g., intellectual property rights, rights of personality).

(b) advertisement referring to the product, coordination of the marketing;[648]

(c) potential establishment and operation of a system of service departments and sets by the distributor;[649]

(d) the distributor shall refrain from, e.g., changing the product or its wrapping or the infringement of business secret;[650]

(e) the distributor's obligation to tolerate in connection with the right of the producer/supplier to control. The result of the violation of the cooperational obligation is the immediate resignation; so in case when the distributor intervenes into the business connections of the commissioner with the intention to capture the market;[651]

(f) the specification of facts, circumstances (e.g., mutual agreement, lapse of time) resulting in the termination of the legal relationship also belongs to the content. In case of the distribution contracts concluded for a definite period of time any member can live with his right of resignation; the unilateral character appears when the natural right of resignation of the distributor is restricted (e.g., he cannot live with this right for a year from the conclusion of the contract). In case of breaching the distribution contract concluded both for a definite and for unlimited period the damaged party terminates the contract with immediate resignation. If the distributor formed a network of marketing losing the distribution right (so the termination of the contract) also affects the sub distributors: the agreements on resale based on these contracts will be ended too (special legal impossibility).[652]

540. The termination of the distribution contract can also cause conducts contrary to the requirement of business fair play:

- the distributor (the brand retailer, dealer) made the obligatory warranty booklet (of his ex-commissioner) without his agreement by copying and using it;[653]
- after the termination of the contract the producer drew the attention of the his business partners to acquire the product from the distributor defined by him;[654]

648. 79/2003. VJ.
649. Fõv. Bír. 19.G.41.403/2010/12.
650. FIT-H-GJ-2007-128.
651. LB-H-GJ-2007-66.
652. FIT 13.Gf.40.534/2010/4.; 14-H-GJ-2007-46.
653. BDT 2007. 1538.
654. 1-H-PJ-2007-620.

– in his corporate name, the distributor still unlawfully used the word brand of the producer realizing usurpation of the brand or he asked the registration of the public brand of the producer unlawfully for his own benefit.[655] The contracting parties can enforce claims arising from this legal situations at courts.

541. The *new Hungarian Civil Code* regulates already – but very shortly – the *distribution contract*: the supplier undertakes to sell specific movable property ('product') to the distributor, and the distributor undertakes to purchase the product from the supplier and to sell it in his own name and on his own behalf. The provisions regarding the distribution contract shall apply mutatis mutandis to the supply of services.[656]

542. The supplier shall have the *right to give instructions* as to the proper distribution of the product. If the supplier gives unreasonable or unsuitable instructions, the distributor shall be obliged to warn him thereof. If the supplier insists on his instruction in spite of the warning, the distributor shall carry out the instruction; any damage resulting therefrom shall be the liability of the supplier. The distributor shall refuse to comply with such instructions if compliance would constitute an infringement of the law or any administrative decision, or it would jeopardize the safety or property of others. The supplier shall be entitled to *check fulfilment* of the contract and his instructions.[657]

543. The parties shall *protect the reputation of the product*. The supplier shall *inform* the distributor of advertisements on the product, and shall – for a fee – make available to the distributor promotional material for *marketing* the product.[658]

544. Under a *franchise contract* the franchisor undertakes to grant rights of use, utilization and exploitation rights relating to assets protected by copyright or industrial property rights, including know-how, and the franchisee undertakes to produce and supply goods and/or services through the use, utilization or exploitation of such assets protected by copyright or industrial property rights, including know-how, and to pay the fee agreed upon; in the process of supply the franchisee shall act in his own name and on his own behalf.[659] The Hungarian Civil Code regulates the distribution and franchise contracts under the same title, as these were related agreements; because of the application of same rules for both contracts the essential differences between these two contracts disappear in the regulation.

655. LB Pfv.IV.21.474/2009/4.; FIT 8.Pf.22.338/2011/8.
656. Section 6:372, s. 6:375 CC.
657. Section 6:374 CC.
658. Section 6:373 CC.
659. Section 6:375 CC.

545. The franchisor shall *ensure* that the franchisee has ongoing and uninterrupted access to the use, utilization and exploitation rights, as are required for running the franchise, during the full term of the contract. The franchisee shall take measures to *protect the know-how* placed at his disposal.[660]

546. If the franchisee is obligated to *obtain the goods* to be sold or supplies of basic materials for the production of goods from the franchisor or from a person designated by the franchisor, and the franchisor fails to fulfil the order of the franchisee, the franchisee shall be entitled to obtain the goods or the basic materials from other sources.[661]

547. The franchisor shall have the right to *give instructions* as regards the production and sale of goods and services, and the protection of the reputation of the network and the goods and services produced and/or sold. If the franchisor gives unreasonable or unsuitable instructions, the franchisee shall be obliged to warn him thereof. If the franchisor insists on his instruction in spite of the warning, the franchisee shall carry out the instruction; any damage resulting therefrom shall be the liability of the franchisor. The franchisee shall refuse to comply with such instructions if compliance would constitute an infringement of the law or any administrative decision, or it would jeopardize the safety or property of others. The franchisor shall be entitled to *check fulfilment* of the contract and his instructions.[662]

548. The parties shall undertake the obligation to *protect the network* established through the rights of use, utilization and exploitation rights granted under the contract relating to assets protected by copyright or industrial property rights, including know-how, as well as the reputation of the goods and services produced and/or sold.[663]

549. Termination of the franchise contract: Either party shall be entitled to terminate a contract concluded for an indefinite period by notice with effect to the last day of the calendar month. The notice period shall be one month during the first year of the contract, two months during the second year and three months during the third and subsequent years of the contract. Upon termination of the contract, *the rights of use*, utilization and exploitation granted to the franchisee relating to assets protected by copyright or industrial property rights, including know-how, *shall cease.*[664]

660. Section 6:377 CC.
661. Section 6:378 CC.
662. Section 6:380 CC.
663. Section 6:379 CC.
664. Section 6:381 CC.

II. Contracts with Middlemen

550. The *engagement-type contracts* are the personal service contract, the consignment contract, the agency contract, the shipping contract and the fiduciary asset management contract in the Hungarian Civil Code.

551. Under a *personal service contract* the agent undertakes to carry out the assignment the principal has entrusted to him, and the principal undertakes to pay the remuneration contracted. If a contract or another legal statement is required for carrying out the assignment, the contract shall function as a power of attorney as well.[665]

552. The agent shall follow the *instructions* of the principal. The agent may disobey the principal's instruction if it is essential for the principal's interest, and the principal cannot be notified in advance. In such a case the principal shall be notified without delay. If the principal gives unreasonable or impracticable instructions, the agent shall be obliged to warn him thereof. If the principal insists on his instruction in spite of the warning, the agent shall be entitled to withdraw from or to terminate the contract, or may carry out the assignment according to the principal's instructions, at the principal's risk. The agent shall refuse to comply with such instruction if compliance would constitute an infringement of the law or any administrative decision, or it would jeopardize the safety or property of others. All costs of the agent incurred in connection with the fulfilment of the instructions shall be reimbursed by the principal. The agent may demand adequate safeguards for carrying out the assignment. If the principal fails to provide adequate safeguards, the agent may refuse to carry out the assignment.[666]

553. The agent shall *inform* his principal of his activities and the status of the assignment upon request, or without a request when deemed necessary. The agent shall inform his principal if employment of another person has become necessary or if the instructions need to be changed due to the emergence of new circumstances. The agent shall notify the principal as soon as he fulfils the assignment.[667]

554. The agent shall be entitled to demand *remuneration* even if his actions brought no results, except if the assignment failed in part or in whole due to the agent's actionable conduct. Remuneration shall be payable at the time the contract is performed. If the contract is terminated before the assignment has been fulfilled, the agent shall be entitled to demand an appropriate fraction of the remuneration agreed upon for his activities. The agent shall be required to advance any *costs* ordinarily required for carrying out the assignment. Upon termination of contract the

665. Section 6:272, s. 6:274 CC.
666. Section 6:273 CC.
667. Section 6:275 CC.

principal shall *exonerate* the agent from obligations assumed in dealings with third persons on the basis of the assignment, and shall *reimburse* his necessary and justified expenses.[668]

555. Under a *consignment contract* the consignment agent undertakes to conclude a sales contract for a movable property in his own name, on the principal's behalf, and the principal undertakes to pay the commission agreed upon. The provisions of consignment contract shall apply to such consignment contract where the consignment agent undertakes the obligation to conclude another contract.[669]

556. A consignment contract that requires the consignment agent to acquire ownership of a real estate property shall be null and void.[670]

557. The sales contract concluded under a consignment contract shall *entitle and bind* the consignment agent in terms of the party contracting with the consignment agent. The consignment agent shall be *responsible* to the principal for the performance of all of the obligations that are undertaken by his contracting partner in the contract, if he has specifically agreed to do so.[671]

558. In respect of *consignment purchases* the consignment agent shall *transfer* to the principal the ownership of movable property acquired in the course of performing the contract as part of the settlement process. In respect of *consignment sales* the consignment agent shall be authorized to *transfer* the ownership of the principal's movable property.[672]

559. The consignment agent shall be entitled to *commission* if the sales contract has been concluded, or if the contract has not been concluded due to reasons within the principal's control.[673]

560. The commission agent may himself conclude a sales contr*act* with the principal, if the market value of the thing can be clearly determined relying on publicly accessible information. In the case of *accession*, the consignment agent shall be obligated to conclude the contract under the terms considered best for the principal. During the process of settlement, the consignment agent shall notify the principal if he himself has concluded the sales contract with the principal. The consignment agent's claim for commission shall not be affected if the sales contract with the principal is concluded by the consignment agent himself. Otherwise, in respect of the consignment agent's accession the provisions on sales contracts shall apply to the relationship between the principal and the consignment agent.[674]

---

668. Section 6:276 CC.
669. Section 6:281 (1), (2) CC.
670. Section 6:281 (3) CC.
671. Section 6:282 (1), (2) CC.
672. Section 6:283 CC.
673. Section 6:284 CC.
674. Section 6:285 CC.

561. If the commission agent concludes the sales contract under conditions more favourable for the principal than the ones set out in the consignment contract, the *benefit* originating therefrom shall accrue to the principal. If the consignment agent makes a sale at a price below the one specified in the consignment contract, he shall *reimburse* the principal for the difference, unless he is able to prove that the sales contract could not have been concluded at the stipulated price, and that by making the sale he saved the principal from losses, and that he was not able to notify the principal in time. If the commission agent *substantially departs from the conditions* stipulated in the consignment contract, he shall notify the principal thereof. Upon receipt of such notice, the principal shall be entitled to reject the sales contract without delay, unless the consignment agent has effected purchase at a price higher than stipulated, but agreed to reimburse the difference.[675]

562. The regulations governing personal service contract shall apply to consignment contracts mutatis mutandis.[676]

563. Under an *agency contract* the agent undertakes to provide services with a view to facilitating the conclusion of a contract between his principal and a third party, and the principal undertakes to pay the fee agreed upon. Unless otherwise provided for in the Hungarian Civil Code, the agent shall not be entitled to conclude the contract he helped negotiating in his principal's name, nor to accept performance under that contract.[677]

564. The agent shall *notify* the principal if he is engaged in providing agency services to a third person. The *fee* shall be payable at the time the mediated contract is concluded and also if the parties conclude the contract after the termination of the agency contract.[678]

565. The Provisions regulating personal service contracts shall apply to agency contracts mutatis mutandis.[679]

566. On the ground of an agency contract the agent may undertake to enter into a long-term relationship and to negotiate – acting independently – contracts for the principal to be concluded with third parties, and to conclude such contract in the principal's name, and the principal undertakes to pay the fee agreed upon (*long-term agency contract*).[680]

675. Section 6:286 CC.
676. Section 6:287 CC.
677. Section 6:288, s. 6:289 CC.
678. Section 6:290, s. 6:291 CC.
679. Section 6:292 CC.
680. Section 6:293 (1) CC.

567. The agent shall be considered as *acting independently* if carrying out the activity by means other than a contract of employment, executive officer relationship or any other relationship invoked by law, court order or administrative decision, granting the right of representation of a legal person.[681]

568. The *long-term relationship* means when the agent:

- is required to negotiate more than one contract;
- is required to negotiate one contract, and to maintain and renew that contract.[682]

569. If the agent is entitled to conclude the contract he has negotiated, his *right of representation* shall cover all legal statements which are usually required in connection with negotiated contracts. This, however, shall not include the right to amend an existing contract, or to accept money or to determine a payment date.[683]

570. If the agency contract is terminated the agent shall be entitled to *indemnification* if deemed justified having regard to all circumstances of significance to the contract, in light of the fact that the termination of the contract deprives the agent of his right to a commission to which he would be entitled in connection with the transactions concluded, or planned to be concluded if the contract remained in force, provided that:

- the agent solicited new clients for the principal through forming new business relations, or expanded existing business relations resulting in at least one new client, if such business dealings produce substantial benefits for the principal even after the termination of the contract; or
- the agent completed the assignment for setting up a long-term relationship, but he is prone to lose regular income due to the termination of the agency contract. The *amount of indemnification* may not exceed one year's average commission the agent had received during the last five years before the contract was terminated, or if the agency contract had existed for less than five years, the average calculated for one year from the sum received during the life of the contract. Claims for indemnification may be enforced within a preclusive period of one year. Indemnification shall not affect the agent's claim for compensation and the fee due on the basis of an agreement containing a restriction imposed upon the agent in exercising economic activities after the time of termination of the contract. Any agreement that had been reached between the parties before the contract was terminated and which contains a clause that derogates from the provisions relating to indemnification to the detriment of the agent shall be null and void.[684]

681. Section 6:293 (2) CC.
682. Section 6:293 (3) CC.
683. Section 6:294 CC.
684. Section 6:298, s. 6:300 CC.

571. The *exclusion of indemnification*: No indemnification shall be paid to the agent if:

- the contract was terminated by the agent, unless termination was based on any circumstance within the principal's control, or for reasons justified by the agent's age or health on account of which the agent's performance could no longer be expected; or
- if, based on an agreement concluded with the principal, the agent transfers his rights and obligations specified in the contract to a third party.[685]

572. The *agreement containing a restriction* imposed upon the agent in exercising economic activities after the time of termination of the contract shall be executed in writing. The agreement containing a restriction imposed upon the agent in exercising economic activities shall be effective for a term of up to two years after the termination of the contract; any clause for a term of over two years shall be null and void. The agreement containing a restriction imposed upon the agent in exercising economic activities shall be null and void inasmuch as it derogates from the geographical area, client base and type of goods fixed in the agency contract.[686]

573. *Financial intermediary* means any person who carries on the activity of:

(a) intermediation of financial services:
- within the framework of supply of special intermediary services for and on behalf of a financial institution – including groups of financial institutions – or more than one financial institution in respect of their non-competing financial services (*special services intermediary*); or
- within the framework of agency activities for and on behalf of a financial institution – including groups of financial institutions – or more than one financial institution in respect of their non-competing financial services (*tied agent*); or
- as a payment services intermediary (*tied intermediary*).

(b) intermediation of financial services:
- within the framework of supply of special intermediary services for and on behalf of several financial institutions in respect of competing financial services (*multiple special services intermediary*); or
- within the framework of agency activities for and on behalf of several financial institutions in respect of competing financial services (*multiple agent*); or
- in the form of brokering activities (*broker*). Supply of payment services by intermediaries may be performed as defined in the Act on Payment Service Providers.[687]

685. Section 6:299 CC.
686. Section 6:301 CC.
687. Act CCXXXVII of 2013 s. 10 (1), (2).

574. Under a *shipping contract* the forwarding agent undertakes to conclude contracts and to make legal statements relating to shipments in his own name and on the principal's behalf, and the principal undertakes to pay the fee agreed upon. The forwarding agent shall be entitled to perform carriage himself.[688]

575. The forwarding agent shall enforce the principal's claims against the carrier and other contractors hired by the forwarding agent, if so instructed by the principal, at the expense and risk of the principal. Furthermore, the forwarding agent shall make statements even in the absence of the principal's instructions, where this is deemed necessary for the protection of the rights of the principal.[689]

576. The forwarding agent shall be entitled to any *freightage discount* granted subsequently and to the referral fees paid by carriers for the consignments delivered.[690]

577. The regulations on consignment contracts shall apply to the relationship of the forwarding agent and the principal, and provisions governing contracts of carriage shall also apply to the obligation to provide information relating to the consignment, to the handling, protection and transport of consignments, to the forwarding agent's lien rights, and also to the period of limitation on claims arising out of or in connection with contracts of carriage.[691]

578. Under a *fiduciary asset management contract*[692] the fiduciary undertakes to manage the assets, rights and receivables entrusted to him by the principal ('assets managed') in his one name and on the beneficiary's behalf, and the principal undertakes to pay the fee agreed upon.[693]

579. The *right to determine the beneficiary* and the conditions for the commencement and termination of beneficiary entitlements lies with the principal. The beneficiary may be identified also by reference to the range of beneficiaries. The principal may provide that after a certain period of time or under certain conditions the assets managed shall – in part or in whole – pass to himself, to his successors or to a specific third party. If the contract contains an entitlement for the fiduciary to designate the person of the beneficiary, the fiduciary shall also be entitled to specify the share to be allotted to that beneficiary. Designating the fiduciary as the sole beneficiary shall be null and void.[694]

580. The assets managed shall not be mixed in any way with the fiduciary's own assets or with other assets he manages, and the fiduciary shall keep separate records

688. Section 6:302, s. 6:304 CC.
689. Section 6:303 CC.
690. Section 6:305 CC.
691. Section 6:309 CC.
692. *See* more about it in: I. Sándor, *A bizalmi vagyonkezelés és a trust, Jogtörténeti és összehasonlító jogi elemzés,* Budapest: HVG Orac, 2014.
693. Section 6:310 CC.
694. Section 6:311 CC.

of such assets (*separation of property*); any provision to the contrary shall be null and void. Components of the assets managed and kept separately from the fiduciary's own assets and from other assets he manages, shown as managed assets shall be deemed to comprise a part of the managed assets until proven to the contrary. Individual assets replacing certain assets, security deposit, reimbursement, or any other value of the like, and the proceeds of such shall comprise a part of the managed assets, even if they are not shown in the records. Individual assets which the fiduciary did not show in the records as part of the assets managed shall be considered to comprise a part of the fiduciary's own personal assets, unless proven to the contrary.[695]

581. The fiduciary's spouse and domestic partner, and personal creditors and creditors of other assets managed by the fiduciary shall not lay claim to any part of the assets managed. The managed assets shall not be included in the fiduciary's estate. The beneficiary and the principal both shall have the right to bring action against the fiduciary's spouse and domestic partner, and personal creditors and creditors of other assets managed by the fiduciary, requesting the separation of the managed assets (*protection of asset managed*).[696]

582. The beneficiary shall have the right under contract to request the fiduciary to release the managed assets and its proceeds. Creditors of the beneficiary shall be entitled to lay claim to the assets of the beneficiary from the point in time when said assets and their proceeds are to be released to the beneficiary.[697]

583. The principal and the beneficiary shall have the right to *check* the fiduciary's activities relating to asset management. The costs of such checks shall be borne by the principal or the beneficiary. The principal and the beneficiary may not give instructions to the fiduciary; any clause to the contrary shall be null and void.[698]

584. Based on the enhanced requirement stemming from the relationship that of which is based upon trust or confidence, the *fiduciary's primary objective* is to serve the beneficiary's best interest. Under the principle of reasonable commercial practices, the fiduciary shall have the obligation to protect the managed assets from foreseeable risks.[699]

585. *Management of the assets* shall cover the exercise of entitlements stemming from the ownership and other rights and receivables entrusted to the fiduciary, and the performance of obligations arising therefrom. The fiduciary shall have the right of disposition over the managed assets according to the conditions and within the limits set out in the contract. If the fiduciary breaches this obligation and unlawfully transfers any part of the assets he manages to a third party, the principal and

695. Section 6:312 CC.
696. Section 6:313 CC.
697. Section 6:314 CC.
698. Section 6:315, s. 6:316 CC.
699. Section 6:317 CC.

the beneficiary shall have the right to recover such asset and to have it reinstated among the managed assets, if the third party did not act in good faith or there was no pecuniary interest; this provision shall also apply when the managed assets are wrongfully encumbered.[700]

586. If the fiduciary is not remunerated for his services, he may request compensation for his justified expenses arising out of or in connection with asset management. The fiduciary shall be entitled to charge his *remuneration* and justified *expenses*, along with other claims arising out of or in connection with asset management directly from the managed assets.[701]

587. If the principal and the beneficiary is the same person, fiduciary asset management shall be established by means of an irrevocable *unilateral statement* made by the principal executed in an authentic instrument. Where fiduciary asset management is created under a *will*, it shall take effect upon the fiduciary's acceptance of the appointment under the conditions set out in the will. The regulations governing fiduciary asset management contracts shall also apply where fiduciary asset management is established by means of a unilateral statement.[702]

588. The provisions regarding personal service contracts shall apply to fiduciary asset management mutatis mutandis.[703]

589. *Liability for subcontractors and agents*: Any person who employs another person to perform his obligations or exercise his rights shall be liable for the conduct of that person as if he himself had carried out the obligation or exercised the right. If the obligor has not been authorized to employ other persons, he shall be liable even for damages that would not have occurred without the employment of such person. The obligor shall be entitled to enforce his rights against subcontractors and agents – for reasons of non-performance – as long as his liability toward the obligee exists.[704]

III. Insurance

590. In Hungary *public law frames of the private insurance business* are laid down in Act LX of 2003 on Insurance Institutions and the Insurance Business.[705] Unless otherwise provided by international agreement, this act had to be applied to:

- insurance activities pursued in the territory of Hungary and activities involved in or closely related to the insurance and the insurance activities and the activities

700. Section 6:318 CC.
701. Section 6:322 CC.
702. Section 6:329 CC.
703. Section 6:330 CC.
704. Section 6:148 CC.
705. With application: T. Papp & T. Jakab, 'The Present Situation of the Insurance System and Insurance Contracts in Hungary', *Wiadomosci Ubezpieczepiawe* 4, 2014, 57–68.

involved in or closely related to the insurance carried on by an insurer established in the territory of Hungary under the authorization of the Act;

- insurance mediation and insurance consulting performed in the territory of Hungary and activities involved in or closely related to the insurance or insurance mediation carried on by an independent insurance intermediary established in the territory of Hungary;
- activities pursued by the Hungarian branches of foreign insurance companies, insurance intermediaries and consultants;
- outsourcing service providers solely with respect to the outsourced activities;
- activities of the body designated to administer the Claims Security Account and the Claims Guarantee Fund, in respect of the activities concerning the administration of the Account;
- supervisory activities of the State Financial Institutions Commission conferred under the Act; and
- the obligations of companies – specified in the Act – that are subject to supervision on a consolidated basis or supplementary supervision.[706]

591. The provisions of the Act LX of 2003 governed insurance, insurance mediation and insurance consulting and/or insurance, insurance mediation and insurance consulting representation activities of resident insurance companies, insurance intermediaries and insurance consultants that are performed abroad but only if the domestic law of the country that provides these services in question does not provide otherwise.[707]

592. In the territory of Hungary, insurance enterprises operated in the form of joint-stock companies, cooperatives, associations or as branch offices of third-country insurance companies.[708]

593. The Act LX of 2003 determined the other participants in the insurance system such as insurance intermediaries, insurance brokers and multiple insurance brokers, insurance agents, principal agents, insurance consultants and the rules of representation of foreign insurance companies, insurance intermediaries and consultants in Hungary.[709]

594. The third part of the Act LX of 2003 contained the rules of authorization (activities, foundation, commencement of insurance operations) and notification (notification requirements of insurance companies, insurance intermediaries and insurance consultants; the regulations of outsourcing; the rules of establishing insurance branch offices in other Member States; the rules governing cross-border activities), provisions concerning the executive employees and other directors of

706. Act LX of 2003 s. 1 (1).
707. *Ibid.*, s. 1 (2).
708. *Ibid.*, s. 10 (1).
709. *Ibid.*, ss 33–53.

insurance companies, the amendment of insurance activities, insurance products and the law applicable to insurance contracts.[710]

595. The Act LX of 2003 provided special rules for legal expenses insurance and for the compulsory insurance.[711] Separate parts dealt with the rules pertaining to the owners, directors and employees of insurance companies, and the insurance company's operating conditions.[712]

596. Among the administrative rules concerning the clients, the Act LX of 2003 mentioned the insurance secrets, business secrets of insurance companies, insurance intermediaries and consultants; the information for policyholders;[713] the proceedings in connection with any infringement of the regulations relating to business-to-consumer (B2C) commercial practises and the complaints handling.[714]

597. The Act LX of 2003 disjointed thoroughly the oversight of the insurance industry, the commission procedures and actions;[715] the emergency situations and the special rules pertaining to liquidation and winding-up procedures.[716]

598. In the end of 2014 the Hungarian Parliament adopted a new act (Act LXXXVIII of 2014 on Insurance Activities) giving new public law frames of the private insurance business, but the regulated legal relations are the same as in the Act LX of 2003; the new act entered into force on 1 January 2016. Its most important aims written in the Preamble are: protecting the insured persons' interests, motivating self-care activities, increasing the confidence in the insurance business and insurance companies, strengthen the role of insurance in the national economy, taking into consideration the legislation compliance requirements of the EU.

599. The former Civil Code of Hungary[717] described the system of 'private' insurance business in the style of the late 1950s legislation.[718] The concept, the terminology – despite the amendments – did not meet the needs of the modern age. The regulation of the insurance contracts was unilateral, consumer protection aspects were not subject to the insurance law legislation. The new Civil Code[719] (entered into force on 15 March 2014) divided the private insurance law by new, modern aspects, by setting down formerly existing definitions that were fixed by other laws in black and white.

---

710. *Ibid.*, ss 54–91.
711. *Ibid.*, ss 103–110.
712. *Ibid.*, ss 115, 116.
713. *Ibid.*, ss 153–167.
714. *Ibid.*, ss 190–207.
715. *Ibid.*, ss 209–215.
716. *Ibid.*, ss 216–226.
717. Act IV of 1959 about the Civil Code.
718. *See* the detailed analysis about this period in: F. Bajai & D. Csabay, *Az állami biztosítás Magyarországon*, Budapest: Közgazdasági és Jogi Könyvkiadó, 1972.
719. Act V of 2013.

600. Under the *insurance contract* the insurer undertakes to provide coverage for the risk specified in the contract, and to provide settlement or benefits for loss arising when a specific future event happens, after the starting date of risk coverage, and the insured person undertakes to pay an insurance premium agreed upon.

601. The insurance company's service covers the payment for the insured person's loss in the amount and in the manner defined in the contract and other policy benefits (indemnity insurance) or the payment of a sum specified in the contract (fixed-sum policies).[720] The main obligation of the insurer is to insure a risk (*praestare* supply: being at the insured person's disposal).[721]

602. The *basic types of the insurance contract* are the *indemnity insurance and the fixed-sum policies*. In case of the indemnity insurance the service of the insurer pays for damages of the insured person to the extent and in the manner determined in the insurance contract, or provides other supply for the insured person.[722] The insured party shall be entitled, under a liability insurance policy, to request the insurance company to exempt him from paying for damages for which he is legally liable in the manner and up to the limit specified in the policy.[723]

603. In connection with *fixed-sum policies*, the written consent of the insured person shall be required for concluding or amending the contract if he himself does not conclude it.[724] *Life insurance* means a type of policy where the insurance company promises to pay a specific sum of money fixed in the contract, or annuity for life or for a specific period of time, upon the insured natural person's death or attainment of a certain age, or at another predetermined time or occurrence of a specific event. Life insurances are, in particular:

(a) term life insurance, that provides no benefits upon expiry and that has no cash surrender value; or
(b) ordinary life insurance other than term life insurance, including unit-linked life assurance policies where investment risk is to be borne according to the contract by the contracting party.[725]

604. *Accident insurance* is a type of insurance where the insurance company promises to pay a specific sum of money or annuity fixed in the contract, or other benefits as contracted upon the insured person's accidental death, health impairment or disability resulting from an accident.[726]

---

720. Section 6:439 of Civil Code (CC).
721. Gy. Wellmann & F. Petrik, *Az új Ptk. magyarázata* VI/VI, Budapest: HVG Orac, 2013, 336.
722. A. Osztovits, *A Polgári Törvénykönyvről szóló 2013. évi V. törvény és a kapcsolódó jogszabályok nagykommentárja*, Budapest: Opten Informatikai Kft., 2014, 1182.
723. Section 6:470 (1) CC.
724. Section 6:475 CC.
725. Section 6:477 CC.
726. Section 6:485 CC.

605. Health insurance is a type of insurance where the insurance company promises to pay benefits as provided for in the contract in the event of the insured person's sickness. The insurance benefits may also cover the costs of healthcare services specified in the contract provided to a person in good health.[727]

606. Insurable interest: An insurance contract may be concluded by any person who has a vested interest in avoiding the occurrence of an insured event under some form of property or personal relationship, or who has a vested interest in the occurrence of an insured event in respect of life insurance policies which comprises assurance on survival to a stipulated age only, birth assurance or marriage assurance, or those who conclude the contract on behalf of an interested person; any indemnity insurance and group fixed-sum policy concluded in contradiction to this provision shall be null and void.[728]

607. Co-insurance: If the insurance risk is covered – in a predetermined percentage – jointly, by more than one insurance company and the insurance services are performed collectively, the contract to take effect shall indicate the name of all insurance companies participating in the co-insurance, including their share in risk coverage; in connection with co-insurance, the service obligations of insurance companies shall be limited by their commitment in the sharing of risks.[729]

608. Group insurance: In this case the insured persons are identified according to their affiliation to a natural group or under the relationship between the insured persons and the contracting party, and the insurance company's risk coverage and the related terms are custom-tailored to the group policyholder.[730]

609. Prohibition of overinsurance: The coverage shall not exceed the value of the insured property; any agreement for coverage higher than the value of the insured interest shall be null and void and the premium shall be reduced accordingly.[731] This provision notwithstanding as an insurance policy can include provisions for the estimated future value of a property and/or for the value of restoration or replacement.[732] In case the insured event happens, the highest amount of settlement the insurance company is liable to pay represents the sum insured.[733]

610. Concurrent insurance: If the same interest is insured by more than one insurance company independently, the insured person shall have the right to submit his claim to one or more of such insurance companies.[734] The insurance company to which a claim is submitted shall be liable to make a settlement payment under the terms and conditions fixed in the document verifying insurance cover and up to

727. Section 6:487 CC.
728. Section 6:440 CC.
729. Section 6:441 (1) CC.
730. Section 6:442 (1) CC.
731. Section 6:458 (1) CC.
732. Section 6:458 (1) CC.
733. Section 6:458 (2) CC.
734. Section 6:459 (1) CC.

the sum insured as specified therein, while reserving the right to lodge a claim for compensation relating to the other insurance companies.[735] The parties may obtain several policies for the same insurable interest and for the same peril, and may accumulate insurance services.[736]

611. Underinsurance: If the amount of coverage is lower than the value of the insured interest, the insurance company shall be liable to cover the loss in such a manner that the amount of insurance is proportionate with the value of the property.[737]

612. Maintaining the amount of the insurance cover: The amount of the coverage for a given period of insurance cover shall be reduced by the amount paid for claims for insured events occurred during the same period, unless the contracting party supplements the premium accordingly.[738]

613. Residual rights: If a life assurance policy is terminated for any reason without payment of the sum insured, the insurance company shall be liable to pay the cash surrender value defined in the policy. The insurance company shall be exempt from payment of the sum insured if the insured person dies in consequence of the wilful conduct of the beneficiary; in this case the cash surrender value can be claimed by the heirs, and the beneficiary shall not have a share. The policy shall be terminated without payment of the sum insured and the insurance company shall return the cash surrender value if the insured person dies in consequence of or in connection with a serious criminal offence he has committed or if the insured person has committed suicide within two years following the time of conclusion of the contract.[739]

614. Waiting period: Where the policy pertains to nursing care services, or if the insurable person suffers in a permanent illness and it was known to both parties at the time the contract was concluded, the waiting period stipulated in the health insurance contract by the parties with respect to such illness may not exceed three years.[740]

615. If the contract is not performed *in writing*, the insurance company shall issue a document so as to verify insurance cover.[741] If the document verifying insurance cover is different from the contracting party's offer and if this difference is not contested by the contracting party without delay upon receipt of the document, the contract shall take effect in accordance with the contents of that document.[742] The

735. Section 6:459 (2) CC.
736. Section 6:476 CC.
737. Section 6:460 CC.
738. Section 6:461 (1) CC.
739. Section 6:484 CC.
740. Section 6:489 CC.
741. Section 6:443 (1) CC.
742. Section 6:443 (2) CC.

offeror shall be bound by the offer for a period of fifteen days from the time when it was made and for sixty days if a health risks assessment is required for the evaluation of the offer.[743]

616. At the time of the *conclusion of the contract*, the contracting party shall disclose to the insurance company all circumstances of which he is or should be aware and that are important in terms of providing the insurance coverage. The contracting party shall satisfy his disclosure obligation by truthfully filling out the questionnaire furnished by the insurance company; leaving the questions unanswered shall not constitute a violation of the disclosure obligation. The contracting party shall be liable to notify the insurance company in writing of any changes in the material conditions.[744]

617. The *coverage of risk* provided by the insurance company shall commence at the time fixed by the parties in the contract or, failing this, at the time the contract is concluded.[745] The parties may agree in writing that the insurance company covers the insurance risk from such a date that is preceding the date of conclusion of the contract (preliminary coverage).[746] The preliminary coverage shall remain in effect until the conclusion of the contract or refusal of the offer but it mustn't exceed ninety days.[747]

618. If the insurance company becomes aware of any material circumstances regarding a contract, or any changes thereof, only after the contract has been concluded, and these circumstances result in a considerable increase in the insurance risk, the insurance company shall be entitled to make a written proposal within fifteen days after gaining knowledge thereof to amend the contract or may terminate the contract in writing with thirty days' notice.[748] If the contracting party does not accept the proposal for amendment or fails to respond to it within fifteen days from the time of receipt thereof, the contract shall be terminated on the thirtieth day following the day of communicating the proposal for the amendment, if the insurance company warned the contracting party of this consequence when the proposal for amendment was made.[749]

619. The first *insurance premium payment* shall be due at a time agreed upon by the parties or, failing this, at the time the contract is concluded and all subsequent premium payments shall be due on the first day of the period to which they pertain. A single premium shall be paid at the time the contract is concluded and the period of insurance cover shall be one year.[750]

743. Section 6:443 (3) CC.
744. Section 6:452 (1), (2) CC.
745. Section 6:445 CC.
746. Section 6:445 (2) CC.
747. Section 6:445 (3) CC.
748. Section 6:446 (1) CC.
749. Section 6:446 (2) CC.
750. Section 6:447 CC.

620. If an insurance event occurs and the contract is terminated, the insurance company shall be entitled to demand payment of the premium for the entire period of insurance cover. In other cases of termination of a contract, insurance companies shall be entitled to claim payment of the premium until such day when risk coverage ends. If there is an overpayment in periodic, the insurance company shall return the surplus.[751]

621. In the event of non-payment of the premium as due, the insurance company shall dispatch a written request for payment to the party in default within thirty days from the due date – indicating the potential legal consequence – with an additional thirty-day deadline from the date when the warning was dispatched. In the event of non-compliance within the additional period, the contract shall be terminated with retroactive effect to the original due date, except if the insurance company forthwith moves to enforce its claim by judicial process.[752]

622. If the contract terminated for non-payment of regular premiums, the contracting party may request the insurance company to reinstate the risk coverage within one hundred twenty days from the time of termination. The insurance company may reinstate the insurance cover under the terms and conditions of the terminated contract, if the overdue premium is paid.[753]

623. If a contract was not concluded by the insured person, the insured person shall be entitled to enter into the contract with a written statement addressed to the insurance company. The insurance company's consent is not required for entering into the contract.[754] Upon entering into the contract the rights and obligations conferred upon the contracting party shall pass to the insured person.[755] If the insured person enters into the contract, the insured person and the contracting party shall be subject to joint and several liability for premium payments due for the current insurance period. The insured person entering into the contract shall be liable to cover the contracting party's expenses arising from the contract, including premium payments.[756]

624. If the insurance event becomes impossible or the insurable interest ceases before the insurance coverage becomes effective, the contract or the relevant part of it shall be terminated.[757] If the insurance event becomes impossible to happen or the insurable interest ceases during the period of risk coverage, the contract or the relevant part of it shall be terminated.[758] The legal effects attached to cases of lapse of interest in the insurance shall not apply if the lapse of interest results solely from the transfer of ownership of the insured property and the property in question was

751. Section 6:448 CC.
752. Section 6:449 (1) CC.
753. Section 6:449 (2) CC.
754. Section 6:451 (1) CC.
755. *Ibid.*
756. Section 6:451 (2) CC.
757. Section 6:454 (1) CC.
758. Section 6:454 (2) CC.

held by the new owner, previously under a different title. In that case, insurance cover shall pass together with ownership and the former and the new owner shall be jointly and severally liable for premium payments due at the time of the transfer of the ownership. The contract may be terminated by either of the parties within thirty days after becoming aware of the transfer of ownership, by giving thirty days' notice.[759]

625. The parties shall be entitled to *terminate* an indemnity insurance contract of indeterminate duration in writing, to take effect at the end of the of insurance cover period *by giving thirty days' notice*. The right to terminate may be excluded for a maximum period of three years; any exclusion of the right to terminate for a period in excess of three years shall be null and void in respect of the part exceeding the three-year period. If a contract covers a period of more than three years and the parties do not stipulate that the contract could be terminated before the specified period lapses, either of the parties shall be entitled to terminate the contract as of the fourth year. If the contract is terminated by the contracting party, the insurance company shall be entitled to demand repayment of any premium discounts based on a commitment for an extended contract term (term discount).[760]

626. The contracting party shall have the right to *terminate the life assurance policy* in writing – if the premium for the first year is paid up – to take effect at the end of the insurance cover period by giving thirty days' notice. The insurance company shall not be allowed to terminate a life assurance policy, with the exception of the substantial increase of the insurance risk.[761]

627. In case of *health insurance contract*, the possibility that the insured person's health deteriorates with age due to natural causes shall not constitute a considerable increase in insurance risk. The insurance company may not terminate a health insurance policy by an ordinary notice.[762,763]

IV. Financial Services

628. The credit and account agreements of the Hungarian Civil Code are the following: the credit contract, the loan contract, the deposit account contract, the current account contract, the payment account contract, the payment service contract, the factoring contract and the financial leasing contract. The Hungarian Civil Code regulates the contractual rules of these agreements, and the 2008/48/EC directive on credit agreements for consumer was implemented by the Act CLXII of 2009 and

759. Section 6:454 (3) CC.
760. Section 6:466 CC.
761. Section 6:483 CC.
762. Section 6:491 CC.
763. *See* more about insurance contract in: K. Kovács & Sz. Kovács, *Indemnification and the Insurance Contract*, In: Business Law in Hungary, ed. I. Sándor, Budapest: Patrocinium, 2016, 398–405.

the 2014/17/EU directive on credit agreements for consumer relating to residential immovable property and mortgage credit was provided in the Government Decree No. 462/2015. (XII. 29.) in Hungary.

629. Under a *credit agreement* the creditor undertakes to ensure the availability of a specific credit limit, and to conclude a loan agreement, contract of suretyship, guarantee contract or conduct other loan operations up to the said credit limit, and the debtor undertakes to pay the fee agreed upon.[764]

630. The creditor shall enter into a contract for loan operations when so requested by the debtor, if the conditions set out in the credit agreement are met. The debtor shall be entitled to call upon the creditor to conclude a contract during the period of availability fixed in the credit agreement.[765]

631. Under a *loan agreement* the creditor undertakes to make available a specific sum of money, and the debtor undertakes to repay that sum to the creditor at a later date with interest.[766]

632. If according to the contract funds from the loan may be drawn within a predetermined period of time following the time of conclusion of the agreement or if certain specific conditions are met, the creditor shall *keep the loan amount available* until said time period or until the conditions mentioned are met. The debtor shall be liable to pay a fee to the creditor on the loan amount kept available, for the duration of keeping it available.[767]

633. The debtor shall not be obligated to draw funds from the loan. If the debtor does not draw funds from the loan, he shall reimburse the creditor for expenses incurred in connection with the conclusion of the agreement.[768]

634. The creditor shall be entitled to *refuse disbursement of the loan* if, due to any material changes in the debtor's circumstances or in the value or enforceability of the collateral, performance of the contract can no longer be expected, and the debtor fails to provide adequate guarantees in spite of being requested to do so.[769]

635. *Complementary loan*: The debtor shall not be required to pay interest and other charges if the parties have expressly provided so or if it follows from the purpose of the agreement or from the circumstances of the case. In this case the provisions on loan agreements shall apply subject to the exception that:

764. Section 6:382 (1) CC.
765. Section 6:382 (2) CC.
766. Section 6:383 CC.
767. Section 6:386 CC.
768. Section 6:385 CC.
769. Section 6:384 CC.

- the creditor shall be entitled to refuse disbursement of the loan due to any material changes in his own circumstances and may move to recover the loan amount already paid out;
- the debtor shall not be liable to pay a fee for keeping the loan amount available.[770]

636. Application of the provisions pertaining to loan agreements:

(a) The regulations governing loan agreements shall apply mutatis mutandis if the subject of the loan is not money but some other fungible property given to the debtor, upon which the debtor shall be liable to return to the creditor property of the same type and quality, in the same quantity at a later date defined in the agreement.
(b) The provisions on loan agreements shall apply mutatis mutandis in those cases where the service provided by one of the parties precedes the money to be provided by the other party, or if payment of the consideration precedes performance of the main subject matter.[771]

637. Under a *deposit account contract* the deposit holder is entitled to deposit a specific amount of money to the bank, and the bank undertakes to accept the sum of money offered by the deposit holder and to repay the same amount at a later date with interest.[772]

638. In the case of *fixed-term* deposits the bank is required to repay the funds held on the account upon maturity or as instructed by the deposit holder. The deposit holder shall be entitled to request repayment of the funds held on the account before the expiry of the term specified in the contract. In the absence of the deposit holder's request, the bank shall not be entitled to repay the funds held on the account before the expiry of the term specified in the contract.[773]

639. The funds not collected upon maturity shall be converted into a deposit of *indeterminate duration*. In the case of deposits for an unfixed term the bank is required to promptly repay the funds held on the account as instructed by the deposit holder.[774]

640. Under a *current account contract* the parties shall assume an obligation to record and settle their enforceable monetary claims arising from a specific relationship in a consolidated account.[775]

---

770. Section 6:388 CC.
771. Section 6:389 CC.
772. Section 6:390 (1) CC.
773. Section 6:390 (2), (3) CC.
774. Section 6:390 (4), (5) CC.
775. Section 6:391 CC.

641. The *balance of a current account* shall be established once a year. The party managing the current account shall communicate the balance to the other party in writing, with an itemized list of transactions. The other party shall be entitled to *contest the balance* or the receivables and payables that serve as the basis for computing the balance, in writing, within a preclusive period of thirty days of receipt of the written communication.[776]

642. The *individual claims on the current account shall cease* to exist and shall be substituted by the current account balance: in the absence of an objection; upon the parties' agreement regarding the items contested; or if the court has ruled on the contest.[777]

643. Under a *payment account contract* the account keeper undertakes to open a current account for the account holder for handling his financial transactions, and the account holder undertakes to pay the fee agreed upon.[778]

644. The account holder and the persons the account holder has authorized and registered with the account keeper shall be authorized to *dispose over the balance* of the payment account. If the payment account is held by more than one person, the account holders shall be authorized to dispose over the payment account jointly.[779]

645. The account keeper shall *accept* the account holder's payment orders and direct debit orders if they clearly indicate the amount of the transaction and the name of the payee. The account keeper shall be obligated to *receive payment transactions* to the account holder's credit or debit in the name of the account holder, and to *handle them* as deposits payable on demand. The account keeper shall provide *monthly statements* to the account holder regarding any sums debited or credited to his account as well as the account balance.[780]

646. The provisions relating to payment account contracts shall apply to securities accounts and safe custody accounts for securities subject to the exception that in these cases ownership claims relating to securities shall be shown on the account.[781]

647. The regulations governing current account contracts shall apply to payment account contracts mutatis mutandis.[782]

776. Section 6:392 (1), (2) CC.
777. Section 6:392 (3) CC.
778. Section 6:394 CC.
779. Section 6:396 (1) CC.
780. Section 6:395 (1), (2), (4) CC.
781. Section 6:398 CC.
782. Section 6:399 CC.

648. Under a *payment service contract* the agent undertakes to pay a certain amount of money to the payee according to the payer's instructions, and the payer undertakes to pay the fee agreed upon.[783]

649. Under a payment service contract the agent undertakes to *pay a certain amount of money* to the payee according to the payer's instructions, and the payer undertakes to *pay the fee* agreed upon.[784]

650. The agent shall be entitled to a *commission* when the funds are: delivered to the payee; credited to the payee's account; or made available to the payee's bank.[785]

651. The provisions regarding personal service contracts shall apply to payment orders mutatis mutandis.[786]

652. Under a *factoring contract* the factor undertakes to pay a certain amount of money, and the debtor undertakes to assign his claim from a third party to the factor; if the obligor fails to satisfy the assigned claim at the time when due, the debtor shall be liable to repay the funds received with interest, and the factor shall be liable to re-assign the claim.[787]

653. The factor shall be required to register the factoring assignment and the debtor's name in the *collateral register*. In the absence of registration the claim shall not pass to the factor in spite being assigned, and the factor shall have the same entitlements on the claim as the lien holder whose lien on the claim has not been registered in the collateral register.[788]

654. The provisions pertaining to the refusal to disburse a loan, to failure to draw funds from the loan and to credit availability shall apply mutatis mutandis.[789]

655. Under a *financial leasing agreement* the lessor undertakes to make available for use, for a limited period of time a thing or a right he owns (hereinafter referred to as 'leased asset'), and the lessee undertakes to accept the leased asset and to make lease payments if the lessee is given the right under the agreement to use the leased asset up to or surpassing its economic lifetime, or – if use is stipulated for a shorter period – to acquire the leased asset at the end of the term of the contract without any consideration or at a price considerably lower than the market

783. Section 6:400 CC.
784. Section 6:401 CC.
785. Section 6:402 CC.
786. Section 6:404 CC.
787. Section 6:405 CC.
788. Section 6:406 CC.
789. Section 6:408 CC.

value prevailing at the time of conclusion of the contract, or the total sum of lease payments reaches or exceeds the leased asset's market value prevailing at the time of conclusion of the contract.[790]

Obligation of registration

656.

(a) If the leased asset is a real estate property, the lessor shall provide for having the lease and the name of the lessee registered in the real estate register at the time of registration of ownership. If at the time the lease agreement is concluded the thing is owned by the lessor, the registration must take place before the time of transfer of possession.
(b) If the leased asset is a movable property or a right, the lessor shall provide for having the lease and the name of the lessee registered in the collateral register.
(c) If ownership of the movable property or the right is recorded in a public register and if hypothecation of the thing is to be registered in the proper registry by law, the lessor shall provide for having the lease and the name of the lessee registered in the proper registry. In the absence of registration, where ownership is acquired from the lessee by a third party in good faith and for consideration: the transferee shall acquire ownership of the movable property, or the right, by way of transfer; and the lessee shall acquire the lien established by the lessee on the movable property or right, even if the lessee has no right of disposition.[791]

657. The lessee shall be required to make *lease payments* for predetermined periods in advance. No lease payments shall be made for the period when the leased asset cannot be used for reasons beyond the lessee's control.[792]

658. The lessee shall, from the date of conclusion of the contract or – in respect of a thing – from the date of taking possession, collect the proceeds of the leased asset, and shall be liable for its encumbrances, costs and for the damages for which no indemnification can be demanded from anyone (*proceeds, burdens, costs, risks, use*). The provisions on lease agreements shall apply to the use and transfer of leased assets mutatis mutandis.[793]

659. The lessee shall be entitled to make available the leased asset for use to a third party subject to the lessor's consent (*assignment of use*). If the lessee has made available the leased asset for use to another person with the lessor's permission, the lessee shall be liable for the conduct of the user as if it was his own. If the lessee made available the leased asset for use to another person without the lessor's permission, the lessee shall be liable for damages that otherwise would not have

790. Section 6:409 CC.
791. Section 6:410 CC.
792. Section 6:414 CC.
793. Section 6:412 CC.

occurred. If the lessee has the right to acquire ownership of or a right to the leased asset (*assignment rights to third parties*), he shall be entitled to transfer this right to a third party without the lessor's consent.[794]

V. Carriage

660. Under a *carriage contract* the carrier undertakes to transport the consignment to its destination and deliver it to the consignee, and the consignor undertakes to pay the fee agreed upon.[795]

661. When so instructed by the consignor, the carrier shall make out the *consignment note* and provide a copy to the consignor or give an acknowledgement of receipt of the consignment. The consignment note made out by the carrier shall, in the absence of proof to the contrary, verify the existence of the contracts of carriage, the receipt of the consignment, and – in the absence of any reservation made by the carrier in the consignment note – that the consignment and its packaging at the time of delivery was apparently in a good condition, and that the amount of the consignments coincides with the one shown in the consignment note, if the consignment note was signed by the consignor and the carrier both, and the consignment note contains: the date and place of receipt of the consignment; the name and address of the consignor, the consignee and the carrier; the place where delivery is effected; a description of the consignment, the type of packaging used, danger classification for the given transport sector, number of the goods, label, number, volume or quantity expressed in any other way.[796]

662. The consignor shall *package* the consignment in a way to provide sufficient protection for the goods and prevent it from jeopardizing the physical safety or property of others, *give information* necessary for handling the consignment on the packaging, or failing this on the consignment itself and *hand over* to the carrier the documents necessary for transporting and handling the consignment.[797]

663. When it is manifest that the *packaging or* the *information* required for handling the consignment is *insufficient*, or if the consignor failed to supply the documents necessary for transporting and handling the consignment, the carrier may refuse to accept the consignment. If the consignor fails to remedy such discrepancies without delay, the carrier shall be entitled to withdraw from the contract.[798]

664. If *discrepancies in the packaging or in the information* required for handling the consignment becomes clear after the consignment is accepted, the carrier shall inform the consignor thereof without delay. In the absence of the consignor's

794. Section 6:413 CC.
795. Section 6:257 CC.
796. Section 6:258 (1), (2) CC.
797. Section 6:259 (1) CC.
798. Section 6:259 (2) CC.

specific instructions as to carriage, the carrier shall not be liable to forward the consignment. If the consignor has given instructions as to carriage, the carrier shall be entitled to request adequate safeguards if there is an imminent risk of loss arising from the discrepancies in the packaging or in the information required for handling the consignment, or if he may be subject to liability in respect of others. If the consignor fails to give instructions or to provide adequate safeguards the carrier shall be entitled to terminate the contract.[799]

665. The carrier shall be required to present means of *transport* at the place and time stipulated in the contract, in a condition suitable for carriage and to commence carriage without delay. *Loading* the consignment shall be the responsibility of the consignor; if the consignee does not unload the consignment, the carrier may do so at the consignor's expense. As regards loading and unloading, the carrier shall have the right to give instructions as to the placement of the consignment.[800]

666. If the consignment contains *dangerous goods*, the consignor shall inform the carrier of the danger classification for the given transport sector of the goods, along with information for avoiding risks. In the absence thereof, the carrier shall be entitled to refuse to accept the goods for carriage.[801]

667. If *carriage* is in any way *obstructed*, the carrier shall immediately notify the consignor and ask for instructions when deemed necessary. The consignor shall pay freight charges up to the amount commensurate until the impediment has occurred, if non-payment of such would result in his enrichment, or if the carrier is able to prove that the impediment occurred in consequence of circumstances beyond his control, that could not have been foreseen at the time of conclusion of the contract, and there had been no reasonable cause to take action for preventing or mitigating the damage.[802]

668. The consignor shall be entitled to *withdraw* from the contract prior to the commencement of carriage.[803]

669. The consignor shall be entitled to *reserve all rights* to the consignment until it is delivered or the consignee receives it. The carrier may demand adequate safeguards in connection with any instruction the consignor has given after the commencement of carriage, if compliance with such instruction is likely to render performance of the carriage more burdensome. If the consignor fails to provide adequate safeguards, the carrier shall act in accordance with the principle of reasonable commercial practices, taking also into account the consignor's and the consignee's interests. In this frame, the carrier has the option to sell the consignment.

799. Section 6:259 (3) CC.
800. Section 6:261 CC.
801. Section 6:260 CC.
802. Section 6:263 CC.
803. Section 6:262 CC.

Unless proven to the contrary, it shall be presumed that the sale of the consignment is conducted under the principle of reasonable commercial practices if:

- the sale is completed in the stock exchange, at a price in effect at the time of sale; or
- the sale takes place under normal market terms usually employed in the commercial sale of the consignment. If the carrier sells or uses the consignment, the consignor shall be notified thereof.[804]

670. The carrier shall be required to *notify the consignee* immediately of the arrival of the consignment. After notification has been received, the right of disposition over the consignment shall pass to the consignee. An *instruction given by the consignee* before the receipt of notice may be taken into consideration by the carrier inasmuch as it does not contradict with the consignor's instructions. The carrier may demand adequate safeguards in connection with any instruction the consignee has given, if compliance with such instruction is likely to make the carrier's obligation more burdensome. The carrier may refuse to carry out the consignee's instruction if the consignee does not provide adequate safeguards.[805]

671. If *freight charges* are to be determined on the basis of information contained in the consignment note, the data in the consignment note shall be considered accurate and appropriate, unless proven to the contrary, even if the carrier has made a reservation on the consignment note showing that he was unable to verify the data. In the event of *loss or destruction* of the consignment in part or in full, the carrier shall be entitled to collect the freight charges or a commensurate part thereof, if able to prove that the loss or destruction of the consignment occurred in consequence of circumstances beyond his control, that could not have been foreseen at the time of conclusion of the contract, and there had been no reasonable cause to take action for preventing or mitigating the damage.[806]

672. The carrier shall be entitled to *statutory lien* up to the amount of freight charges and expenses on the things he gained possession of in connection with carriage, or which are at his disposal on the basis of documentary evidence. The lien shall also cover other overdue and uncontested claims of the carrier from the consignor arising from the contracts of carriage.[807]

673. Any contract term limiting or excluding the *carrier's liability* shall be null and void, also if it pertains to damages caused deliberately or as a result of gross negligence. If the carrier makes shipping arrangements for the consignment using different modes of transport, each mode of transport shall be implemented in accordance with the rules of the given transport sector. If the place where the damages have occurred cannot be identified, the provisions of the Civil Code for carriage

804. Section 6:264 (1)–(4) CC.
805. Section 6:265 CC.
806. Section 6:266 CC.
807. Section 6:267 CC.

contract shall apply to the carrier's liability. If the consignor is a foreigner, the amount of compensation for which the carrier is liable may not exceed the highest amount of compensation that may be awarded under the law of the consignor's home state. The consignment may be considered lost when it has not been delivered within thirty days after the prescribed period of carriage. If the consignment is recovered following the payment of damages, the carrier shall notify the consignor within the shortest possible time, upon which the consignor shall have the right of disposition over the consignment.[808]

674. The *consignor* shall be *liable* toward the carrier for the loss or damage resulting from discrepancies in packaging, or from the lack or inaccuracy of, or any flaws in the data, information and/or documents relating to the consignment.[809]

675. The *period of limitation for claims* arising out of or in connection with contracts of carriage shall be one year, except for damages caused deliberately or as a result of gross negligence. The initial date of this period shall be the date on which the consignment is delivered to the consignee or the date on which the consignment should have been delivered to the consignee. These provisions shall also apply if the carrier makes shipping arrangements for the consignment using different modes of transport.[810]

676. The regulations governing works contracts shall apply to contracts of carriage mutatis mutandis.[811]

Carriage by land, river and air

677.

- 120/2016. (VI. 7.) government decree regulates the transport of goods on public roads and Hungary joined the international agreement CMR (*Convention relative au contrat de transport international de merchandises par route*);
- 32/2009. (II. 19.) government decree provides regulation the transport of goods by railway and Hungary implemented the international agreement CIM-COTIF (*Convention Internationale concernant le transport des merchandises per chemin de fer*);
- the Act CXLI of 2005 proclaimed the international agreement on transport contracts of goods on inland waters (CMNI, *Convention de Budapest relative au contrat de transport de merchandises en navigation*);
- 26/1999. (II. 12.) government decree controls the transport of goods by air and Hungary pronounced the international agreement of Montreal by Act VII of 2005.

808. Section 6:268 CC.
809. Section 6:269 CC.
810. Section 6:270 CC.
811. Section 6:271 CC.

VI. Other Services

Works contracts

678.

(a) Under a *works contract* the contractor undertakes to perform activities to achieve the result agreed upon and the customer undertakes to accept delivery of and pay the contracted fees for such works.[812]
(b) Under a *design contract* the contractor undertakes to provide design services and to deliver the resulting plans and designs, and the customer undertakes to accept delivery of and pay the contracted fees for such.[813]
(c) Under a *construction contract* the building contractor undertakes to carry out building and installation works and to deliver the works, and the customer undertakes to accept delivery of and pay the contracted fees for such works.[814]
(d) Under a *research contract* the researcher undertakes to perform research activities, and the customer undertakes to accept the results achieved and pay the contracted fees.[815]
(e) Under a *contract for travel services* the contractor undertakes to make arrangements for travel and for accommodations at points of excursion and to provide the related services, and the customer undertakes to accept the services and to pay the contracted fees.[816]
(f) Under an *agricultural services contract* the contractor undertakes to keep the customer's animals and to grow crops on the customer's land, and the customer undertakes to pay the contracted fees for such services.[817]
(g) Under a *public service contract* the service provider undertakes to provide services of general economic interest, and the user undertakes to pay a fee.[818]
(h) *Carriage contract* (*see* from 437 until 455).

Lease contracts

679.

(a) Under a *lease agreement* the lessor undertakes to convey temporary use of a thing, and the lessee undertakes to accept the thing and pay the lease charge.[819]

812. Section 6:238 CC.
813. Section 6:251 (1) CC.
814. Section 6:252 (1) CC.
815. Section 6:253 (1) CC.
816. Section 6:254 (1) CC.
817. Section 6:255 (1) CC.
818. Section 6:256 (1) CC.
819. Section 6:331 (1) CC.

(b) Under a *leasehold contract* the lessee shall be entitled to use temporarily an economically viable thing or to exercise an economically viable right, and to collect the proceeds thereof, and he shall be obliged to pay appropriate rent therefor.[820]

(c) Under a *lending arrangement* the lender undertakes to make available for use, for a limited period of time and not for direct or indirect economic or commercial advantage, a specific thing, and the borrower shall accept the thing.[821]

Deposit agreements

680.

(a) Under a *deposit contract* the depositary undertakes to safeguard the movable property to which the contract pertains and to return it when the contract is terminated, and the depositor undertakes to pay the fee agreed upon.[822]

(b) *Collective deposit contract*: If the object of deposit is a fungible property and if according to the agreement the depositary is entitled to safeguard in the same place the fungible property of several different depositors together, without having to separate them according to depositors or to identify them individually, the depositors shall become the co-owners of such fungible properties of the same type and quality and, when the deposit is terminated, the depositary shall be required to return property of the same type and quality as the property deposited in the proportion due to the depositor according to his share of ownership.[823]

(c) *Exceptional deposit contract*: If the item deposited is a fungible property and, according to the contract, the depositary is entitled to use and dispose over the deposited property, the depositary shall acquire ownership and shall be liable to return to the depositor property of the same type and quality, in the same quantity when the deposit contract is terminated.[824]

(d) *hotel deposit contract,* etc.

Guarantee contracts

681.

(a) Under a *contract of suretyship* the surety undertakes the obligation of performance to the creditor in the event of non-performance by the principal debtor.[825]

---

820. Section 6:349 (1) CC.
821. Section 6:357 (1) CC.
822. Section 6:360 CC.
823. Section 6:366 (1) CC.
824. Section 6:367 CC.
825. Section 6:416 (1) CC.

(b) The *guarantee contract* and the statement of guarantee means a guarantor's commitment under which payment is to be made to the creditor subject to the conditions laid down in the statement.[826]

Livelihood agreements

682.

(a) Under a *maintenance agreement* the person owing maintenance undertakes to provide care to the person to whom maintenance is owed and to ensure his sufficient living conditions, and the maintenance creditor undertakes to provide compensation.[827]
(b) Under a *life-annuity contract* the annuity provider undertakes to provide a specific sum of money or other fungible property to the annuitant periodically, and the annuitant undertakes to provide compensation.[828]

826. Section 6:431 (1) CC.
827. Section 6:491 (1) CC.
828. Section 6:497 CC.

Chapter 10. Commercial Securities

§1. General Observations

I. Theoretical Categorization of Security Institutions

683. From a theoretical point of view, legal institutions used to secure a claim under Hungarian law could be divided into two main categories: personal securities like surety and guarantee, and in rem securities like lien and sale goods, or the right to purchase a good for security purposes. In cases of personal securities, the secured claim could be satisfied from the total assets of the person giving the security; in cases of in rem securities, the person giving the security can only lose a defined asset, e.g., the pledged property, the good sold or purchasable for security purposes.

II. Structure of Regulation

684. A major structural reform took place on 15 March 2013, when Act No. V of 2013 on Civil Code (the New Civil Code; NCC) entered in force. Contracts concluded before this date are subject to Act No. IV of 1959 on the Civil Code (the Old Civil Code; OCC); contracts concluded after this date are subject to the NCC. Therefore, the two systems of regulation are applicable in parallel, depending on the date of origin of the security.

685. The OCC regulated all securities in Part Four (Obligations), Title I (Contracts), Chapter XXIII (Collateral Commitments for Securing Contracts). Eight kinds of legal institutions were regulated in this chapter of the OCC: earnest money ('*foglaló*'), contractual penalty ('*kötbér*'), warranty ('*jótállás*'), bank guarantee ('*bankgarancia*'), stipulation of forfeiture a right ('*jogvesztés kikötése*'), lien ('*zálogjog*'), suretyship ('*kezesség*') and security deposit ('*óvadék*').

686. In the NCC these legal institutions are not regulated in a single chapter. Lien ('*zálogjog*') is regulated in Book Five (Rights in Rem), Part III (Limited Rights in Rem), Title VII (Lien), and security deposit ('*óvadék*') became a part of lien (a pledge with right for direct satisfaction). Earnest money ('*foglaló*'), contractual penalty ('*kötbér*'), and stipulation of forfeiture a right ('*jogvesztés kikötése*') are regulated in the Book Six (The Law of Obligations), Part II (General Provisions on Contracts), Title XI (Confirmation and Amendments of Contracts), in Chapter XXVI (Confirmation of Contracts). Suretyship ('*kezesség*') and guarantee ('*garancia*') are regulated in Book Six (The Law of Obligations), Part III (Contract Types), Title XXI (Security Contracts), in Chapter LX (Contract of Surety) and Chapter LXI (Guarantee).

687. There are some connecting regulations, in particular Act No. CXLI of 1997 on the Land Registry (LRA), Act No. CCXXI of 2013 on the Security Interest Register (SIRA), the (XII. 29.) FVM Regulation on the implementation of the LRA, and the 18/2014. (III. 13.) KIM Regulation on Detailed Rules of the Security Interest Register.

§2. LIEN

I. Definition of Lien

688. Under right for lien, the lienor has the right to satisfy his or her specified claim (claim under lien, '*zálogkövetelés*') before all others by selling a specified asset or assets owned by lienee (pledged property, '*zálogtárgy*'), in case specified conditions occur (the right of satisfaction opens), generally, if the obliged person did not perform his or her obligations under the secured legal relationship.

II. Parties of the Relationship

689. The parties of this legal relationship are the lienor ('*zálogjogosult*') and the lienee ('*zálogkötelezett*'). The obliged person ('*kötelezett*'), who is obliged to perform the secured obligation, is not necessarily a subject of this legal relationship. When the obliged person and the lienee are not the same person, the former is called the personally obliged person ('*személyes kötelezett*'), and the latter is called the in rem obliged person ('*dologi kötelezett*').

690. The lienor of an independent lien shall be only a financial institution or, temporarily, the lienee itself (cf. NCC § 100 (8)). Otherwise, both the lienor and the lienee could be any natural person as well as any entity having legal capacity. However, there are special rules in case the lienee is considered to be a consumer.

691. One or more lienors could act as a lienors' agent ('*zálogjogosulti bizományos*') who can exercise the rights of the lienor(s) under the lien legal relationship in his or her own name, and should perform the duties of the lienor(s) universally and jointly with the lienor(s). The lienor's agent could also conclude the lien contract on behalf of the lienor(s) in his or her own name. Where a lienor's agent is acting instead of the lienor(s), only the name of the lienor's agent is registered in the relevant registry.

III. Types of Lien

692. There are two main types of lien, namely mortgage (*hypotheca*, '*jelzálog*') and pledge (*pignus*, '*kézizálog*'). The fundamental difference between the two types of lien is who possesses the pledged property between the founding of lien and the opening of the right of satisfaction.

693. In case of pledge, the pledged property is possessed by the lienor or a third person, called the lien holder ('*zálogtartó*'), who effectively possesses the pledged property as a deposit. In case of pledge, the pledged property could be only a collateral thing, or money, or securities (e.g., bill of exchange, share, bond, etc.). A special sub-type of pledge is the security deposit ('*óvadék*'), where the pledged property is money, payment account balances, or securities traded on the stock exchange, or any other securities whose market price is listed publicly, or securities embodying pecuniary claims whose market price can be determined at that time independently of the parties and under conditions fixed in the securities, and where the lienor has the right of direct satisfaction.

694. In case of mortgage, the pledged property is possessed by the lienee, who could also use and utilize it, before the opening of the right of satisfaction. Every type of property can be pledged in the form of a mortgage, but immovables can be pledged only in this form. A special sub-type of mortgage is the independent lien ('*önálló zálogjog*'), where the lienor is a financial institution, the pledged property is an immovable, and the lien has, in theory, a non-accessory nature, so the claim under the lien could exist without or independent of a secured claim. Indeed, under the law in force, the independent lien is rather an *independently transferable* lien, which has accessory features originating from the so-called security agreement. (For details *see* below.)

695. The NCC had introduced a new type of lien, namely the separated lien, which meant a fiduciary transfer of a normal accessory lien. A major amendment of the NCC in 2016 abolished this type of lien and made it possible to transform the existing separated lien into a normal accessory or independent lien.

696. From a theoretical point of view, the lien could be imposed on individually specified pledged property, or on a pledged property specified as a group of assets described by some features. The former does not mean that the pledged property is a single asset, but rather that the pledged assets are specified individually.

697. Where the lien is imposed on more than one individually specified asset, as a default all of the assets could be used to satisfy the whole secured claim; this is the so-called lien with jointly and severally liability ('*egyetemleges zálogjog*'), and the relevant register, except the security interest register, shall indicate that the lien is lien with jointly and severally liability. In case of a lien with jointly and several liability, the lienor shall have the right to determine the order of enforcement; however, the right to satisfaction covers only as many pledged properties as necessary to provide satisfaction.

698. Where the pledged property is defined as a group of assets described by some features, the lien shall at all times pertain to those things, rights, and claims identified by said features, over which the lienee has the right of disposition; this type of lien is often called a 'floating lien' ('*lebegő zálogjog*').

IV. The Creation of a Lien

699. Under § 5:87 of the NCC, the preconditions for the creation a lien are (I) establishing the lien and (II) the existence of the right of disposition of the lienee over the pledged property. Under § 5:88 of the NCC, the establishment of a lien needs (1) a contract or a statutory provision to establish a lien under which (2) (a) the possession of the pledged property is transferred to the lienor or lien holder in case of pledge or (b) the lien is registered in the appropriate registry in case of mortgage. (These two are collectively the so-called in rem transactions.)

A. The Lien Contract

700. The lien contract (*'zálogszerződés'*) is an arrangement between the lienee and the lienor to found a lien on a specific item and – except for an independent lien – to secure a specific claim. Under the contract of pledge, the lienee undertakes the obligation to take the necessary steps for founding the lien in this respect. These steps are to transfer possession of, or control over, the pledged property to the creditor in the case of pledge; to grant approval for the registration of a mortgage; and either to inform the obligor of a hypothecated claim in writing on having the lien established or to make out a statement thereof and deliver it to the lienor, whichever method is chosen by the lienor.

701. It is debated in Hungarian jurisprudence whether the lien contract is a real security contract subject to the general rules of contracts or an in rem agreement subject to the general rules of the limited rights in rem. At stake in this dispute is whether the parties could deviate in their contract from the rules of the NCC. In failing to found a lien, the lien contract also binds the parties, so the rights and obligations established under the NCC with respect to the lienor and the lienee shall also apply to the parties with respect to each other.

702. A lien contract shall be concluded in written form independent of the type of lien. In case of pledge, the lien contract may be replaced by a security issued by the creditor authorizing the holder of such document to obtain the pledged property in exchange for the sum indicated in the security, within the time limit specified in the security.

703. The (a) pledged property and (b) the secured claim or – in case of an independent lien – (3) a specified frame of amount shall be specified in the lien contract.

1. The Pledged Property

704. The pledged property shall be any merchantable asset with commercial value. With the exception of an ownership share in a joint property or a share of the lienee of an asset that is owned by more than one person or a specific part of a divisible claim, a fraction or part of a thing or a right may not be pledged as security.

705. The pledged property shall be specified in a clear and identifiable manner, in particular by its individual identification number, by its specific substantive features, etc. The pledged property may also be described by type and quantity. The description may also include some assets that do not yet exist, or over which the lienee has still no right of disposition.

706. The scope of the lien extends not only to the pledged property but also to all its components and, in case of doubt, to all its accessories. The scope of the lien also could extend to the products, produce, and progeny of the thing and to other benefits of the pledged property, except a third person (e.g., beneficial owner) is entitled to them.

707. A claim secured by a lien could be also a pledged property (*subordinated lien*). The subordinated lien covers the lien and the claim it secures.

2. The Secured Claim

708. The lien could secure one or more pecuniary claims, existing or future, conditional or unconditional, of a specific amount or of an amount that can be determined. If the secured claim is not a pecuniary claim, the lien secures the claim for damages or other pecuniary claim resulting from the failure to satisfy the claim. A lien cannot be created to secure a claim that cannot be enforced before a court.

709. The secured claim shall be specified in a manner by which it could be identified at the time of opening of the right to satisfaction, especially with an indication of the – one or more – underlying legal relationship and its specified amount, or in any other way suitable for the identification of the secured claim. The description may also extend certain claims that do not yet exist.

710. The scope of liability of the lienee is adjusted to the size of the secured claim. It does not mean that the secured claim and the claim under the lien, or their amounts, are the same, but their amounts shall change in straight proportions. The liability of the lienee shall include the interest on the claim, the costs of enforcing the claim and the lien as well as reasonable costs spent on the pledged property.

3. Frame of Amount

711. If the parties set a limit up to which the lienor may seek satisfaction from the pledged property, the lien shall guarantee the claim and the associated costs up to that limit (‘*keretbiztosítéki zálogjog*’). In case of an independent lien, there is always such a limit.

B. In rem Transactions

1. Transfer of Possession

712. In establishing a pledge, the transfer of possession should be effective, so the lienee should lose actual exclusive physical control over the pledged property, but transfer of possession may also be satisfied if possession is maintained jointly by the lienor and the lienee. While the transfer of possession is an in rem legal institution, it has contractual features. The transfer of possession shall be realized upon the conveyance of physical control of the thing on the basis of an agreement for this purpose.

2. Registration

713. In establishing a mortgage, the appropriate registry could be (1) the land registry (‘*ingatlan-nyilvántartás*’) for immovables, (2) the ship registry for ships and other watercraft, (3) the aircraft registry for planes and other aircrafts or (4) the security interest register (‘*hitelbiztosítéki nyilvántartás*’) for other assets.

714. The security interest register is actually an IT application that contains security interest registered by its obligor, and by which the registered user can make security interest declarations. The registration of a user needs the assistance of a civil law notary, and the security interest register is administered by the National Chamber of Civil Law Notaries. The registration of a lien requires that the lienor or the lienee make a declaration on founding a lien indicating the lienor the lienee and the pledged property and that the other party (i.e., the lienee or the lienor) make a declaration consenting to the founding of a lien.

V. Transfer of the Lien and/or the Secured Claim

715. As a default, the lien and the secured claim cannot be transferred independently. If the lienor transfers the secured claim to a third person, the lien shall also be transferred to this third person. If the parties agreed to transfer the secured claim without the lien, the lien ceases to exist, except the lien secures also other claims of the lienor, when the lien secures thereafter only the claim still owned by the lienor. If only a part of the secured claim is transferred, the previous and the new lienor shall receive the same rank for the lien in proportion to their respective claims. The lien – except independent liens – may be transferred or encumbered together with the secured claim.

716. In case of an independent lien, there is no direct connection between the lien and the secured claim, so the lien could be transferred independently from the claim it secured. Indeed, the connection between the independent lien and the claim secured by it is established in the so-called security agreement, which should be concluded besides the lien contract in written form and contains criteria for opening the right to satisfaction, generally the preconditions of termination of the independent lien. As a default, the right to satisfaction opens by termination, after six months elapses following the termination, under the NCC. A third person who acquires the independent lien as a lienor or the pledged property as a lienee became a party to the security agreement.

VI. Relationship Between Parties Before the Opening of the Right to Satisfaction

717. The content of the legal relationship between parties before the opening of the right to satisfaction depends on the type of lien.

A. General Rules on Pledge

718. In case of pledge, the pledged property could be possessed by the lienor, who could handle it as a deposit under the rules applicable to the synallagmatic deposit contract, but the lienee or the personal obligor cannot reclaim the pledged property during the existence of the lien, except he or she offers adequate other assets in replacement, if this does not jeopardize the right to satisfaction. The lienor should not use or utilize the pledged property or give it into the possession of a third person, except this is necessary to protect the lienee from any damages or losses. If the lienor uses or utilizes the pledged property or gives it into the possession of a third person, he or she becomes liable for any damages or losses that would not occur without it. The lienee and the personal obligor are entitled to check the condition and use of the pledged property.

719. If any loss in value of the pledged property could jeopardize satisfaction of the claim, the lienor shall call for the lienee to restore the condition of the pledged property or to provide adequate new pledged property or additional security covering the loss of value within a specified time limit. The lienee is entitled to any insurance settlement, compensation, or other value received in exchange for the pledged property to restore the pledged property, provided this does not jeopardize the satisfaction of the secured claim. If the lienee fails to take one of these actions, the lienor, acting in the name of and on behalf of the lienee, is entitled to sell the pledged property to prevent further depreciation. The creditor shall be entitled to sell the pledged property without warning and without setting a time limit, if any insurmountable obstacles exist or if any further delay in waiting for the debtor's action is likely to result in further depreciation.

720. In changing of the value of a security deposit or of a divisible pledged property whose value can be clearly determined relying on publicly accessible information or of the secured claim, the lienee is required to provide additional security, and the lienor is required to release proportionally the excessive amount of the pledged property to the lienee.

B. General Rules on Mortgage

721. In case of mortgage, the pledged property could be possessed by the lienee, who is also entitled to use and utilize it in a manner corresponding to its proper function, but the lienee is required to keep it in good condition. The lienee of a lien registered in the security interest register on a pledged property specified by detailed description is entitled to process, convert, merge, or mix the pledged property within the framework of prudent management.

722. The lienor is entitled to check the condition and use of the pledged property. In case the lienee or a third person is endangering the integrity of the pledged property, the lienor is entitled to exercise the rights of a person who is in a situation threatening damage. If any loss in value of the pledged property could jeopardize satisfaction of the claim, the lienor shall exercise the same rights as the lienor of a pledge in analogous situation.

C. Special Rules on Pledged Claim

723. After the debtor of a pledged claim is notified in writing concerning the establishment of a lien with an indication of the pledged claim and the lienor, the termination or such amendment of the underlying contract between the lienee and the obligor of the pledged claim, which may have a detrimental effect on the lienor's right to satisfaction or otherwise diminishes the value of the pledged property, is ineffective in relations of the lienor. However, termination or amendment of the contract shall take effect if the lienor declares his or her consent to the lienee and to the obligor. The obligor of the pledged claim could evoke such objections and counterclaims against the lienor that are based on legal grounds still existing at the time of notification against the lienee.

724. The obligor of the pledged claim shall perform the claim to the lienee until he or she gets a performance instruction containing the lienor's name and registered office or home address, or habitual residence, or account number for a natural person. After that, the obligor shall perform to the lienor. The lienor is entitled to give an effective performance instruction after the opening of the right to satisfaction; before this date the lienee is entitled to give it, but when the notification contains the name of lienor, the lienee could give a performance instruction in favour of the lienor. The performance instruction shall not affect the rights and obligations the payment service provider has under the account or deposit contract in terms of the account holder.

725. At the lienor's request, the lienee shall produce the documents necessary for enforcing the pledged claim. If the maturity of a pledged claim depends on the legal statement of the lienee or on a condition to be met by him or her, the lienor shall be entitled to make the legal statement or to satisfy the condition required for maturity.

VII. Enforcement of the Lien

726. There are multiple ways to enforce the right to satisfaction under Hungarian law. Generally, the lienor can choose from these, but there are some restrictions of this right. First, when a lienee is considered to be a consumer, the lien can be enforced only by judicial enforcement processes, except the lienor exercises his or her right to direct satisfaction in respect of security deposit, or enforces a pledged right or claim against its obligor, or acts under a written agreement concluded with the lienee after the opening of the right to satisfaction. Second, in case of a mortgage on payment account balances, which shall be enforced only by way of judicial enforcement. Third, if the pledged property is subject to a judicial enforcement process or an insolvency process, the right to satisfaction can be exercised only within these processes.

727. There are two main ways by which the right to satisfaction could be enforced: (1) by judicial enforcement and (2) by means other than judicial enforcement.

A. *Judicial Enforcement*

728. The processes of judicial enforcement are regulated by Act No. LIII of 1994 on judicial enforcement (JEA). There are three different means of judicial enforcement: (a) initiating an action before the court to enforce the lien, and then a judicial enforcement process under the final Judgment of the court by issuing an enforcement certificate by the court under § 15 (1) a) of the JEA; (b) initiating a judicial enforcement process by issuing an enforcement clause on a public document by a civil law notary under § 23/C of the JEA; and (c) initiating a judicial enforcement process by issuing an enforcement clause on a public document to simplify enforcement of the lien by a civil law notary under § 204/B of the JEA.

B. *Other Means*

729. There are two different ways of enforcement outside of judicial enforcement under § 5:127 of the NCC: (a) selling the pledged property by the lienor to a third person; and (b) acquiring the pledged property by the lienor.

1. Selling the Pledged Property to a Third Person

730. The lienor is entitled to transfer the ownership of the pledged property instead and in the name of the lienee.

731. In case of mortgage, after the opening of the right to satisfaction, the lienor has the right to take the possession of the pledged property for the purpose of sale.

The lienor should call on the lienee to release the pledged property into his possession by the time limit specified, at least ten days in the case of collaterals, at least twenty days in the case of immovables, and at least three months in the case of residential estates. Failure to take possession shall have no bearing on carrying out the sale of the pledged property.

732. The lienor shall send notice in writing concerning his intention to sell the pledged property ten days before the time of sale to every person concerned, e.g.: the lienee; the personal obligor; the persons having guaranteed the personal obligor's performance; beneficiaries of registered in rem rights on the pledged property, if the pledged property has been registered; and persons who sent notice in writing claiming to hold some right on the pledged property, with proof attached, more than ten days before the date of the lienor's notice. In the prior notice, the lienor shall specify the name of the lienor and the lienee, the pledged property to be sold, the amount of the claim enforced and the associated costs, the reason for and the date of the opening of the right to satisfaction, the planned mode of sale, and the place and date of the public sale, or if sold by other means, the date after which the sale will take place. The lienor is entitled to sell the pledged property without prior notification if the pledged property is perishable, or if its value is likely to diminish considerably upon any delay, or if it is traded on the stock exchange.

733. The lienor shall act in accordance with the principle of reasonable commercial practices, and in due observation of the lienee's and/or the personal obligor's interest. The pledged property could be sold in its original conditions or after commercially justified processing or conversion, privately or publicly. If the lien is established on more than one pledged property to secure the same claim, they may be sold together or separately. Unless proven to the contrary, it shall be presumed that the sale of the pledged property is conducted under the principle of reasonable commercial practices if the sale is completed on the stock exchange at a price in effect at the time of sale; or if the sale takes place under normal market terms usually employed in the commercial sale of pledged properties. The lienor may acquire ownership of the pledged property he is selling in the case of public sale, or if the pledged property is traded on the stock exchange.

734. After the sale, the lienor, acting as the seller, is required without delay to distribute the purchase price received plus the proceeds collected, minus the costs arising out of or in connection with the safeguarding, maintenance, processing, conversion, and sale of the pledged property, taking into consideration the ranking of the liens and the amounts of the claims secured by such liens among the holders of the liens on the pledged property, and to pay the remaining amount to the lienee. The lienor, in order to comply this obligation, shall send a written statement to the lienee and to all persons to whom prior notification is to be sent.

2. Acquisition of the Pledged Property by the Lienor

735. An agreement concluded before the opening of right to satisfaction under which the lienor acquires the ownership of the pledged property is invalid and has no effect. Nonetheless, the lienor, after the opening of the right to satisfaction, could acquire ownership of the pledged property under a bid made in written form after this date. This bid shall contain a financial plan to satisfy the claims of the lienor and other beneficiaries of rights on the pledged properties, and should be sent to the lienee and to all persons to whom prior notification is to be sent in case of selling the pledged property to a third person. If the lienee accepts this bid and the other notified persons do not object to it within twenty days, a sales contract is created between the lienor and the lienee on the pledged property, and the lienor is required to satisfy besides his or her own claim, all claims of other beneficiaries from the sales price under the beforehand-sent financial plan.

736. In case of security deposit, the lienor has the right to direct satisfaction, which means that the lienor is entitled to acquire ownership of the pledged property by way of a unilateral statement addressed to the lienee up to the amount of the secured claim at date of opening his right to satisfaction. The lienor shall settle accounts in writing with the lienee immediately after exercising direct right to satisfaction and pay the amount remaining after the secured claim is satisfied to the lienee. To that end, money and payment account balances shall be taken into account at their nominal value, whereas securities shall be taken into account at market value or at a price that can be determined at that time independent of the parties.

737. The lienor of a lien on a pledged claim or right has also the right to enforce the pledged claim by giving a performance instruction to the obligor of the claim or enforcing the claim by judicial processes after the date of maturity of the claim, instead of the original beneficiary of the claim. Hereinafter, the money received as performance of the pledged claim should be handled as a security deposit; other things received as performance are handled as a pledged property. If the claim on which the lien is founded is secured by a lien or surety, the lienor, as lienor of the subordinated lien, may also exercise the rights arising out of or in connection with the lien or surety to the extent the lienor is entitled to exercise these rights. The lienor of the subordinated lien shall exercise his or her rights in such a way as not to endanger recovery of the lienor's secured claim. The lienor has a lien on any sum received by the lienor of the subordinated lien upon satisfaction thereof in excess of the claim secured by that subordinated lien in security for any settlement claim the lienor may have against the lienor of the subordinated lien.

VIII. Termination of the Lien

738. A pledge ceases to exist if (1) the lienor waives his or her pledge and returns the pledged property to the lienee; (2) the pledged property is destroyed without any replacement; (3) the lienor loses possession of the pledged property, except when he or she brings an action in rem or a possessory action without delay; (4) the secured claim ceases to exists or any legal relationship that may result in a secured claim in the future is terminated; (5) the lienor sells the pledged property or acquires ownership of the pledged property as exercising of his or her right to satisfaction.

739. In general, a mortgage ceases to exist if (1) the lienor waives his or her lien and the mortgage is cancelled in the relevant register; (2) the pledged property is destroyed, or the pledged right or claim ceases to exist without any replacement; (3) the secured claim ceases to exists or any legal relationship that may result in a secured claim in the future is terminated; (4) the secured claim lapses; (5) the lienor sells the pledged property or acquires ownership of the pledged property as exercising of his or her right to satisfaction.

740. In both cases, if the secured claim ceases to exist, the lien shall remain in force nonetheless for guaranteeing the recovery claim accruing to the obligor who satisfied the claim, to the lienee, or to a third party. The lien also shall remain in force to guarantee the secured claim if the same person becomes the lienee and the lienor.

741. There are different grounds for termination of an independent lien, namely if (1) the security agreement is not concluded; (2) the purpose indicated in the security agreement for establishing the independent lien failed permanently; (3) the security agreement ceased to exist; (4) the claim that can be satisfied from the pledged property under the security agreement ceased to exist; (5) any other reason indicated in the security agreement for the termination of the independent lien. Furthermore, the independent lien does not cease to exist automatically. If one of the aforementioned grounds occurs, the lienee has a right to choose between two options. The lienee is entitled to call for the lienor to give consent in written form to (1) the lienee or a financial institution assigned by the lienee being registered in the land registry as the beneficiary of the independent lien, or (2) the independent lien being deleted from the land registry.

§3. Suretyship

I. Definition of Suretyship

742. Under a suretyship contract, the surety undertakes the obligation to perform a certain sum of money to the creditor in event of the obligor not performing his or her obligation. The scope of liability of the lienee is adjusted to the size of the secured claim. It does not mean that the secured claim and the claim under the suretyship, or their amounts, are the same, but their value shall change in straight proportions.

II. Parties of the Relationship

743. The parties to this legal relationship are the creditor (‘*hitelező*’) and the surety (‘*kezes*’). The obligor (‘*kötelezett*’), who is obliged to perform the secured obligation, is not necessarily a party of this legal relationship. The obliged person and the surety cannot be the same person, except the obligor has a limited liability under the relationship on which the secured claim is based and undertakes an unlimited liability as a surety for his or her own debt.

744. Both the debtor and the surety could be any natural person, as well as any entity having legal capacity. However, there are special rules in case the surety is considered to be a consumer. These special rules cannot be applicable when the surety is an executive officer or a member with majority control of the obligor legal person.

III. Suretyship Contract

745. The suretyship contract shall be concluded in written form. In any suretyship contract, the secured claim should be specified. The secured claim could be one or more pecuniary claims, existing or future, conditional or unconditional, of a specific amount or of an amount that can be determined at the time of maturity, or any other claims of monetary value. The secured claim cannot be an invalid claim, and surety securing a claim that cannot be enforced by judicial process cannot be enforced before the court. If the surety is considered to be a consumer and is liable for all claims of the obligor toward the creditor, or all obligations of the obligor arising from specific relationship (so-called global suretyship), the contract shall only be considered valid if the highest amount of debt for which the consumer is liable is specified in the contract.

746. In case a surety is considered be a consumer, the creditor shall inform the consumer before the contract of suretyship is concluded of the rights and obligations of the surety, and about specific risks inherent to the debtor’s circumstances or to the nature of the liability of which the creditor is aware. In case the creditor fails to comply with this obligation, the surety shall be entitled to cancel the contract without a time limit.

747. The suretyship can also be originated under legal rules (so-called statutory suretyship). The provisions on contracts of suretyship shall apply to statutory suretyship *mutatis mutandis*.

IV. Content of Legal Relationship

A. *Liability of Surety*

748. The payment obligation of a surety shall be adjusted to the value of the secured obligation. The obligation of a surety shall not and cannot subsequently exceed the original obligation; however, it shall cover the consequences of the debtor's non-performance and shall include collateral claims that fall due after the suretyship is undertaken. The surety shall be liable for court costs and for the costs of enforcement only if he or she has been called on by the creditor to perform without result prior to taking legal action.

749. The surety is entitled to count in the obligor's counterclaims, besides his or her own, the creditor's claims, and to evoke the obligor's objections besides his or her own. After the suretyship is undertaken, the debtor's waiver of the right of objection shall not apply to the surety.

750. Any respite of payment afforded in insolvency proceedings opened against the obligor does not affect the surety's obligation. Any settlement reached in insolvency proceedings opened against the obligor shall not affect the surety's obligation, if the creditor informed the surety of the terms of the settlement before it was concluded. After being informed, the surety is entitled to satisfy the creditor's claim; following satisfaction, the surety shall replace the creditor in the insolvency proceedings. In the event of failure to provide the said information, the obligation of the surety shall be reduced to the level set out in the settlement.

751. In case of a surety without objection of rank order, the liability of the surety, who has undertaken to be a surety for a fixed period of time, is terminated following expiry of the time period. In case of a suretyship for an indefinite time period securing all existing and future obligations of the obligor toward the creditor (so-called global suretyship), the surety shall be entitled to terminate the contract of suretyship by giving at least three months' termination notice.

752. If the creditor waives any right securing the claim, or if the claim has become otherwise irrecoverable for reasons attributable to the creditor, or if recovery becomes increasingly burdensome, the surety shall be exonerated inasmuch as he or she could have received satisfaction based on his or her claim for reimbursement against the obligor.

B. *Objection of Rank Order*

753. In general, the surety is entitled to refuse the performance as long as the creditor demonstrates that he or she had attempted to recover the debt from the obligor, but that did not lead to a result within a reasonable timeframe (objection of rank order; '*sortartás kifogása*'). This does not prevent bringing a joint action against the obligor and the sureties.

754. The surety cannot refuse the performance (suretyship without objection of rank order; '*készfizető kezesség*') if (1) recovering the debt from the obligor is considerably impeded due to changes in the obligor's address, habitual residence, place of business, or registered office; (2) the creditor conducted enforcement proceedings on the obligor's assets to recover other claims, and the enforcement procedure has been unsuccessful; (3) the obligor was granted a respite of payment in insolvency proceedings, or in a liquidation process initiated against the obligor; or (4) the parties have ruled out it in the suretyship contract.

755. If suretyship expressly covers that part of the debt that cannot be recovered from the obligor (compensating suretyship; '*kártalanító kezesség*'), the creditor is entitled to demand payment from the surety after an enforcement proceedings on the obligor's assets to recover the secured claim has been unsuccessful.

C. Enforcing the Suretyship

756. The creditor shall inform the surety without delay in the event that (1) the obligor fails to perform; (2) the date of performance of a secured claim changes; (3) the obligor's circumstances change in a way that may negatively affect the surety's claim for reimbursement against the obligor. The information shall include the extent of the secured claim existing at the time the information is provided. Furthermore, in case of global suretyship, the creditor shall also inform the surety without delay if the extent of the secured claim has increased by 20% since the time the suretyship was undertaken, or since information was last provided.

757. If the obligor fails to fulfil the secured claim, the creditor shall call for the surety to perform his or her obligation under suretyship. Then the surety shall inform the obligor without delay of receipt of the request for payment, and shall ask for information as to the extent of the secured claim and on the objections and claims the obligor may have in respect to the creditor. The surety shall without delay (1) perform to the creditor, and shall forthwith notify the obligor of performance without delay; or (2) refuse performance, and shall forthwith notify the debtor and the creditor of its refusal to perform, indicating the reasons.

D. Claim to Reimbursement

758. The surety, having performed his or her duty, has generally the right to reimbursement against the obligor under the legal relationship between them. Therefore, after the surety's performance, the creditor shall forthwith deliver to the surety all documents and shall provide all information that may be necessary for the surety to recover his or her claim for the obligor. If the creditor's claim is satisfied by a person who guaranteed performance of the surety's obligations, that person shall also be entitled to enforce, up to the amount of the claim, all those rights the surety would have had in the event of satisfying the creditor's claim.

759. If suretyship is undertaken by more than one person for the same secured claim, the sureties are subject to joint and several liability toward the creditor. If suretyship is concurrently undertaken by more than one person independently, in their relationship the sureties are liable in the sequence they have undertaken to provide suretyship. The surety who had objection of rank order against the creditor shall also call for it in respect to the surety who satisfied the creditor's claim. If suretyship is jointly undertaken by more than one person, in their relationship the sureties shall be subject to liability in proportion to their exposure. If the same claim is secured by suretyship and by lien established by a person other than the obligor, the liability of the surety and the lienor, and their relationship, are governed by the provisions on multiple sureties.

§4. GUARANTEE

I. Definition of Guarantee

760. In case of guarantee, the guarantor undertakes by a written unilateral statement or a written contract the obligation to perform payment to the beneficiary or creditor, if the conditions laid down the written statement of guarantee are proved. The obligation of the guarantor undertaken in the statement of guarantee is independent of the obligation for which he has promised to respond, even if there is a reference of a general character made in the statement of guarantee to the guaranteed obligation, so the guarantor may not enforce the same objections that can be made by the debtor against the creditor.

II. Parties to the Relationship

761. The parties to this legal relationships are the creditor (*'hitelező'*) and the guarantor (*'garantőr'*). The obligor (*'kötelezett'*), who is obliged to perform the secured obligation, is not necessarily a subject of this legal relationship. The obliged person and the guarantor cannot be the same person, except the obligor has a limited liability under the relationship in which the secured claim is based and undertakes an unlimited liability as a surety for his or her own debt.

762. The creditor may not transfer the right to call upon to pay under the statement of guarantee without the guarantor's consent; however, he or she is entitled to designate a person to whom payment is to be made by the guarantor. The right to call upon to pay passes to the creditor's successor.

763. Under the OCC, the guarantor could be only a bank or other financial institution. Under the NCC, both the debtor and the guarantor can be any natural person, as well as any entity having legal capacity. However, natural persons considered to be consumers cannot be guarantors; his or her obligation is valid as a consumer's suretyship without objection of rank order.

III. Content of Legal Relationship

764. The guarantor has an abstract liability strictly regulated by the statement of guarantee. The guarantor shall perform payment under the guarantee if the creditor requested payment in writing, strictly abiding by the requirements specified in the statement of guarantee. The guarantor is entitled only to invoke all objections originating from the written statement of guarantee, or otherwise those the guarantor has on his or her own right against the creditor.

765. The guarantor shall inform the debtor without delay of receipt of the request for payment, in order that the debtor may inform him or her about any accidental suspicious circumstances. After the request for payment is received, the guarantor shall without delay (1) perform to the creditor, and notify the debtor of performance; or (2) refuse performance, and notify the debtor and the creditor of its refusal to perform, indicating the reasons.

766. The guarantor has the right to refuse performance or to recover payments already performed, only in that case, when based on the information at the guarantor's disposal, the creditor exercises his or her right to call on to pay in a manner that is manifestly fraudulent or in bad faith. The request of payment shall be considered to be in a manner that is manifestly fraudulent or in bad faith when, in particular (1) any of the documents submitted to the guarantor is forged; (2) the debtor has already performed the obligation for which the guarantor has undertaken liability, or the creditor is not entitled to the sum requested for other reasons; (3) the creditor's intentional behaviour prevented performance of the obligation for which the guarantor has promised to answer; or (3) the obligation for which the guarantor promised to answer has been declared invalid by court decision, unless the guarantee covers such instance as well.

767. The guarantor is entitled to terminate an open-term guarantee contract after three years by giving at least three months' notice.

§5. Other Institutions Used for Securing a Claim

768. There are some other institutions that are not peculiar to purpose of securing a claim but are used for this purpose in practice.

I. Fiduciary Transactions

769. When the OCC was in force, a practice developed under which a claim, especially originating from a loan or a financial leasing contract, could be secured by fiduciary transaction, namely founding a purchase option, transfer of ownership or cession for security purpose.

770. Under § 6:99 of the NCC, any clause in which a consumer undertakes an obligation for the transfer of ownership, other right or claim for the purpose of security of a pecuniary claim, or for the right to purchase, shall be null and void. This rule should be applied not only to a contract between a consumer and a businessman but also to contracts between consumers. Otherwise, a clause in which the obligor undertakes an obligation to found a purchase option or to transfer an asset for security purpose is valid.

771. In case of founding a purchase option for security purposes, the purchase option could be exercised only in the case where the obligor of the secured claim does not perform its obligations within the validity period of the options. In the founding contract, the sales price should be exactly specified, and the creditor shall without delay give the remaining sum of money to the obligor, after having counted his or her claim into the sales price.

772. In case of transfer of assets for security purposes, the owner or beneficiary transfers the ownership or other own right or claim to the creditor under the condition, if the debtor performs his duty, that the owner can repurchase his previously sold assets. In the founding contract, the resale price should be exactly specified, and the creditor shall without delay give his or her counted claim into the resale price.

II. Retention of Property Rights

773. Section 6:216 of the NCC provides the possibility for the seller to retain his or her property rights until the purchase price is paid in full under a written agreement between the parties to the sales contract.

774. In the case of retention of property rights relating to real estate property, the seller shall have it recorded in the real estate register in the form of an entry showing the fact of retention of title and the name of the buyer. In the case of retention of property rights relating to collaterals, the seller shall have it registered in the security interest register showing the fact of retention of title and the name of the buyer, or in the relevant registry if ownership of the property sold is recorded in a public register and if hypothecation of the thing is to be registered in the proper registry by law.

775. In the absence of registration, the collateral sold is acquired from the buyer by a third person acting in good faith, and the lien founded on the collateral sold by the buyer for a third party would be created even if the buyer has no right of disposition.

Part II. Economic Law

Chapter 1. General Principles

776. In the socialist period of Hungary the economic law was a branch of law regulating the economy of society.[829] The material of economic law consisted of the collective ownership and the connecting contractual system at that time.[830] Asztalos László thought so that the parallel of economic and civil laws ripped vertically the private law in two.[831]

777. However the conception of *economic law had a very short phase in Hungary:*[832] nowadays there is not any independent economic law, it does *not exist in Hungary*. The object and the method of the regulation are same in commercial and economic – but also inside of private law[833] – the phrase of economy law is not used in Hungary (only a few times as synonym of commercial law).

778. Following from the lack of economic law in Hungary the basic principles, the institutional framework, the state shareholdings, etc. are the same as in commercial law.

829. Gy. Vadas & A. Weltner, *Gazdasági jog*, Budapest: Magyar Magánalkalmazottak Szabad Szakszervezete kiadása, 1949, 5.
830. M. Világhy & Gy. Eörsi, *Magyar polgári jog*, Budapest: Tankönyvkiadó, 1965, 22; Lábady, *supra* n. 56, 36.
831. Asztalos, *supra* n. 58, 18; Boóc & Sándor, *supra* n. 59, 17; Bíró & Lenkovics, *supra* n. 61, 21; Lábady, *supra* n. 56, 35.
832. Kecskés, *supra* n. 52, 44.
833. Világhy & Eörsi, *supra* n. 830, 8.

Chapter 2. Law of Establishment and Supervision of Economic Activities

779. Follow from the lack of economic law in Hungary the law of establishment and supervision of economic activities are identical with the commercial law institutes.

Chapter 3. State Incentives for Economic Activities

780. State incentives for economic activities include:

- tax benefit;
- non-repayable financial grants;
- subsidies on interest and leasing or factoring fees;
- State guarantee for purposes of obtaining credit or a bank guarantee;
- investment in venture capital funds or acquiring shares in capital companies or other enterprises.

781. As to the objectives of State aid, the following categories are established by law:[834]

- horizontal objectives (e.g., R&D, innovation, reorganisation, culture, protection of the environment, export-credit insurance and guarantee);
- regional subsidies;
- sectoral subsidies (e.g., car manufacturing, coal and steel industry, transport);
- aid under TFEU Article 107 (2) and (3) and under TFEU Article 108 (2);
- aid for public services provided;
- aid under Commission Regulation 651/2014/EU;
- aid for the development of broadband infrastructure;
- fishery;
- agriculture, rural development and forestry.

782. State aid may be provided as part of an aid programme (e.g., Supporting the Hungarian sport sector via tax benefit scheme) or as an ad hoc aid.

783. State aid is primarily regulated by the law of the EU, including TFEU Article 107, Council Regulation (EU) No. 2015/1588 of 13 July 2015 on the application of Articles 107 and 108 of the Treaty on the Functioning of the EU to certain categories of horizontal State aid as well as Commission Regulation (EU) No. 651/2014 of 17 June 2014 declaring certain categories of aid compatible with the internal market in application of Articles 107 and 108 of the Treaty.

784. The State Aid Monitoring Office (SAMO), organised within the Prime Minister's Office, is responsible for State aid control (except for agricultural, fishery, forestry and rural development cases).

785. The SAMO has the task to ensure that State aid in Hungary is granted in accordance with the State aid rules of the Union. The legal background for implementing State aid control is Government Decree No. 37/2011. (III. 22.) on procedures relating to State aid measures under TFEU Article 107 (1) and the regional

834. Government Decree No. 37/2011. (III. 22.) on procedures relating to State aid measures under TFEU Art. 107 (1) and the regional aid map, Annex I.

aid map. The Government Decree contains procedural rules relating to prior notification, sets out the rules for cumulation of aid coming from different sources, defines the Hungarian regional aid map and prescribes the obligatory elements of the aid measures.

786. The procedural rules oblige all aid grantors to notify their aid plans in advance to SAMO, which is responsible for assessing the compatibility of each aid proposal with relevant EU laws and regulations. In its preliminary opinion SAMO can recommend modification of the given measure to make it compatible with the EU rules. In cases where the approval of the Commission is necessary, if SAMO finds that the rules of an aid measure do not comply with the EU rules, the notification cannot be submitted to the Commission unless the Government specifically instructs SAMO to do so. SAMO will keep the aid grantor informed of any additional questions and decisions of the Commission concerning the notified aid plan.

787. The regional aid map of Hungary specifies the maximum allowed aid intensity (the proportion of aid measured against total expenses) for the different regions depending on their level of economic development. Allowed aid intensity ranges from 50% in the least developed regions to 20% in the more developed regions. Aid intensity may be increased by an additional 10% for medium and 20% for small enterprises.

788. Rules on State involvement in capital companies and other enterprises are provided in Act CXCVI of 2011 on national assets (NAA) and Act CVI of 2007 on State assets (SAA). The State may participate in economic activities only with assets that are not the exclusive property of the State and are marketable. The State may perform economic activities within the limits of budgetary authorisation by the National Assembly and with the objective of facilitating the exercise of its public functions and may take only reasonable economic risks. The same rules apply to local governments.

789. The State or a local government may found or participate only in economic entities where its liability does not exceed its financial contribution.[835] The State may not invest in economic entities that are not transparent or have non-transparent members (owners) with at least 25% of the shares.[836] An entity is deemed transparent:

- by definition (e.g., the State, local governments, State-owned enterprises, churches, international organisations); or
- if its ownership structure and actual owners may be ascertained and it has its tax residence in the EU, EEA or OECD Member State or in a country that concluded with Hungary an agreement on the avoidance of double taxation.[837]

835. SAA Art. 29 (1); NAA Art. 9 (2).
836. NAA Art. 8 (1).
837. NAA Art. 3 (1) 1.

790. State assets are managed by the Hungarian National Asset Management (HNAM) Inc. It exercises ownership rights over state assets of over HUF 17 trillion and ownership supervision over more than 500 state-owned business associations, of which it directly exercises ownership rights over about 450 companies. Some of the key companies supervised by HNAM Inc. are MVM Hungarian Electricity Ltd., a major Hungarian energy group, Szerencsejáték Ltd., a dominant player in the market of games of chance, regional transport companies providing local road transport services and Volánbusz Zrt., as well as the water utilities companies and the waste management holding.

Chapter 4. Competition Law

791. In Hungary, the first legal regulation of competition was Act V of 1923, which incorporated the main characteristics of the German Act against Unfair Competition.[838] After the democratic change of regime, competition rules have been further developed by Act LXXXVI of 1990 on the Prohibition of Unfair Market Practices, which was an important step forward regarding the harmonisation of Hungarian competition law with European Community law principles.[839] Thereafter, Act LVII of 1996 on the Prohibition of Unfair and Restrictive Market Practices has entered into force (HCA[840] which has been further amended as well.

792. The HCA covers all substantive fields of Hungarian competition law,[841] including classical antitrust issues,[842] prohibition of unfair competition, prohibition of the unfair manipulation of business decisions, and relevant procedural law applicable by the GVH and the courts.

793. The provisions on the prohibition of unfair competition in Chapter II of the HCA are enforced by the courts. In case of other infringements (e.g., unfair manipulation of business decisions, restrictive agreements, abuse of dominant position) and control of the concentration of undertakings, the GVH applies the provisions of the HCA in its competition supervision proceedings.

794. The GVH is an autonomous government body that applies the provisions of Hungarian national and EU competition law. The efficiency and uniformity of law enforcement related to EU competition law are assisted by cooperation within the European Competition Network (ECN), which consists of the European Commission as the EU competition authority and the competition authorities of the Member States.

795. The GVH is seated in Budapest. The chief executive of the GVH is the president. The president shall be nominated by the prime minister and appointed by the president of the republic. The two vice presidents of the GVH shall be nominated by the president of the GVH to the prime minister, who will forward them to the president of the republic. The vice presidents, one of whom shall be assigned to fill the office of president of the Competition Council, shall be appointed by the president of the republic. The terms of the president and the vice presidents are six years. The terms of these officers may be renewed but the term of the president of the Competition Council may be renewed only once.

838. Gesetz gegen den unlauteren Wettbewerb, 'UWG', 1909.
839. *See*: T. Tóth, *Competition Cases from the European Union – Hungary.* In: Kokkoris, Ioannis (ed.): *Competition Cases from the European Union*, Sweet & Maxwell: London, 2010, pp. 629–672.
840. *See* for more details: P. Miskolczi BodnárB., *A versenytörvény magyarázata* [The commentary of the Competition Act], KJK-Kerszöv: Budapest, 2002.
841. *See* for more details: Cs. I. Nagy, *Competition Law in Hungary*, Wolters Kluwer: The Hague, 2016.
842. *See* for more details: Gy. Boytha. & T. Tóth (ed.), *Versenyjog*. PKE JÁK, Budapest, 2010.

796. The Competition Council consists of members and the president of the Competition Council. The Competition Council shall make its decisions independently, in accordance with the law, and in conformity with their own convictions, and they may not be influenced or instructed during their decision-making.

797. Investigators are public officials acting within the responsibilities of the GVH who participate in sectoral inquiries, in notification (including notifications of contraction) and/or complaint proceedings, and in competition supervision proceedings in the interest of the effectiveness of the proceedings as well.

§1. ANTITRUST LAW

I. Restrictive Practices

798. Agreements and concerted practices between companies, as well as the decisions of the association of companies, which aim to prevent, restrict, or distort economic competition or which may display such an effect, are prohibited.[843] The typical restrictive actions are the following:

(1) fixing purchase or sales prices, and defining other business conditions directly or indirectly;
(2) restricting manufacture, distribution, technical development, and investment, or keeping them under control;
(3) dividing the sources of supply and restricting the freedom of choice, as well as excluding specific trading parties from the purchase of goods;
(4) dividing the market, excluding any party from selling;
(5) preventing any party from entering the market; and
(6) making the conclusion of a contract conditional on undertaking a commitment that does not form part of the subject of the contract.

799. There are vertical agreements between undertakings[844] operating on different levels of the production and distribution chain (e.g., between manufacturers and distributors) and horizontal agreements between competitors. In principle, both agreements are prohibited and void[845] according to the HCA. Certain restrictive agreements, however, are exempted from the prohibition.

800. With the exception of hardcore infringements, agreements of minor importance are not prohibited. An agreement is regarded as of minor importance if the combined share of the parties to the agreement and of the companies that are not independent from such parties does not exceed 10% in the market in question. In

843. *See* for consequences: B. Berke, *Büntető közigazgatás és bírósági felülvizsgálat.* In: *Viva Vox Iuris Civilis, Tanulmányok Sólyom László tiszteletére*, Budapest, 2012, 41–76.
844. *See* for more details: L. Darázs., *Vertikális kartellek* [Vertical restraints]. Complex, Budapest, 2007.
845. *See* for more details: L. Darázs., *A kartellek semmissége* [The automatic invalidity of restrictive agreements]. Complex, Budapest, 2009.

case the undertakings engaged are not independent of each other, their agreement does not qualify as restrictive under the HCA.

801. An agreement that has beneficial effects on the economy and at the same time allows consumers a fair share of the resulting benefit does not fall under the scope of the prohibition. Apart from individual exceptions, block exemption regulations may be applied. It may occur that the undertakings have to prove their agreement's qualification for exemption in a competition supervision proceeding, which is carried out by the Competition Council of the GVH.

802. The most serious restrictive agreements are the so-called hardcore cartels. Hardcore cartel agreements create direct or indirect fixing of prices, other business terms and conditions, or relate to the allocation of the market. Therefore, neither an exception nor an exemption can apply to them.

803. Decisions made by the associations of undertakings that have the object or effect of restricting competition are also prohibited. In fact, these associations are capable of affecting their member undertakings' market behaviour, therefore the association itself qualifies as a market actor.

II. A Leniency Policy

804. In cartel cases,[846] leniency policy is available. The leniency policy is based on the assumption that certain undertakings involved in secret agreements would be willing to end their participation and provide information about the existence and operation of the cartel, but they are afraid of penalties. The leniency policy grants immunity or reduction of fines for undertakings that participate in a cartel but also actively assist in its detection.

805. Leniency policy can be initiated by the submission of an application for leniency. Since 1 July 2014, it is not required to use a form for filing a leniency application. The most essential requirements of leniency applications are stipulated by Article 78/A and 78/B of the HCA.[847]

III. Monopolies and Abuse of Dominant Position

806. Dominant position can be obtained only in a relevant market because, as a 'step zero' of the analysis, the market has to be clearly defined. Relevant market means – in a geographic sense – the area in which the conditions of competition are

---

846. *See* for more details: Cs. I. Nagy, *Kartelljogi kézikönyv. A közösségi és a magyar kartelljog kézikönyve* [Handbook of Restrictive Agreements. Handbook of Restrictive Agreements in Community and Hungarian Competition Law]. HVG Orac, 2006.

847. *See also*: ECN Model Leninency Programme (As revised in November 2012) http://ec.europa.eu/competition/ecn/mlp_revised_2012_en.pdf.

adequately homogenous. The other aspect that has to be taken into account is the relevant market of goods in which the goods are interchangeable from the perspective of consumers.

807. An undertaking has a dominant position in the relevant market if it can conduct its economic activity largely independently of other market participants, without the need to substantially take into account the market policies of its competitors, suppliers, and business partners. In other words, the undertaking has a significant market power, so its dominant position is sustainable and, for that reason, it is capable of excluding competitors from the market, as well as influencing the price on the market. Having a dominant position in itself is not prohibited; it simply means that the undertaking concerned has a leading role on the market. However, the prohibition applies to abusing this dominance on the market.

808. In particular, the following criteria shall be considered for the assessment of dominant position:

(1) costs and risks regarding entering or exiting the relevant market, and the implementation of the technical, economic or legal background;
(2) assets, financial strength, and income of the company; and
(3) structure of the relevant market, ratios of market shares, conduct of the participants of the market, and economic influence exercised by the company.

809. Dominant position can be abused,[848] in particular, through the following activities:

(1) fixing purchase or sales prices unfairly in business relations, including where general contract terms and conditions apply or forcing the acceptance of adverse terms and conditions on the other party;
(2) restricting production, distribution, or technical development to the disadvantage of final trading parties;
(3) refusing to establish or maintain business relations without any justification;
(4) influencing the other party's business decisions;
(5) withdrawing goods from general circulation, or withholding goods without justification;
(6) tying of goods;
(7) discriminating against certain business partners unduly;
(8) forcing competitors off the relevant market, or using excessively low prices to prevent competitors from entering the market; and
(9) creating a market environment that is unreasonably disadvantageous for the competitors.

848. *See* for more details: Cs. I. Nagy, *Competition Law in Hungary*, Wolters Kluwer: The Hague, 2016.

IV. Mergers and Acquisitions

810. Merger control is the control of concentrations of undertakings, which is coordinated by the GVH. There are areas to which separate legal norms apply. These may determine additional rules concerning the control of concentrations, which is enforced either by the GVH (e.g., Act on Medicines) or a sectoral supervisory authority (e.g., Act on Credit Institutions, Act on Radio and Television Broadcasting).

811. A concentration arises when:

(1) two or more previously independent companies merge, or one partly or fully merges into another;
(2) a company or more companies jointly acquire the right of direct or indirect control of a previously independent company; and
(3) several independent companies jointly establish a company to be controlled by them that is capable of functioning as an independent company.

812. Substantial changes to the HCA (hereinafter referred to as 'Amendment') regarding merger control entered into force on 15 January 2017.[849] The new rules, according to the Amendment, set up the current regime of the notification system. Contrary to the former authorisation system, GVH must be notified of mergers if, in the preceding business year, the undertakings concerned achieved a combined turnover of more than HUF 15 billion (approximately EUR 50 million) and the turnovers of at least two of the groups concerned exceeded HUF 1 billion (approximately EUR 3.2 million).

813. The Amendment creates a new regime for mergers that do not meet the HUF 15 billion and the new HUF 1 billion thresholds but the GVH still shall be notified if:

(1) it is not obvious that the concentration does not significantly reduce competition on the relevant market, particularly by creating or strengthening a dominant position; and
(2) the combined turnover of the groups of companies concerned exceeded HUF 5 billion (approximately EUR 16 million).

814. Mergers falling under this new regime are not subject to any standstill obligation, and the GVH may only investigate them within six months after the implementation of the concentration (whereas concentrations that must be notified for meeting the HUF 15 billion and HUF 1 billion thresholds may be investigated for five years).

---

849. *See* for more details: T. Tóth, *A versenytörvény újdonságai az összefonódások ellenőrzése és a kártérítési perek tekintetében.* Jogtudományi Közlöny 2017/5, pp. 243–255.

815. Formerly, the thresholds for companies registered in Hungary were calculated on the basis of their worldwide turnovers. However, pursuant to the Amendment, such companies' thresholds are also calculated on the basis of the turnover achieved in Hungary only.

816. Concentrations first need to be notified to the GVH in a simplified form. Following that notification, the GVH has to decide within eight days whether to initiate an investigation, otherwise the concentration can be implemented. The administrative fee for such notifications amounts to HUF 1 million (approximately EUR 3,200).

817. Previously, dawn raids were only available for the investigation of alleged abuses of a dominant position or restrictive agreements but, according to the Amendment, dawn raids are also available in merger cases.

818. The purpose of these provisions is to put every merger, takeover, and acquisition that is economically significant under supervision. The GVH prohibits the concentration if the concentration constitutes a significant obstacle to the competition in the relevant market, particularly in consequence of the creation or strengthening of a dominant position. The concentration shall be assessed by weighing the advantages and disadvantages, in particular:

(1) the structure of the relevant markets, the existing or potential competition, the purchase and sales opportunities on the relevant markets;
(2) the costs and risks, as well as the technical, economic, and legal requirements for entering and exiting a market;
(3) foreseeable impact of the concentration on competition in the relevant markets;
(4) the market position and strategy of the companies affected, their economic and financial capacities, business policies, competitiveness on national and foreign markets; and
(5) the effect of the concentration on the suppliers and trading parties.

819. It is fundamental for the assessment of the restrictive effect whether the merger in question is between competitors (horizontal) or trading parties (vertical). In some cases, portfolio effects can be expected although there is no market on which both participants of the concentration are present (e.g., in case of complementary products). If a concentration results in an overall improvement in the property status, financial strength, and profitability of an undertaking with a strong position on the market of a product, conglomerate effects arise, which enable this undertaking to apply restrictive strategies (e.g., tying) on the market of another product.

820. In the notification procedure, if the considerable reduction of competition resulting from a concentration can be effectively prevented by fulfilling specific conditions (e.g., disposal of specific business units or assets, termination of control over any indirect participant), the GVH does not prohibit the concentration, but renders the implementation of the concentration subject to compliance with specific prior or subsequent conditions. If any prior condition is set, the concentration can be put into effect only upon compliance with that condition.

§2. Law of Unfair Competition and Trade Practices

I. Unfair Competition

821. According to the HCA, it is prohibited to conduct economic activities in an unfair manner, in particular, in a manner violating or jeopardising the lawful interests of customers or competitors, or in a way that is in conflict with the requirements of business integrity.[850]

822. The prohibition of unfair competition also includes infringements upon, or jeopardising the good reputation or credibility of any competitor by communicating untrue facts, or by misrepresenting true facts with any false implication.

823. Moreover, it is forbidden to gain access to or use trade secrets in an unfair manner, and to disclose such secrets to unauthorized parties, or to make them available to the public.

824. Without gaining prior consent of the competitor, easily interchargeable goods or services may not be produced, placed on the market, or advertised with such an appearance, packaging or marking, by which the competitor or its goods and/or services are recognised.

825. It has to be underlined that the above-mentioned practices typically result in a lawsuit between competitors, as private rather than public interests are infringed by them. Thus, these cases belong to the sole competence of the courts.

II. Prohibition of the Unfair Manipulation of Business Decisions

826. The state intervenes in the actions of economic actors in favour of consumers by legal acts adopted in various fields of law. Private enforcement and the proceedings of the GVH are the main areas of competition consumer protection.[851]

827. The prohibition of the unfair manipulation of business decisions related provisions are placed in Chapter III of the HCA.

---

850. *See* for more details: P. Miskolczi Bodnár, *A versenytörvény magyarázata* [The commentary of the Competition Act], KJK-Kerszöv: Budapest, 2002.
851. *Ibid.*

828. The most important prohibition forbids the misleading of trading parties in economic competition. Another important prohibition deals with the unjustified restriction of the freedom of consumer choice. Through these provisions, the HCA aims to ensure the fairness of competition and the freedom of consumer choice, as a result of which no market actor would obtain unfair advantage in competition.

829. The misleading actions mostly appear as communications, typically through advertising or any kind of information qualifying as communication (e.g., an inquiry via telephone, call for participation in lottery or even a contractual offer if no other information is available about the product). The information is misleading if it contains false information, deceives the persons to whom it is addressed or whom it reaches in any way, or conceals material information that may be required for taking a business decision, or provides such information in an unclear, ambiguous, or untimely manner, and thereby affects the economic behaviour of trading parties.

830. Material information that may influence the decision of the consumer covers in particular:

(1) essential characteristics of the goods, such as:
   (a) execution, composition, technical features;
   (b) quantity;
   (c) geographic or commercial origin;
   (d) method and date of manufacture;
   (e) availability, form, and time of delivery;
   (f) knowledge required for use and maintenance;
   (g) benefits to be expected from their use;
   (h) compliance with the requirements set out in the relevant legislation;
   (i) dangers, risks, impact on health;
   (j) expected environmental impact and energy efficiency indicators; and
   (k) results and material features of tests or checks;
(2) the price of the goods, or the manner in which the price is calculated (e.g., discounts);
(3) any other contractual condition relating to the supply of the goods; and
(4) nature, attributes, and rights of the business entity or his agent.

The list of practices in the HCA is non-taxative, therefore the GVH is free to intervene whenever it reveals unlawful practices.

§3. Consequences of Violations and Enforcement Possibilities

I. Rules for the Procedure of GVH

831. In the framework of public enforcement, the GVH enforces the provisions of the HCA and EU competition law in competition supervision proceedings. The main procedural rules are contained in the HCA and Act CL of 2016 on General

Public Administration Procedures (hereinafter referred to as 'Code'), including the initiation, performance, and conclusion of the competition supervision proceeding. The competition supervision proceedings of the GVH may be initiated ex officio or on application.

832. The GVH commences competition supervision proceedings ex officio against suspected infringements based on Hungarian and EU competition law provisions.

833. Competition supervision proceedings consist of an examination phase followed by the proceeding of the Competition Council. The examination phase ends when the investigator's report is presented to the Competition Council.

834. During the competition supervision proceeding, the GVH has the possibility to use the following investigative measures: request for information; hearing of witnesses; access to documents; on-site inspection without prior notification (based on a judicial authorisation) at the headquarter of the undertaking; or even in private rooms and cars of the staff.

835. In the decision regarding proceedings initiated against unfair manipulation of consumer choice, abuse of a dominant position or restrictive agreements, the Competition Council may:

(1) establish the fact of infringement;
(2) order the infringement to be terminated;
(3) prohibit continuation of the illegal conduct;
(4) prescribe certain obligations in connection with the infringement;
(5) order the publication of a statement of remedy in connection with any unlawful communication;
(6) declare a conduct to be legal;
(7) impose a fine; and
(8) issue a warning and impose the obligation of compliance with competition law in order to prevent infringements.

836. In decisions regarding merger cases, the Competition Council:

(1) shall establish that the concentration does not significantly reduce competition in the relevant market, or impose a condition, or prohibit the concentration;
(2) shall authorise the extension of the one-year transitional period, or shall refuse the request thereof;
(3) shall order the company to fulfil its commitment of compliance; or
(4) may determine that aggregate exemption does not apply to a specific agreement.

837. By means of commitment injunctions issued during the proceedings, the intended effect may be achieved without any serious intervention. If the undertaking makes a commitment to ensure compliance of its practices with legal provisions, the Competition Council make those commitments binding for the party.

838. Moreover, the GVH also conducts proceedings commenced on application but in case an undertaking fails to submit an application, the GVH may initiate a proceeding ex officio as well. In its decision, the Competition Council may grant or reject the application (e.g., the extension of the duration of a temporary acquisition).

839. Through the submission of a complaint or an informal complaint, any person may draw the attention of the GVH to specific infringements. The GVH initiates a proceeding if the complained situation may infringe the provisions laid down in the HCA or EU competition law in favour of the public interest. Upon request of the complainant, the GVH does not forward his/her identification data to the undertakings concerned.

840. As the proceedings of the GVH start ex officio, the complainant does not become a party, even if the GVH initiates its proceeding based on the document submitted by the complainant. A complaint can be made by submission of a standard form published by the GVH. The form can be downloaded from the homepage of the GVH.

841. The GVH shall handle any submission that does not fulfil the requirements of a complaint as an informal complaint. Hence, even handwritten notes or letters, or e-mails can be used for making informal complaints. At the same time, however, also the assessment of informal complaints is carried out by a simplified procedure.

II. Procedure Before Courts in Competition Cases

A. Court Supervision in Administrative Cases

842. The Hungarian Parliament adopted Act I of 2017 on the new Code of Administrative Procedure Before Court.[852] These rules, together with the Code, resulted in a new model of administrative procedure and court system in Hungary and led to a number of other changes in Hungarian legislation from 1 January 2018.

843. Under public enforcement procedures (in other words: in administrative cases), the measures and decisions adopted by the investigator of the Competition Council may be appealed. The appeal is heard by the competent Competition Council in chambers. The decision adopted by the Competition Council may not be

852. *See* procedural questions of this topic: J. Dán, *A bírósági felülvizsgálat örökzöld kérdései a GVH gyakorlatában.* In: K. Gombos (ed.), *A versenyjog legújabb fejleményei európai uniós kitekintéssel.* Dialóg Campus, Budapest, 2017, pp. 75–95.

appealed, however, judicial review may be requested. The appeal against the investigator's decision or the claim for judicial review of the Competition Council's decision may be submitted by the client or any person in respect of whom the decision contains provisions, and by the notifier, to whom the decision has to be delivered.

844. The Competition Council's administrative decision can be attacked before the Administrative and Labour Court. The judgment of this court can be appealed and challenged later before *Kúria* (the Supreme Court of Hungary) with a plea for supervision. The plea for supervision is an extraordinary appeal, which can be submitted under limited circumstances. In proceedings conducted by courts, there is a possibility of the reduction of fines as well.[853]

B. Legal Proceedings Instituted by the GVH

845. If the GVH detects that any decision of an authority violates the freedom of competition, it shall call upon the authority affected to reverse or withdraw the decision. If the authority affected fails to comply within thirty days, the GVH may file an action with the court requesting the review of the decision adopted by the authority affected that is alleged to violate the freedom of competition. After a period of one year following the operative date of the decision, no such petition may be submitted, and in the case of missing the above deadline, no application for extension may be submitted. The Budapest Metropolitan Tribunal has competence to hear the above-specified cases.

846. The GVH may request information from an agency that has adopted an administrative decision in the first or second instance that violates the freedom of competition concerning administrative decisions adopted in proceedings similar to the one contested.

847. The GVH may submit an action of public interest in order to enforce civil claims of a wide range of consumers. These actions can only be submitted if a competition supervision procedure has already been initiated by the GVH.

C. Private Enforcement

848. Apart from public enforcement carried out by the GVH, private enforcement is also available in competition cases. Consequently, actions against infringers of competition law may take two forms. On the one hand, the GVH commences proceedings in order to safeguard the public interest by terminating and sanctioning the violation. On the other hand, the persons whose rights were infringed can submit civil law claims and thus directly enforce the provisions laid down in the HCA and Act V of 2013 on the Civil Code (hereinafter referred to as 'Civil Code').

853. *See* EU dimension of this topic: E. R. Simon, *Versengő alapjogok.* In: K. Gombos (ed.): *A versenyjog legújabb fejleményei európai uniós kitekintéssel.* Dialóg Campus, Budapest, 2017, pp. 57–63.

1. Competition Supervision Proceedings Carried Out Directly by Courts

849. Claims in connection with unfair competition (Chapter II of the HCA) may be filed directly with the competent tribunal (ordinary general court). In such cases, regional high courts serve as courts of appeal.

850. In these cases, the plaintiff may demand:

(1) the establishment of the infringement;
(2) discontinuation of the infringement and restraint from further infringements;
(3) amends for the infringer's action by way of a statement or another appropriate manner;
(4) termination of the unlawful situation;
(5) reinstallment of the former status quo (in *integrum restitutio*);
(6) deprivation or destruction of illegally manufactured or supplied goods;
(7) damages and compensation for any violation of personality rights; or
(8) disclosure of information on the parties participating in the manufacturing and marketing of the products involved.

851. Cases related to public procurement procedures fall under the scope of Act CXLIII of 2015 on Public Procurement, which contains different procedural provisions.

852. Claims for damages and compensation arising from the breach of provisions of Chapter II of the HCA may be filed with the courts of regular competence on the basis of the general rules of the Civil Code and Act CXXX of 2016 on the Code of Civil Procedure (hereinafter referred to as 'Civil Procedure Act').

2. Procedural Rules in Other Civil Cases

853. In civil lawsuits on issues related to the application of provisions on restrictive agreements, abuse of dominant position and Articles 101 and 102 of the Treaty on the Functioning of the European Union (TFEU),[854] the competent court shall notify the GVH and the GVH, as *amicus curiae*, may submit its (written or oral) observations.

854. If, during any stage of the hearing, the GVH notifies the court that it has launched a competition supervision proceeding in the case, the court shall suspend the hearing of the case until the decision in the competition supervision proceeding becomes final and legally binding.

---

854. *See* for more details: Gy. Boytha (ed.), *Versenyjogi jogsértések esetén érvényesíthető magánjogi igények* [Private claims enforceable in case of competition violations]. HVG Orac, Budapest, 2009.

855. If the case in question was heard by the GVH, the decision of the GVH establishing the infringement shall be binding upon the court.

856. Claims arising from the breach of prohibition of agreements restricting economic competition (Chapter IV of the HCA) or the prohibition of abuse of dominant position (Chapter V of the HCA) or Articles 101 and 102 of the TFEU may be submitted to tribunals of regular competence as well. In such cases, regional high courts serve as courts of appeal.

857. In these cases, there are derogations from the Civil Code[855] regarding claims for damages resulting from any infringement of competition law (e.g., in the field of burden of proof, disclosure of evidence, term of limitation of claims). There are also specific procedural rules to be followed (e.g., joinder of actions for damages, suspension of the proceeding if the GVH or the European Commission launched proceedings related to actions for damages under competition law, or until the conclusion of the alternative dispute resolution procedure).

858. In this field, EU Directive 2014/104 on antitrust damages actions ('Damages Directive') resulted in several changes[856] in the Hungarian legislation.[857]

859. The changes include that leniency applicants will be liable for the damage caused to their own direct or indirect purchasers or suppliers, even if they received full immunity. In addition, courts are able to order the disclosure of certain information based on a reasoned request subject to certain exceptions (e.g., privileged communication).

860. As a result of the changes, applicants for damages are able to benefit from a rebuttable presumption concerning the passing-on defence (i.e., the defendant will need to prove that the price increase has been passed on) and also the 10% Presumption under Hungarian competition law (i.e., the defendant will need to prove that the price increase was less than 10%).

---

855. *See* for more details: Á. Fuglinszky, *A versenyjogi jogsértések esetén alkalmazható polgári jogi jogkövetkezmények.* In: Kisfaludi, András (ed.), *Versenyjogi jogsértések – magánjogi jogkövetkezmények.* ELTE Eötvös Kiadó, Budapest, 2012.

856. *See* for more details: P. Miskolczi Bodnár, *Versenyjogsértéssel okozott károk megtérítése – egy a magyar jog számára iránymutató irányelv átültetése.* In: K. Gombos (ed.), *A versenyjog legújabb fejleményei európai uniós kitekintéssel.* Dialóg Campus, Budapest, 2017, pp. 19–47; K. Gombos, *A versenyjog legújabb fejleményei – európai uniós kitekintéssel.* In: K. Gombos (ed.), *A versenyjog legújabb fejleményei európai uniós kitekintéssel.* Dialóg Campus, Budapest, 2017, pp. 9–18; L. Jerney, *A kartelljogi jogsértések magánjogi jogkövetkezményei.* In: K. Gombos (ed.), *A versenyjog legújabb fejleményei európai uniós kitekintéssel.* Dialóg Campus, Budapest, 2017, pp. 49–56.

857. *See* Act CXXIX. of 2017.

3. Civil Claims Connected to the Unfair Manipulation of Business Decisions

861. The competence of the GVH for protection of public interest shall not prevent the enforcement of individual civil claims for any infringement of the provisions of prohibition of the unfair manipulation of business decisions (Chapter III of the HCA) before the court. In court proceedings opened for any violation of these provisions, the burden of proof regarding the business practice lies with the party engaged in the relevant business practice. In these cases, specific procedural rules (notification to court, *amicus curiae*) shall apply *mutatis mutandis.*

4. Procedure Related to EU Competition Law

862. Since the accession of Hungary to the EU, EU competition law[858] is directly applicable to Hungarian undertakings as well. Furthermore, the GVH and Hungarian courts must apply EU competition law[859] according to EC Regulation 1/2003 in each case regarding restrictive agreements and abuse of a dominant position.

863. If the competent Hungarian court opens a case, in which Article 101 or 102 of the TFEU are affected, it has a notification obligation towards the European Commission. The European Commission may submit its (written or oral) observations as *amicus curiae*. The final decisions taken in these cases have to be sent to the European Commission through the Hungarian minister of justice.

858. *See* for more details: I. Vörös, *Az európai versenyjogok kézikönyve* [The handbook of European competition laws]. Logod Bt. Budapest, 1996; B. Berke, *Az Európai Unió gazdasági joga II.* Eötvös Kiadó, Budapest, 2013, 7–194; R. Whish & D. Bailey, *Competition Law.* Oxford University Press, Oxford, 2015.

859. *See* for more details: T. Tóth, *Az Európai Unió versenyjoga* [Competition law of the European Union]. Wolters Kluwer, Budapest, 2014.

Chapter 5. State Regulation of the Conditions of Commercial Transactions

§1. Price and Supply Regulation

864. The history of institutional price control by the government in peacetime can be traced back to the 1930s by the establishment of the Government Commission on Prices and later the Hungarian Royal Office for Materials. Such offices operated under various names (for most of the time as National Material and Price Control Office) until 1990 when price control functions, in general, were taken over by the Ministry of Finance.

865. The current system of price control is divided into a general price control mechanism and special price control mechanisms designed for specific commodities and services.

866. The general price control mechanism is regulated by Act LXXXVII of 1990 on setting prices (ASP). The regulator may set prices on its own initiative or on the request of the seller of the commodity or the service provider. In the latter case the request must be accompanied by a proposal related to the official price. The regulator may establish minimum or maximum prices for the commodity or service. The price may be set by determining the price itself or determining the method applicable for the calculation of the price. Minimum prices must be set so as to cover expenses of an efficiently operating enterprise taking into account subsidies and contributions. Maximum prices must be set so as to provide for a profit necessary for the operations of the enterprise. The regulator may consult economic chambers on the situation related to turnover and prices in the relevant market.

867. Official prices and terms related thereto must be promulgated by law. Official prices may not be applied with retroactive effect. In exceptional cases, the law raising the official maximum price might provide for the incorporation of the new price into existing contracts. The parties, however, may agree on the maintenance of the agreed contractual price.

868. Any agreement related to the provision of commodities or services with an official price that sets a price below the minimum price or a price above the maximum price is void. In such cases the agreed price is substituted with the official price.

869. The practical relevance of ASP is limited because it is applicable only to commodities and services listed in the Annex to the law. The Annex currently includes only one item: commercial price margin for human medicines applied in ambulant care covered by national health insurance. ASP provides, however, that the Government may establish price control for a maximum period of six months for items not listed in the Annex if a change in tax, financial or other regulations affect the national economy in a way that has impact on prices as well.

870. There are a growing number of special price regulation regimes for specific commodities and services. The main characteristic of these regimes is that independent regulatory authorities or professional self-governing communities play a determining role in price control. The most important special price regulation regimes are listed below:

– Wine communities may introduce protective minimum prices for the purchase of wines from producers.[860]
– There exists a separate system for market intervention for certain agricultural products in the framework of the Common Organisation of Agricultural Markets.[861]
– The Minister for Innovation and Technology sets prices for electricity provided by universal service providers, including network access fee, system usage fee and service fee.[862] As far as system usage fee and network access fee is concerned by non-universal service providers, prices are set by the Hungarian Energy and Public Utility Regulatory Authority.[863]
– The Minister for Innovation and Technology sets prices for natural gas provided by universal service providers, including network access fee, system usage fee and service fee.[864] As far as system usage fee and network access fee is concerned by non-universal service providers, prices are set by the Hungarian Energy and Public Utility Regulatory Authority.[865]
– The Minister for Innovation and Technology sets price calculation schemes and maximum prices for the provision of district heating while local governments are authorised to set network access fees.[866]
– The Minister for Innovation and Technology sets prices for the provision of water as a utility, sewage disposal and water treatment on the proposal of the Hungarian Energy and Public Utility Regulatory Authority.[867]
– The Minister for Innovation and Technology sets price calculation schemes for some universal postal services and for postal services related to the delivery of official documents.[868]

860. ASP Art. 1 (2) c).
861. *See* Act XVI of 2003 on the organisation of agricultural markets.
862. Authorisation by Act LXXXVI of 2007 on electricity (Arts 141 and 170 (2) 1.); regulation by Decree No. 4/2011 (I.31.) by the Minister of National Economic Development on price calculation in universal service of electricity.
863. Decree No. 15/2016 (XII.20.) by the Hungarian Energy and Public Utility Regulatory Authority on system usage fees, network access fees and additional fees for electricity.
864. Authorisation by Act XL of 2008 on the provision of natural gas (Arts 103 (1) and 133 (1) 3.); regulation by Decree No. 4/2011 (I.31.) by the Minister of National Economic Development on price calculation in universal service of electricity.
865. Decree No. 13/2016 (XII.20.) by the Hungarian Energy and Public Utility Regulatory Authority on system usage fees, network access fees and additional fees for the provision of natural gas.
866. Authorisation by Act XVIII of 2005 on the provision of district heating (Arts 6 (2) b) and 60 (2) b)); regulation by Decree No. 50/2011 (IX.30.) by the Minister of National Economic Development.
867. Authorisation by Act CCIX of 2011 on the provision of water utilities (Art. 65).
868. Authorisation by Act CLIX of 2012 on postal services (Art. 78 (3)); regulation by Decree No. 67/2012 (XII.15.) by the Minister of National Economic Development.

871. The Minister for Innovation and Technology is constrained in the exercise of his powers to set official prices for certain utilities by Act LIV of 2013 on the decrease of utility prices:

- natural gas: max. 93.5% of the prices applicable on 1 November 2013;
- electricity: max. 94.3% of the prices applicable on 1 November 2013;
- water and sewage: max. 90% of the prices applicable on 1 November 2013;
- district heating: max. 96.7% of the prices applicable on 1 November 2013.

872. A special system of supply and price control is applicable to the sale of tobacco products that may be sold to final consumers by concessionary retailers only. Wholesale distributors must allow for a profit margin of 10% to 15% depending on the tobacco product and the type of wholesale distributor.[869]

873. As an atypical price control measure, banks and financial institutions must allow account holders two cash withdrawals every month free of charge in the maximum value of HUF 150,000. In order to ensure application of this provision, banks may not set cash withdrawal limits below HUF 75,000 per transaction and HUF 150,000 per diem.[870]

§2. Consumer Law

I. Institutional Aspects, General Principles, and Representation of Consumer Interests

874. Hungarian consumer protection law is heavily influenced by EU legislation. According to Article 169 TFEU the EU shall contribute to protecting the health, safety and economic interests of consumers, as well as to promoting their right to information, education and to organise themselves in order to safeguard their interests. In this area the EU may act by adopting internal market measures under Article 114 TFEU or measures which support, supplement and monitor the policy pursued by the Member States.

875. A selected list of EU legislation and implementing measures by Hungary can be found in the table below:

869. Act CXXXIV of 2012 on combatting smoking by minors and the retail sale of tobacco products (Art. 15/E).
870. Act LXXXV of 2009 on payment services (Arts 14/A and 36/A).

EU Legislation	*Implementing Measures by Hungary*
Directive 85/374/EEC on the approximation of laws concerning liability for defective products	Civil Code Article 6:550–6:559
Directive 93/13/EEC on unfair terms in consumer contracts	Civil Code Article 6:102–6:105
Directive 2005/29/EC on unfair commercial practices	Act LVII of 1996 on the Prohibition of Unfair Trading Practices and Unfair Competition
Directive 2006/114/EC on misleading and comparative advertising	Act XLVIII of 2008 on the Basic Requirements and Certain Restrictions of Commercial Advertising
Directive 2011/83/EU on consumer rights	Government Decree No. 45/2014. (II. 26.) on detailed rules for contracts concluded between consumers and traders
Directive 2008/48/EC on credit agreements for consumers	Act CLXII of 2009 on consumer credit agreements

876. Act CLV of 1997 on consumer protection declares as its main objective the promotion of consumer interests related to safe goods and services, proper information and education, effective legal remedy, interest representation through consumer organisations as well as safeguarding consumers' economic and financial interests.

877. Consumer relations are established between a business party and a consumer. A business party may be any person acting for purposes which are inside his trade, business or profession. The consumer may be any natural person acting for purposes which are outside his trade, business or profession. For the purposes of consumer conciliation proceedings, NGOs, churches, micro, small and medium enterprises, housing cooperatives and condominiums are also considered consumers when acting outside their trade, business or profession.

878. Minors, i.e., persons under the age of 18 years, are considered vulnerable consumers and are provided special protection. The sale of alcoholic beverages, tobacco products and sexually explicit products as well as the provision of gambling services for minors is prohibited.

879. The top institution responsible for consumer protection is the Ministry for Innovation and Technology (as the successor of the Ministry of National Economic Development that took over the functions of the National Authority for Consumer Protection from 1 January 2017).[871] The Ministry for Innovation and Technology is

871. Government Decree No. 378/2016 (XII.2.) on legal succession related to the revision of central offices and ministerial auxiliary bodies and the transfer of certain public functions.

responsible for strategic management, including supervision of consumer laboratories or the Hungarian branch of European Consumer Centre (ECC). District government offices are the first-instance authorities for consumer affairs and Pest County Government Office serves as the appeal body with overall national jurisdiction.

880. Regional chambers of commerce and industry maintain consumer conciliation bodies. The conciliation bodies deal primarily with the out-of-court settlement of consumer disputes relating to the application of rules on the quality and safety of goods and services and product liability, and to the conclusion and implementation of contracts. The aim of the Conciliation Body procedure is to settle disputes between consumers and undertakings by agreement and failing this to reach a ruling in the interests of enforcing consumers' rights quickly, effectively and simply. The bodies have no jurisdiction in disputes for which a rule establishes the competence of some other authority. Members of the conciliation bodies are appointed by the chamber and by consumer protection organisations on the basis of parity.

881. There are a number of consumer protection NGOs operating in Hungary. Consumer protection organisations are entitled to initiate legal proceedings in the public interest if the alleged violation of consumer protection provisions affects a broad group of consumers whose members are not yet identified individually but may be ascertained based on the circumstances. Such right is also given to the Prosecution Service.

882. All companies falling under the scope of the Accounting Act that are not considered SMEs are required to employ a qualified consumer protection specialist. The consumer protection specialist monitors the company's relevant activities, organises education and training programmes and serves as a contact point to the consumer protection authority, consumer conciliation bodies and consumer organisations.

II. Consumer Information

883. Act CLV of 1997 on consumer protection regulates in detail information requirements related to the price of the product or service. The consumer must be informed in writing about the sale price and unit price of the product and service rendered. The price must be provided in HUF with the indication of the currency. The indicated price must be the one to be actually paid by the consumer, including VAT and other additional expenses. If there are more than one prices indicated on the product, the consumer must pay the lowest price. Both producer and seller are responsible for the proper indication of price on the product sold. If the producer failed to comply with its obligations, the seller must remedy the situation.

884. The general rule on packaging is that it must ensure the quality and quantity of the product and facilitate its transfer. Special packaging rules are applicable to a number of consumer products and most of them also include information requirements (e.g., in the case of foodstuff, medicines or tobacco products).

885. Business parties must inform the consumer about their seat, postal and e-mail address, phone number and website as well as the place where consumer service is provided if it is not the seat of the business party. In case of a consumer dispute, the consumer must be informed about the possibility of consumer conciliation.

886. Business parties providing public services or utilities as well as designated business parties must operate consumer service facilities. Consumer service facilities may be provided in premises open to the public or as a call centre. Consumer service must be organised in a way that it is accessible at least on one working day a week for a continuous period of twelve hours between 7 a.m. and 9 p.m. Consumers must be able to make an appointment in advance via phone or the internet for a date not later than five days after contact. In case of a call centre, processing of the consumer complaint must commence no later than five minutes after the establishment of the call.

887. Business parties providing public services or utilities must operate a public website containing at least the following information:

- name and seat of the business party;
- geographic scope of the services provided;
- prices and fees and their method of calculation;
- laws and regulations applicable to the activities;
- procedures related to consumer complaints;
- contact details and links to consumer protection authorities, conciliation bodies and consumer organisations;
- access to consumer services, location, opening hours, contacts;
- general terms and conditions.

III. The Safety of Goods and Services

888. Liability for defective product is regulated by Article 6:550–6:559 of the Civil Code. The provisions implement Council directive 85/374/EEC on the approximation of the laws, regulations and administrative provisions of the Member States concerning liability for defective products.

889. The producer is liable for damage caused by a defect in his product. 'Producer' means the manufacturer of a finished product, the producer of any raw material or the manufacturer of a component part and any person who, by putting his name, trade mark or other distinguishing feature on the product presents himself as its producer. Without prejudice to the liability of the producer, any person who imports into the Community a product for sale, hire, leasing or any form of distribution in the course of his business shall be deemed to be a producer and shall be responsible as a producer.

890. Where the producer of the product cannot be identified, each supplier of the product shall be treated as its producer unless he informs the injured person, within thirty days from the receipt of the inquiry by the injured person, of the identity of the producer or of the person who supplied him with the product. The same shall apply, in the case of an imported product, if this product does not indicate the identity of the importer, even if the name of the producer is indicated.

891. For the purposes of product liability provisions 'damage' means:

(a) damage caused by death or by personal injuries;
(b) damage to, or destruction of, any item of property other than the defective product itself, with a lower threshold equivalent to EUR 500 according to the official exchange rate of the Hungarian National Bank, provided that the item of property:
   (i) is of a type ordinarily intended for private use or consumption; and
   (ii) was used by the injured person mainly for his own private use or consumption.

892. A product is defective when it does not provide the safety which a person is entitled to expect, taking all circumstances into account, including:

(a) the presentation of the product;
(b) the use to which it could reasonably be expected that the product would be put;
(c) the time when the product was put into circulation;
(d) the state of scientific and technical knowledge;

893. A product shall not be considered defective for the sole reason that a better product is subsequently put into circulation. The injured person is required to prove the defect.

894. The producer shall not be liable if he proves:

(a) that he did not put the product into circulation; or
(b) that, having regard to the circumstances, it is probable that the defect which caused the damage did not exist at the time when the product was put into circulation by him or that this defect came into being afterwards; or
(c) that the product was neither manufactured by him for sale or any form of distribution for economic purpose nor manufactured nor distributed by him in the course of his business; or
(d) that the defect is due to compliance of the product with mandatory regulations issued by the public authorities; or
(e) that the state of scientific and technical knowledge at the time when he put the product into circulation was not such as to enable the existence of the defect to be discovered (not applicable for damages caused by proper use of medicines); or

(f) in the case of a manufacturer of a component, that the defect is attributable to the design of the product in which the component has been fitted or to the instructions given by the manufacturer of the product.

895. The producer may not, in relation to the injured person, limit or exclude his liability.

896. A limitation period of three years applies to proceedings for the recovery of damages. The limitation period shall begin to run from the day on which the plaintiff became aware, or should reasonably have become aware, of the damage, the defect and the identity of the producer. The rights conferred upon the injured person are extinguished upon the expiry of a period of ten years from the date on which the producer put into circulation the actual product which caused the damage unless the injured person has in the meantime instituted proceedings against the producer.

IV. Consumer Contracts

897. The consumer contract covers contractual relations between business party and consumer (B2C relationships).[872] The *business party* means any person acting for purposes which are inside his trade, business or profession; the *consumer* has the meaning of any natural person acting for purposes which are outside his trade, business or profession.[873]

898. The Hungarian Civil Code provides regulation for business-to-business contractual obligations (the ground is the contract law of business partners), and only exceptionally for B2C relations of agreements. The 45/2014. (II. 26.) government decree regulates the detailed provisions of contracts between business party and consumer (*especially the rules of off-premises and distance contracts*).

The special rules for consumer contracts among general provisions on contract of Hungarian Civil Code

899.

(a) *Conclusion of Contracts with Standard Terms and Conditions*: Any term granting the right to the business party to demand extra payments in addition to the consideration due for the fulfilment of the primary commitment shall form part of the contract only if the consumer has expressly accepted it after having been informed thereof (*terms allowing extra claims from consumers to become part*

872. *See* more about it in: V. Szikora, *Magyar fogyasztóvédelmi jog – európai kitekintéssel*, Debrecen, FOME, 2010, 53–249.
873. Section 8:1 (1) 3, 4 CC.

of the contract).[874] In connection with an electronic contract that involves a consumer and a business party any agreement derogating from the provisions of the Hungarian Civil Code shall be null and void.[875]

(b) *Interpretation of contract*: If the meaning of a standard contract term or the contents of the contract term which has not been individually negotiated cannot be clearly established, the interpretation that is more favourable to the party entering into a contract with the person imposing such contract term shall prevail; in connection with a contract that involves a consumer and a business party, this provision shall also apply to the interpretation of any contract term.[876]

(c) *Invalidity*:

(i) Any clause of a contract that involves a consumer and a business party that derogates from the provisions of this Act on consumer rights to the detriment of the consumer shall be null and void (*unfair clause in consumer contracts*).[877]

(ii) In a contract that involves a consumer and a business party, any disclaimer by a consumer of a statutory right shall be considered null and void (*consumer disclaimers*).[878]

(iii) As regards contracts which involve a consumer and a business party, the provisions relating to standard contract terms shall also apply to the contract terms which have been drafted in advance by the business party and which have not been individually negotiated. The burden of proof to verify that a contract term has been individually negotiated lies with the business party. As regards contracts which involve a consumer and a business party, where a standard contract term or any contract term which has been drafted in advance by the business party and which has not been individually negotiated shall be regarded as unfair if they are not drafted in plain and clearly understandable language, solely on that basis (*unfair contract terms in consumer contracts*). Any unfair contract term that has been incorporated into a contract that involves a consumer and a business party shall be null and void; nullity may be invoked in favour of the consumer.[879]

(iv) *Other unfair terms in consumer contracts*: In contracts which involve a consumer and a business party a contract term shall, in particular, be considered unfair if its object or effect is to:

- give the business party the exclusive right to interpret any contract term;
- give the business party the exclusive right to determine whether performance is in conformity with the contract;
- provide that the consumer is bound by the contract when the business party is not;

874. Section 6:79 CC.
875. Section 6:85 (2) CC.
876. Section 6:86 (2) CC.
877. Section 6:100 CC.
878. Section 6:101 CC.
879. Section 6:103 CC.

- entitle the business party to withdraw from or terminate the contract on a discretionary basis without giving the same right to the consumer;
- exclude the consumer's right to recover at the time the contract is terminated the services already performed without compensation, except where the contract is terminated on the grounds of non-performance;
- exclude or limit the right to offset claims that the consumer may have against the business party against what the consumer may owe to the business party;
- allow the business party to transfer its debts to a third party without the consumer's consent;
- limit the business party's obligation to be bound by commitments undertaken by its authorized agents;
- exclude or hinder the consumer's right to take legal action or exercise any other legal remedy, particularly by requiring the consumer to take disputes exclusively to an arbitration system not foreseen generally in legal provisions, restrict the evidence available to the consumer or impose on the consumer a burden of proof which should legally lie with the other party;
- alter the burden of proof to the detriment of the consumer.[880]

(v) In contracts which involve a consumer and a business party the contract term shall, in particular, be considered unfair, until proven otherwise, if its object or effect is to:

- declare a specific conduct of the consumer as making a contract statement, or the failure to make one, if the time limit available for performing that conduct is unreasonably short;
- subject the consumer in making statements to particular formalities that are unreasonable;
- extend a contract of fixed duration unless the consumer indicates otherwise, in cases where contract terms provide for an unreasonably early deadline for making such statement;
- enable a business party to alter contract terms unilaterally without a valid reason which is specified in the contract, in particular to increase the monetary consideration fixed in the contract, or to allow the business party to alter unilaterally the terms of a contract where there are serious grounds laid down in the contract for doing so, provided that in such cases the consumer is not free to withdraw from or to terminate the contract;
- enable a trader to alter unilaterally without a valid reason any characteristics of the services to be provided as contracted;
- allow a business party to be bound by commitments subject to compliance with a particular condition the fulfilment of which depends exclusively on the business party, except if the consumer is free to withdraw from or to terminate the contract;

880. Section 6:104 (1) CC.

- allow a period of over forty-five days for the business party to satisfy its debt or to provide an inappropriately determined deadline for the performance of its service, and for the acceptance of the consumer's contract statement;
- exclude or limit the remedies available to the consumer against the business party in the case of non-performance;
- exclude the consumer's right to recover any payment made under contract in case of the consumer's non-performance or if his performance is not in conformity with the contract if the business party is not bound by similar obligations;
- order the consumer to pay a disproportionately high amount if he fails to perform obligations or fails to perform as stipulated by the contract.[881]

(vi) In the event of limited invalidity of a consumer contract, the entire contract shall fail only if the contract cannot be performed without the invalid part.[882]

(d) *Performance*: In contracts that involve a consumer and a business party any term excluding the early settlement of a monetary debt, and any term imposing extra charges on the consumer apart from the costs directly related to early settlement shall be null and void.[883]

(e) *Non-performance*:

- *Lack of conformity:* In connection with contracts that involve a consumer and a business party, in the absence of proof to the contrary, any lack of conformity detected by the consumer within six months of the date of performance shall be presumed to have existed at the time of delivery, unless this presumption is incompatible with the nature of the thing or the nature of the lack of conformity. In the case of contracts that involve a consumer and a business party, if notification of the lack of conformity is made within two months of the time it is detected, it shall be deemed to have been made in good time. In connection with contracts that involve a consumer and a business party, the obligee's right to warranty shall lapse after two years from the delivery date. If the things supplied under a contract that involves a consumer and a business party are second-hand, the parties may agree on a shorter limitation period, however, the limitation period may not be less than one year in this case either.[884]
- Any clause of a contract that involves a consumer and a business party that derogates from the provisions of this Chapter on warranties and commercial guarantees to the detriment of the consumer shall be null and void.[885]
- *Product liability claims*: In case of lack of conformity of any movable property sold by a business party to a consumer the consumer shall have the right to demand from the manufacturer (shall mean anyone who manufactures

881. Section 6:104 (2) CC.
882. Section 6:114 (2) CC.
883. Section 6:131 CC.
884. Section 6:158 (1), s. 6:162 (2), s. 6:163 (3) CC.
885. Section 6:157 (2) CC.

and places the product on the market) to have the product repaired or – if repair is not possible within a reasonable period of time and without harming the consumer's interest – to provide a replacement. A product shall be deemed defective if it does not meet the requirements related to conformity in effect at the time of placing on the market, or it does not meet the specifications provided by the manufacturer. The manufacturer shall be relieved of product guarantee obligation if able to prove that he manufactured or placed the product on the market in the course of operations other than in the course of its business activity or for purposes relating to his profession; the state of scientific and technical knowledge at the time when he put the product into circulation was not such as to enable the existence of a defect to be discovered; or the defect in the product was caused by the application of a regulation or a regulatory provision prescribed by the authorities. The consumer shall be required to inform the manufacturer of any lack of conformity without delay (if notification of the lack of conformity is made within two months of the time it is detected, it shall be deemed that notification was made in due time); the consumer shall be liable for any damage that results from late notification. The manufacturer shall remain subject to product liability for a period of two years effective from the date of placing the given product on the market; this deadline shall apply with prejudice. If the product's ownership is transferred, product liability may be enforced by the new owner against the manufacturer.[886]

The particular provisions for consumer contracts among special rules on express contracts of Hungarian Civil Code

900.

(a) *Sales contract*: If the seller is a business party and the buyer is a consumer, and the seller undertakes to dispatch the thing to the buyer, risks shall pass to the buyer when he or a third party named by the buyer has acquired the physical possession of the thing.[887] If the seller is a business party and the buyer is a consumer unless otherwise agreed by the parties the seller shall place the thing at the buyer's disposal without delay upon the conclusion of the contract, at the latest within thirty days. In the event of late performance by the seller, the buyer shall have the right to set an additional time for performance. If the seller fails to perform within such additional period, the buyer shall be entitled to withdraw from the contract. The buyer shall be entitled to withdraw from the contract without setting an additional time for performance if the seller refused the performance the contract, or according to the agreement of the parties or due to the imminent purpose of the service, the contract had to be performed at a definite time and none other.[888]

886. Section 6:168–6:170 CC.
887. Section 6:219 CC.
888. Section 6:220 CC.

(b) *Carriage* contract: At the time of handing over the thing to the carrier, risks shall pass to the buyer if the carrier was hired by the buyer, provided that the carrier was not recommended by the seller.[889]

(c) *Consumer suretyship*: In the case of consumer suretyship, the creditor shall inform the consumer before the contract of suretyship is concluded of the rights and obligations of the surety and about specific risks inherent to the debtor's circumstances or to the nature of the liability, of which the creditor is aware. In the event if the creditor fails to comply with this requirement, the surety shall be entitled to withdraw from the contract without a time limit. If the consumer guarantee covers all liabilities of the debtor toward the creditor, or all obligations of the debtor arising from specific relationship, the guarantee shall be considered valid if the highest amount of debt the consumer guarantees is specified in the contract. In the event of the debtor's delay, the creditor shall forthwith notify the surety thereof, in the absence of notification the surety shall not be liable for damages caused by such late performance or for interest on late payment. The provisions on consumer guarantees shall not apply if the surety is an executive officer or a member with majority control of the debtor legal person.[890]

(d) *Consumer guarantee*: If the guarantor is a consumer, the statement of guarantee shall function as a first-loss guarantee.[891]

(e) *Consumer pledge agreement*: If the lienor (mortgagee) is a natural person and the pledged property is primarily used for a purpose which is not required for the pursuit of profession, private entrepreneurial activities or business operations of the lienor, furthermore, the claim secured by a pledge is not a result of the lienor's profession, private entrepreneurial activities or business operations, the provisions of pledge agreements shall apply subject to the following exceptions:
   - the property pledged may be an individually determined asset that is owned by the lienor, or an asset which the lienor will acquire by means of a loan or respite of payment the lien holder has provided;
   - the definition of the secured claim shall include the sum as well.[892] In connection with a consumer pledge agreement, the lien holder shall be allowed to sell the pledged property only publicly, unless the parties agreed on an alternative sales method after the effective date of the right to satisfaction, and shall not acquire ownership of the pledged property as a mode of satisfaction, with the exception of collateral security.[893] The prior notification shall be sent at least ten days, in the case of consumer pledge agreement, at least thirty days before the sale.[894]

(f) *Insurance* contract: If the contracting party is a consumer, the contract shall be performed also if the insurance company does not respond to the offer within

889. Section 6:219 CC.
890. Section 6:430 CC.
891. Section 6:438 CC.
892. Section 5:90 CC.
893. Section 5:128 CC.
894. Section 5:131 (1) CC.

fifteen days of the time of receipt thereof, or sixty days if a health risk assessment is required for the evaluation of the offer, provided that the offer was made on the insurance company's own standard offer sheet for the type of policy in question, upon receipt of the relevant statutory information, containing the tariffs applicable. In this case the contract shall be executed – under the conditions contained in the offer – with retroactive effect to the date on which the offer is conveyed to the insurance company and comes into effect on the day following the expiry of the risk assessment period.[895] So the contract is concluded by the implicit conduct of the insurance company at a consumer agreement.[896] *Unilaterally cogent rules of retail insurance contracts*: If the contracting party is a consumer, the contract shall be allowed to derogate from the provisions of the Hungarian Civil Code only to the benefit of the contracting party, the insured person and the beneficiary, where such provision pertains:

- to the insurance company's implicit conduct in a consumer contract;
- to any considerable increase in insurance risk;
- to the consequences for non-payment of premiums;
- maintaining the amount of insurance cover;
- to the obligation to prevent and mitigate damages;
- to the obligation of disclosure and notification of changes and the obligation of reporting the occurrence of an insured event;
- to any composition between the insured person and the injured party;
- to premium payment obligation when the contract is terminated;
- to the insurance company's exemption from settlement obligation;
- to claims for compensation.[897] *Unilaterally cogent rules of retail fixed-sum insurance policies and health insurance policies*: If the contracting party is a consumer, the contract shall be allowed to derogate from the exclusion of derogation only to the benefit of the contracting party, the insured person and the beneficiary with respect to fixed-sum and health insurance policies.[898]

901. There are *atypical* – outside of the Hungarian Civil Code – *consumer contracts*[899] with specific obligations:

(a) *distance contract*: In the frame of distance selling scheme organized for offer of contracting product or service the parties conclude the contract without their simultaneous presence so that in favour of concluding contract the contracting parties use exclusively instruments facilitating communication between absent legal entities;[900] the 2011/83/EU directive on consumer rights was implemented by Government Decree No. 45/2014. (II. 26.) in Hungary.

895. Section 6:444 (1), (2) CC.
896. L. Vékás, *A Polgári Törvénykönyv magyarázatokkal*. Budapest, Complex, 2013, 905.
897. Section 6:455 CC.
898. Section 6:456 CC.
899. *See* more about it in: T. Papp, *Atipikus szerződések*. Budapest, Opten Informatikai Kft., 2015, 96–222.
900. 45/2014. (II. 26.) Government Decree s. 4 (10).

(b) *consumer contract in connection with electronic commercial services*: Electronic commercial services are all services in connection with the information society, online. It means a sales or service contract where the business party, or the business party's intermediary, has offered goods or services on a website or by other electronic means and the consumer has ordered such goods or services on that website or by other electronic means;[901] at the regulation of the Hungarian Civil Code the codifiers considered the 2000/31/EC directive.

(c) *off-premises contract*: Such contract:
- is concluded at the simultaneous physical presence of contracting parties, but in off-premises place of business party; or
- for which the consumer makes an offer at the simultaneous presence of contracting parties, but in off-premises place of business party; or
- is concluded in premises of business party or by using exclusively instruments facilitating communication between absent legal entities immediately after that the business party entered into relations with the consumer at the simultaneous physical presence of contracting partners in off-premises place of business party; or
- is concluded in the course of journey organized by the business party in order to sell or propagate products or services for consumer;[902] the 2011/83/EU directive on consumer rights was implemented by Government Decree No. 45/2014. (II. 26.) in Hungary.

(d) *consort contract*: The consort agreement is an agreement with the purpose of taking part in the consumer-group. According to the consort agreement, the consumer acquires the proprietary right of the tangible asset/real property assigned in advance by the consumer himself in a certain period of time agreed before and by the assistance of the organizer in a way that:
  (i) from the day when the agreement was concluded the consumer has to pay once or periodically a set amount of fee for the organizer at the expiration stated in advance;
  (ii) the date of entitlement to conclude a purchase agreement is defined by the result of the selection held at regular intervals among the members of the consumer-group;
  (iii) the goods are chosen by the consumer – after designating him/her as beneficiary and the consumer concludes the purchase agreement – by the collaboration of the organizer referring to obtaining, selecting the goods and preparing the purchase agreement – with the owner;
  (iv) the payment of the price for the owner (or for the contractor entrusted with producing the goods) – up to the actual contractual value valid on the day of the selection of the consumer – is charged to the periodical monthly instalments provided by the consumers, administrated separately by the different consumer-groups and kept separately from the financial assets of the organizer. Therefore the essential of the consort agreement is the following:

901. Act CLV of 1997 on Consumer Protection s. 2 p).
902. 45/2014. (II. 26.) Government Decree s. 4 (14).

- the agreement is concluded by one organizer and many consumers separately in order to acquire the ownership of certain goods (the consumer cannot buy on his financial assets);
- therefore a single registration fee and periodical payments are paid by the consumers for the organizer, who purchases the goods wished to be bought by the consumer;
- at regular intervals one of the consumers entitled to acquire the ownership is selected;
- in consequence of the above-mentioned, the purchase agreement can be concluded between the selected consumer and the owner of the certain goods under the condition that the price is financed from the common payments of the consumers being parties of the consort agreement by the organizer, and this transaction is continually repeating until the last consumer can get the chosen goods (chain of purchase until a fixed date: in case of tangible asset not more than sixty months, in case of real property and building materials not more than one hundred twenty months).[903]

(e) *timesharing contract*: Timeshare agreement is a contract that aims to the acquisition of the right to use an accommodation for a period of time on a rotating basis and according to this agreement the consumer, in return for consideration, directly or indirectly acquires the right from the marketer for more than one year to use one or more properties repeatedly for recreation or housing aims for a definite period of time. By the contract the consumer:
- acquires the right of use for a definite aim (recreation/housing) for one year (or for a longer – maybe definite period of time);
- in a definite period of the year which was laid down before (e.g., for a week or for ten days), repeated annually (in general at the same time, for the same period so in the definite hotel on the same days of the same month every year);
- covering one or more buildings (e.g., hotel) and its rooms and accessories (e.g., tennis court, swimming pool, sauna, etc.);
- acquired from the owner of the property (that can be a company too) directly or indirectly from the marketer (if different from the owner) or agency dealing with resales (RDO – Resort Development Organization – a company with membership that deals with secondary selling);[904] the 2008/122/EC directive on the protection of consumer in respect of certain aspects of timeshare, long-term holiday product, resale and exchange contracts was implemented by the Government Decree No. 141/2011. (VII. 21.) in Hungary.

---

903. T. Papp, *Atipikus jelenségek szerződési jogunkban, Atypical Phenomena in Our Contract Law.* Szeged, Lectum Kiadó, 2009, 39–40.
904. Papp, *supra* n. 635, 109.

V. Sales Promotion and Commercial Practices

902. The Act XLVIII of 2008 on the Basic Requirements and Certain Restrictions of Commercial Advertising Activities determines the definition of *commercial advertising*: any form of communication, information or the making of a representation in any form with the aim or having the direct or indirect effect of promoting the supply of goods of a fungible nature that are capable of being delivered, including natural resources that can be utilized as capital goods, including money, securities and financial instruments, and services, immovable property, rights and obligations, or in connection with this objective, the representation of the name, the trademark or the activities of a producer of goods or a provider of services.[905,906]

General advertising prohibitions and restrictions

903.

(a) No advertisement may be disseminated if it contains violence, or if it encourages any conduct that is likely to jeopardize personal or public safety.[907]
(b) No advertisement of sexual services may be disseminated and also such advertisement is prohibited that is aimed to arouse sexual interest may be disseminated.[908]
(c) Advertising is prohibited for goods whose production or marketing is illegal.[909]
(d) The dissemination of subliminal advertising is prohibited.[910]
(e) No advertisement of free gifts, discounts, bonuses, financial advantages and drawings may be disseminated in connection with direct sales by party plan provided for in the Trade Act.[911]

Restrictions and prohibitions relating to the advertisement of certain goods

904.

(a) Weapons, ammunition, explosives and other means which are considered extremely dangerous to public safety may not be advertised.[912]
(b) No advertisement may be disseminated relating to dogs which are considered dangerous according to specific other legislation, nor to animal fights.[913]

---

905. *See* more about it in: K. Pázmándi, *Magyar fogyasztóvédelmi és reklámjog*. Budapest, HVG Orac, 2010; Szikora, *supra* n. 872, 251–288.
906. Section 3 d).
907. Act XLVIII of 2008 s. 7 (1).
908. *Ibid.*, s. 9 (2), (3).
909. *Ibid.*, s. 10.
910. *Ibid.*, s. 11.
911. *Ibid.*, s. 12.
912. *Ibid.*, s. 14 (1).
913. *Ibid.*, s. 15.

(c) The advertisement is prohibited relating to human organs or tissues for any purpose whatsoever.[914]
(d) Advertising of tobacco products is prohibited.[915]
(e) No advertisement may be disseminated addressed to children and young persons containing a presentation to enter any games of chance.[916]

905. The Act XLVII of 2008 on the Prohibition of Unfair B2C Commercial Practices shall apply to unfair B2C commercial practices, before, during and after a commercial transaction in relation to goods, and it lays down the requirements relating to codes of conduct applicable to such commercial practices, as well as the provisions for proceedings in cases of infringements of these codes of conduct.[917]

906. *Unfair commercial practices* shall be prohibited. A commercial practice shall be unfair if:

– it is contrary to the requirements of professional diligence, i.e., the trader acting in commercial practices fails to use the standard of special skill and care which a trader may reasonably be expected to exercise, commensurate with honest market practice and/or the general principle of good faith (*requirements of professional diligenc*e); and
– it materially distorts or is likely to materially distort the economic behaviour with regard to the product of the average consumer whom it reaches or to whom it is addressed, using this practice to impair the consumer's ability to make an informed decision and thereby causing the consumer to take a transactional decision that he would not have taken otherwise (*materially distort the economic behaviour of consumers*);
– which are *misleading* or are *aggressive*. The Schedule of the Act XLVII of 2008 on the Prohibition of Unfair B2C Commercial Practices contains the list of those commercial practices which shall in all circumstances be regarded as unfair.

907. A commercial practice shall be regarded as *misleading* if it contains false information and is therefore untruthful or in any way, including overall presentation, deceives or is likely to deceive the average consumer, even if the information is factually correct, in relation to one or more of the following elements, and in either case causes or is likely to cause him to take a transactional decision that he would not have taken otherwise:

(a) the existence or nature of the goods, taking into account the statutory provisions relating to the names of products;
(b) the main characteristics of the goods, in particular: their execution, composition, technical features, accessories; their quantity; their geographical or commercial origin; their method and date of manufacture or provision; their

914. *Ibid.*, s. 16.
915. *Ibid.*, s. 19 (1).
916. *Ibid.*, s. 21 (1).
917. Section 1 (1); *see* more about it in: Szikora, *supra* n. 872, 289–328.

availability, delivery; their usage, facts regarding use and maintenance; their fitness for purpose, results to be expected from their use, benefits; their dangers, risks; their environmental impact; their impact on health; the way they are controlled or tested and the results;

(c) the price of the goods or the manner in which the price is calculated, or the existence of a specific price advantage or discount;

(d) tax exemption, tax allowance or the use of other tax advantage provided in connection with the goods;

(e) the need for a service, part, replacement or repair in connection with the goods;

(f) aftersales customer assistance and complaint handling provided in connection with the goods;

(g) the nature, attributes and rights of the business party or his agent, such as his identity and assets, his qualifications, status, approval, affiliation or connection and ownership of industrial, commercial or intellectual property rights or his awards and distinctions;

(h) the extent of the business party's commitments, the motives for the commercial practice and the nature of the sales process, any statement or symbol in relation to sponsorship or approval of the business party or the product;

(i) the consumer's rights or the risks of unfavourable legal outcomes he may face in connection with the transaction;

(j) a commercial practice which creates confusion with any business party or its corporate name, or with any products, trademarks, trade names or other distinguishing marks of such business party;

(k) non-compliance by the business party with commitments contained in codes of conduct by which the business party has undertaken to be bound, where the commitment is not merely aspirational but is firm and is capable of being verified, and the business party indicates in a commercial practice that he is bound by the code, if taking account of the factual context it causes or is likely to cause the average consumer to take a transactional decision that he would not have taken otherwise;

(l) taking account of all its features and circumstances and the limitations of the communication medium, it omits or conceals material information that the average consumer needs, according to the context, to take an informed transactional decision, or provides such information in an unclear, unintelligible, ambiguous or untimely manner, or fails to identify the commercial intent of the commercial practice if not already apparent from the context and thereby causes or is likely to cause the average consumer to take a transactional decision that he would not have taken otherwise (*misleading omission*).[918]

908. A commercial practice shall be regarded as *aggressive* if, in its factual context, taking account of all its features and circumstances, by harassment, coercion, including the use of physical force, or undue influence for exploiting a position of power in relation to the consumer so as to apply pressure, it significantly impairs or is likely to significantly impair the average consumer's freedom of choice or conduct and the consumer's ability to make an informed decision with regard to the

918. Act XLVII of 2008 s. 6, s. 7 (1).

product and thereby causes him or is likely to cause him to take a transactional decision that he would not have taken otherwise. In determining whether a commercial practice is aggressive, account shall be taken of:

- the timing, location, nature or persistence of the commercial practice;
- the use of threatening, frightening or abusive language or behaviour in commercial practices;
- the exploitation by the trader acting in commercial practices of any specific misfortune or circumstance of such gravity as to impair the consumer's Judgment, of which the trader is aware, to influence the consumer's decision with regard to the product;
- any onerous or disproportionate non-contractual barriers imposed by the trader acting in commercial practices where a consumer wishes to exercise rights under the contract, including rights to terminate a contract or to switch to another product or another trader;
- any threat to take any action that cannot legally be taken.[919]

Unfair commercial practices

909.

(1) Claiming to be a signatory to a code of conduct when the business party is not.[920]
(2) Claiming that a code of conduct has an endorsement from an administrative authority, public or other bodies which it does not have.
(3) Displaying a trust mark, quality mark or equivalent without having obtained the necessary authorization.
(4) Claiming that a business party (including his commercial practices) or a product has been approved, endorsed or authorized by a public or other body, or administrative authority when he/it has not or making such a claim without complying with the terms of the approval, endorsement or authorization.
(5) Making an invitation to purchase products at a specified price without disclosing the existence of any reasonable grounds the trader may have for believing that he will not be able to offer for supply or to procure another trader to supply, those products or equivalent products at that price for a period that is, and in quantities that are, reasonable having regard to the product, the scale of advertising of the product and the price offered (bait advertising).
(6) Making an invitation to purchase products at a specified price and then:
    (a) refusing to show the advertised item to consumers;
    (b) refusing to take orders for it or deliver it within a reasonable time; or
    (c) demonstrating a defective sample of it, with the intention of promoting a different product (bait and switch).

919. *Ibid.*, s. 8.
920. Act XLVII of 2008 Schedule.

(7) Falsely stating that a product will only be available for a very limited time, or that it will only be available on particular terms for a very limited time, in order to elicit an immediate decision and deprive consumers of sufficient opportunity or time to make an informed choice.
(8) Undertaking to provide aftersales service to consumers with whom the business party has communicated prior to a transaction in a language which is not an official language of the Member State where the business party is located and then making such service available only in another language without clearly disclosing this to the consumer before the consumer is committed to the transaction.
(9) Stating or otherwise creating the impression – whether in itself by way of presentation of the product in the commercial communication – that a product can legally be sold when it cannot.
(10) Presenting rights given to consumers in law as a distinctive feature of the business party's offer.
(11) Using editorial content in the printed or electronic media to promote the sale or other forms of use of a product where a business party has paid for the promotion without making that clear in the content or by images or sounds clearly identifiable by the consumer (advertorial).
(12) Making a materially inaccurate claim concerning the nature and extent of the risk to the personal security of the consumer or his family if the consumer does not purchase the product.
(13) Promoting a product similar to a product made by a particular manufacturer in such a manner as deliberately to mislead the consumer into believing that the product is made by that same manufacturer when it is not.
(14) Establishing, operating or promoting a pyramid promotional scheme where a consumer gives consideration for the opportunity to receive compensation that is derived primarily from the introduction of other consumers into the scheme rather than from the sale or consumption of products.
(15) Claiming that the business party is about to cease trading or move premises when he is not.
(16) Claiming that products are able to facilitate winning in games of chance.
(17) Falsely claiming that a product is able to cure illnesses, dysfunction or malformations.
(18) Passing on materially inaccurate information on market conditions or on the possibility of finding the product with the intention of inducing the consumer to acquire the product at conditions less favourable than normal market conditions.
(19) Claiming in a commercial practice to offer a competition or prize promotion without awarding the prizes described or a reasonable equivalent.
(20) Describing a product as 'gratis', 'free', 'without charge' or similar if the consumer has to pay anything other than the unavoidable cost of responding to the commercial practice and collecting or paying for delivery of the item.
(21) Including in marketing material an invoice or similar document seeking payment which gives the consumer the impression that he has already ordered the marketed product when he has not.

(22) Falsely claiming or creating the impression that the business party is not acting for purposes relating to his trade, business, craft or profession, or falsely representing oneself as a consumer.
(23) Creating the false impression that aftersales service in relation to a product is available in a Member State other than the one in which the product is sold.
(24) Creating the impression that the consumer cannot leave the premises until a contract is formed.
(25) Conducting personal visits to the consumer's home ignoring the consumer's request to leave or not to return.
(26) Making persistent and unwanted solicitations by telephone, fax, e-mail or other remote media or equivalent means of communication, except in circumstances and to the extent justified to enforce a contractual obligation.
(27) Requiring a consumer who wishes to claim on an insurance policy to produce documents which could not reasonably be considered relevant as to whether the claim was valid, or failing systematically to respond to pertinent correspondence, in order to dissuade a consumer from exercising his contractual rights.
(28) Including in an advertisement a direct exhortation to children to buy advertised products or persuade their parents or other adults to buy advertised products for them.
(29) Demanding immediate or deferred payment for or the return or safekeeping of products supplied by the business party, but not solicited by the consumer except where the product is a substitute supplied in conformity with Article 7 (3) of Directive 97/7/EC (inertia selling).
(30) Explicitly informing a consumer that if he does not buy the product or service, the business party's job or livelihood will be in jeopardy.
(31) Creating the false impression that the consumer has already won, will win, or will on doing a particular act win, a prize (award, reward or other equivalent benefit), when in fact either there is no prize or taking any action in relation to claiming the prize or other equivalent benefit is subject to the consumer paying money or incurring a cost.

910. Liability for any violation of the prohibition of unfair commercial practices shall lie with the business party directly connected with the promotion, sale or supply of goods to which the commercial practice in question pertains. The business party shall be held liable also if the commercial practice is carried out under contract by another person acting on behalf of or for the business party in question. Liability for any infringement arising in connection with the representation of commercial communication shall also lie with the person who uses means suitable for the publication of commercial communication to disseminate commercial communication, and with the person professionally involved in producing or creating commercial communication in the context of his economic activities, or in providing other related services, with the exception if the infringement originates from the carrying out of the instructions of the business party mentioned. The aforesaid persons shall bear joint and several liability with the business party mentioned for damages resulting from such unlawful commercial practices.[921]

911. A code of conduct may not promote unfair commercial practices. Liability for any infringement of this provisions lies with the person or persons drawing up the code of conduct, or the person or persons in charge of the review of the codes or for monitoring the enforcement of the codes by the business entities that have decided freely to adhere to such codes.[922]

VI. Consumer Redress

912. The *consumer dispute* means any dispute between a consumer and a business party arising from, or in connection with, the conclusion and performance of a sales or service contract, and any dispute regarding the quality and safety of goods, the application of product liability regulations and the quality of services in the absence of a sales or service contract between a consumer and a business party.[923,924]

913. Consumers shall be able to lodge their *complaints* concerning the activities and the conduct of the business party or any person acting on behalf of or for the business party relating to the sale and supply of products to consumers, including any negligence, orally or submitted in writing to the business party. Oral complaints shall be investigated without delay and, if possible, shall be remedied immediately. If the consumer is in disagreement with the way the complaint is handled, or if the complaint cannot be investigated immediately, the business party shall proceed without delay to record the complaint and its position regarding the compliant in a report and shall provide a copy to the consumer. The business party shall assign an individual identifier to each oral complaint made through the phone or other means of electronic communications. Unless otherwise provided by any directly applicable legislation of the EU, the business party shall effectively reply to written complaints within thirty days of receipt, and shall provide for its communication; if the business party rejects the complaint, it must do so in a reasoned statement. The business party shall retain the complaint report and a copy of the reply for a period of five years and shall present it to the competent authorities for inspection when so requested. When a complaint is rejected, the business party shall inform the consumer affected in writing concerning the authority or arbitration body, as applicable, where he may seek remedy.[925]

921. Act XLVII of 2008 s. 9 (1)–(3).
922. *Ibid.*, s. 5, s. 9 (4).
923. *See* more about it in: Szikora, *supra* n. 872, 329–362.
924. Act CLV of 1997 s. 2 s).
925. *Ibid.*, s. 17/A (2)–(4), (6)–(8).

914. The enterprises engaged in the pursuit of public service activities and other companies defined in specific other legislation shall set up a *customer service centre* for handling customer relations, investigating and handling complaints and for providing information to consumers at a location which is open for customers.[926]

915. The *arbitration board* signifies a body registered by the organ (person) provided for in Act CLV of 1997 established on a long-term basis for the purpose of resolving consumer disputes within the framework of alternative dispute resolution procedures.[927] The arbitration board functions as an independent body attached to the competent county (Budapest) chamber of industry and commerce. The competence of the arbitration board shall cover the settlement of consumer disputes out of court. The arbitration board's responsibilities shall include to attempt to reach a conciliation agreement for the settlement of the dispute or, failing this, to adopt a decision in the case to enforce consumer rights simply, efficiently and practically and under the principle of cost-efficiency. The arbitration board shall provide advice upon the consumer's or the business party's request on the rights and obligations of the consumer.[928] The arbitration board attached to the competent Budapest chamber of industry and commerce shall function as the national online dispute resolution platform provided for in Regulation (EU) No. 524/2013 of the European Parliament and of the Council of 21 May 2013 on online dispute resolution for consumer disputes and amending Regulation (EC) No. 2006/2004 and Directive 2009/22/EC.[929] The arbitration board of jurisdiction by reference to the consumer's home address or temporary residence shall have competence to conduct the proceedings.[930] The arbitration board shall proceed in a panel of three; if according to the chairman of the board the consumer dispute is a simple case, a sole board member shall be appointed to hear the case. However, if so requested by both parties, the arbitration board shall hear such cases in a panel of three as well.[931] A precondition for opening arbitration board proceedings is that the consumer has attempted to settle the case directly with the business party affected. Arbitration board proceedings are opened upon the consumer's request, the request shall be submitted to the chairman of the arbitration board in writing.[932] Within eight days of the opening of the proceedings, the chairman of the arbitration board shall review whether the board has jurisdiction and competence over the case and, in the event that the board does not have jurisdiction or competence, shall forward the case without delay to the appropriate body of jurisdiction and competence and shall notify the requesting party accordingly.[933] In the event that the board's jurisdiction and competence is established, the chairman shall set a hearing date for the parties within sixty days of the opening of the proceedings.[934] The chairman shall in due time notify the parties

926. *Ibid.*, s. 17/B (1).
927. *Ibid.*, s. 2 o).
928. *Ibid.*, s. 18 (1), (2).
929. *Ibid.*, s. 19.
930. *Ibid.*, s. 20 (1).
931. *Ibid.*, s. 25 (1), (4).
932. *Ibid.*, s. 27, s. 28 (1), (2).
933. *Ibid.*, s. 29 (2).
934. *Ibid.*, s. 29 (3).

regarding the scheduled time of the hearing, or if he plans to lodge a motion to proceed without hearing, with a copy of the request and shall request the parties to file their recommendation concerning the person they wish to delegate to the panel of arbitrators within eight days of receiving the said notice, otherwise the chairman of the arbitration board shall appoint such member ex officio.[935] In the notice, the business party affected shall be requested to file a written statement (*response*) within eight days of receipt of the notice with regard to the legitimacy of the consumer's claim, the circumstances of the case, and acceptance of the decision of the panel as binding (ad hoc submission). In the statement the business party shall indicate the facts and evidence in support of its position and shall attach any documents (or copies thereof), the contents of which it relies on as evidence. The business party shall be advised that representation in the hearing is mandatory by a person duly authorized to conclude a settlement, and, in the event of its failure to file a statement regarding the merits of the case, the panel shall pass its decision based on the information at its disposal.[936] The chairman shall send a copy of the response of the business party to the consumer without delay, or if there is not sufficient time to do so, shall present it at the hearing. If the business party fails to file a response, the panel shall continue the procedure, however, it shall not be construed as acceptance of the requesting person's claims.[937] In the proceedings the presiding umpire of the panel shall attempt to negotiate an agreement between the parties: the panel shall approve the negotiated settlement by resolution if it is in conformity with legal regulations, otherwise, or if there is no agreement, it shall continue the proceeding.[938] The panel shall decide on the merits of the case by a simple majority of votes. The council shall conclude the proceedings within ninety days of the time of opening (in justified cases, the presiding umpire shall have powers to extend this time limit by no more than an additional thirty days).[939] In the absence of a negotiated settlement the panel of arbitrators shall:

- adopt a binding resolution if the request is found substantiated, and the business party affected has undertaken to be bound by the decision of the arbitration board in a standard statement of submission – filed at the arbitration board or the chamber, or contained in its commercial communication – or in a statement filed at the time of the opening of the proceedings or, at the latest, before the decision is adopted; or
- makes a recommendation if the request is found substantiated, however, the business party affected has refused to be bound by the decision of the arbitration board in a statement filed at the time of the opening of the proceedings or did not declare its position concerning the decision of the arbitration panel in terms of submission.[940] The panel of arbitrators shall refuse the consumer's request if it considers upon the hearing that the request is unsubstantiated.[941] The costs of the

935. *Ibid.*, s. 29 (5).
936. *Ibid.*, s. 29 (8).
937. *Ibid.*, s. 29 (9), (10).
938. *Ibid.*, s. 30 (1).
939. *Ibid.*, s. (4), (5).
940. *Ibid.*, s. 32.
941. *Ibid.*, s. 32/A.

proceedings shall be borne by the party against whom the resolution was passed.[942] The panel shall deliver its resolution or recommendation on the day when adopted and send within thirty days one copy of the written decision or recommendation to each of the parties.[943] The resolution or recommendation of the panel of arbitrators is adopted without prejudice to the consumer's right to have his claim enforced in the court of law. The binding resolution or recommendation of the panel may not be appealed; however, annulment of the resolution by court order may be requested.[944] In the event that the business party fails to comply with the panel's recommendation, the arbitration board shall be entitled to publish, without indicating the name of the consumer, a brief description of the dispute and the outcome of the proceedings within sixty days of the time of delivery of the recommendation to the business party in question.[945] In the event of the business party's failure to discharge the binding resolution of the panel, or the negotiated settlement approved by resolution within the prescribed time limit, the consumer may request the court to append an enforcement clause to the panel's resolution, of which the chairman of the arbitration board shall be informed simultaneously.[946]

916. Legal recourse in the public interest: The consumer protection authority or the associations for the protection of consumers' interests may file for civil action on behalf of consumers against any person who was found guilty by the consumer protection authority of any violation of the consumer protection regulations – personally unknown – consumers whose general identity, however, can be established relying on the circumstances of the infringement. No action may be brought after three years following the time of commission of the aforementioned infringement, or following the statute of limitation prescribed in specific other act for the civil claims of consumers if this is shorter; this deadline shall apply with prejudice. If, with respect to the consumers affected by the infringement, the legal grounds for the claim and the amount of damages demanded, or the overall contents of the claim in the case of other claims, can be clearly established irrespective of the individual circumstances of the consumers affected by the infringement, the consumer protection authority or the associations for the protection of consumers' interests may request the court to award such claims and order the business party in question to satisfy these claims, or failing this, to request the court to declare the infringement covering all consumers indicated in the claim. If according to the court's decision the violation was established covering all consumers indicated in the claim, the consumers affected may file charges against the infringer and are required to verify only the amount of damages and that the damage is the direct result of such infringement. The court's decision shall specify the consumers who are affected by the violation and are therefore entitled to demand satisfaction based on the judgment, and shall determine the data required for their identification. The recourse exercised by

942. *Ibid.*, s. 33 (3).
943. *Ibid.*, s. 33 (5).
944. *Ibid.*, s. 34 (1), (2).
945. *Ibid.*, s. 36 (1).
946. *Ibid.*, s. 36 (3).

the consumer protection authority or by the associations for the protection of consumers' interests is without prejudice to the consumers' right to bring civil action independently against the infringer.[947]

917. Bringing action in the public interest: When the illegal actions of a business party affect a wide range of – personally unknown – consumers whose general identity, however, can be established relying on the circumstances of the infringement, or causing substantial harm, and the case falls within the jurisdiction of the court, the public prosecutor or the associations for the protection of consumers' interests shall have the right to bring action. The organizations entitled to bring action may also demand:

- the termination of the infringement and the prohibition of the offender from any further violation of the law;
- the termination of the injurious situation and the restoration of the previous state. This recourse is without prejudice to the consumers' right to bring civil action independently against the infringer.[948]

918. Public-interest proceedings in connection with unfair standard contract terms: As regards contracts which involve a consumer and a business party, an action may be brought for the annulment of an unfair contract term that has been incorporated into a contract by the public prosecutor, the minister, autonomous administrative agencies, government agencies, the director of the head office, the heads of the Budapest and county government agencies, economic and trade organizations or interest-representation bodies and associations for the protection of consumers' interests within the scope of consumer interests they protect, and organizations set up for the protection of consumers' interests under the laws of any Member State of the EEA. In public-interest proceedings, the court shall establish the annulment of an unfair contract term in favour of all of the parties with which the party imposing the condition has a contractual relationship, and shall order the party who applied the contract term in question to take measures for having a public notice on declaring the contract term unfair published at his own cost. Moreover, an action may be brought in the public interest to request to have a standard contract term or condition declared unfair, that has been defined for consumer contracts and made available to the general public, regardless of whether the term or condition in question had in fact been applied or not. If the court finds the contested standard contract term unfair, the court ruling may also contain a clause banning the party who made it available to the public from the further use of such. Furthermore, the lawsuit may be brought against any party who publicly recommends the use of any unfair standard contract term or condition that has been defined for consumer contracts and made available to the general public.[949]

947. *Ibid.*, s. 38 (1)–(4).
948. *Ibid.*, s. 39 (1), (3), (4).
949. Section 6:105 CC.

919. The consumer protection authority shall have jurisdiction in connection with any infringement of the provisions relating to the *prohibition of unfair commercial practices*. The NBH, acting within its function as supervisory authority of the financial intermediary system, shall have jurisdiction in connection with any violation of the provisions relating to the prohibition of unfair commercial practices if the commercial practices in question relate to such activities of the business party that is conferred under the competence of the NBH. The GVH shall have jurisdiction in connection with any infringement of the provisions relating to the prohibition of unfair commercial practices if the commercial practices in question exert material influence upon competition.[950]

VII. Miscellaneous

920. No advertisement may be disseminated if it encourages any conduct that is likely to jeopardize the natural or man-made environment.[951]

921. The advertisement is prohibited if it is capable of harming the physical, intellectual or moral development of children and young persons.[952]

922. The advertisement is forbidden if it displays sexuality in a gravely indecent manner, meaning, in particular, the open display of sexual intercourse or genitals (pornographic advertisement).[953]

923. No advertisement may be disseminated relating to alcoholic beverages that:

- is addressed to children or young persons;
- depicts children or young persons;
- encourages immoderate consumption of alcohol or presents abstinence from the consumption of alcoholic beverages or moderation in a negative light;
- links the consumption of alcohol to enhanced physical performance or to driving;
- creates the impression that the consumption of alcohol contributes towards social or sexual success;
- claims that alcohol has therapeutic qualities or that it is a stimulant, a sedative or a means of resolving personal conflicts;
- claims that alcohol has therapeutic qualities or that it is a stimulant, a sedative or a means of resolving personal conflicts;
- places emphasis on high alcoholic content as being a positive quality of the beverages. The advertisement is prohibited relating to alcoholic beverages on the outside of the first page of any printed media, or on the home page of a website; in theatres or cinemas before 20:00 hours, as well as immediately preceding any programs for children or young persons, during the full duration thereof, and

950. Act XLVII of 2008 s. 10 (1)–(3).
951. Act XLVIII of 2008 s. 7 (2).
952. *Ibid.*, s. 8 (1).
953. *Ibid.*, s. 9 (1).

immediately afterwards; on goods which have been clearly designed and manufactured for the purpose of a toy, including the packaging of such goods; and in public education and healthcare institutions, or on any outdoor advertising media situated within a two hundred-meter radius from the entrance thereof.[954]

924. The advertisement is forbidden relating to abortions, institutions carrying out abortions, nor to means and procedures for carrying out abortions.[955]

925. No advertisement relating to funeral and related services may be disseminated in health care institutions, on the walls or fences of health care institutions, and in cemeteries except in designated areas.[956]

926. The consumer protection authority shall have jurisdiction in connection with any infringement of the provisions relating to commercial advertising.[957]

927. A notification or complaint may be submitted to the *GVH* by anyone when detecting any infringement falling within its the competence. The proceedings for investigating a notification or complaint shall not comprise part of competition control proceedings.[958]

928. The GVH may file for civil action on behalf of consumers against a business entity engaged in any infringement falling within its competence, where such illegal action results in a grievance that affects a wide range of consumers that can be established relying on the circumstances of the infringement.[959]

929. In the interest of educating the general public concerning competition, and for promoting the implementation of regulations designed to enhance the consumer's ability to make an informed decision and to support competition in a law abiding way, and enhancing the consumers' awareness in their decision-making practices, the GVH shall promote the dissemination of competition culture and the improvement of consumer information so as to enable consumers to make informed decisions, contributing to the development of trade circles addressing the economic and legal aspects of competition and the consumers' right to make informed decisions – in particular by fostering scientific and educational programs relating to competition law and to competition and consumer protection policy, and by supporting the training of experts in the fields of competition law, competition and consumer protection, and by improving consumer information so as to enable consumers to make informed decisions and for the protection of such right.[960]

---

954. *Ibid.*, s. 18.
955. *Ibid.*, s. 17.
956. *Ibid.*, s. 22 (1).
957. *Ibid.*, s. 24 (1).
958. Act LVII of 1996 s. 43/G (1), (2).
959. *Ibid.*, s. 92.
960. *Ibid.*, s. 33 (4).

Selected Bibliography

Asztalos, László. *Polgári jog, Általános rész, Személyek,* (Budapest: Tankönyvkiadó, 1988).

Auer, Ádám. 'A felelős társaságirányítás hatása a jogi személyek elméletére', *Jogtudományi Közlöny* 4 (2013).

Bajai, Ferenc & Dezső Csabay (eds). *Az állami biztosítás Magyarországon,* (Budapest: Közgazdasági és Jogi Könyvkiadó, 1972).

Balásházy, Mária, Kinga Pázmándi & Tamás Sárközy. *Business Law,* (Budapest: Typotex, 2008).

Bárdos, Péter & Attila Menyhárd. *Commercial Law,* (Budapest: HVG Orac, 2008).

Barta, Judit, Zoltán Fazakas et al. *A kereskedelmi szerződések alapvető szabályai,* (Budapest: Patrocinium, 2015).

Berke, Barna. Az Európai Unió gazdasági joga II. Eötvös Kiadó, (Budapest: 2013), 7–194.

Berke, Barna. Büntető közigazgatás és bírósági felülvizsgálat, In: Viva Vox Iuris Civilis, Tanulmányok Sólyom László tiszteletére, (Budapest: 2012), 41–76.

Bíró, György & Barnabás Lenkovics. *Általános tanok (Magyar polgári jog),* (Miskolc: Novotni Kiadó, 2000).

Miskolczi Bodnár, Péter. A versenytörvény magyarázata. KJK-Kerszöv, Budapest, 2002. [The commentary of the Competition Act].

Miskolczi Bodnár, Péter. Versenyjogsértéssel okozott károk megtérítése – egy a magyar jog számára iránymutató irányelv átültetése. In: Gombos, Katalin (ed.), A versenyjog legújabb fejleményei európai uniós kitekintéssel. (Budapest: Dialóg Campus, 2017), pp. 19–47.

Boóc, Ádám & Sándor, István. *Előadásvázlatok a polgári jog általános tanaiból,* (Budapest: Patrocinium, 2012).

Boóc, Ádám. *General Principles of the Hungarian Private Law,* In: Business Law in Hungary, ed. István Sándor, (Budapest: Patrocinium, 2016).

Boytha, Györgyné & Tóth, Tihamér (ed.). Versenyjog. PKE JÁK, (Budapest: 2010).

Boytha, Györgyné (ed.). Versenyjogi jogsértések esetén érvényesíthető magánjogi igények. HVG Orac, (Budapest: 2009) (Private claims enforceable in case of competition violations).

Csehi, Zoltán. *Civil Associations and Foundations,* In: Business Law in Hungary, ed. István Sándor (Budapest: Patrocinium, 2016).

Csőke, Andrea. *A határokon átnyúló fizetésképtelenségi eljárások* (Cross-border Insolvency Procedures). (Budapest: HVG Orac, 2016).

Selected Bibliography

Dán, Judit. A bírósági felülvizsgálat örökzöld kérdései a GVH gyakorlatában. In: Gombos, Katalin (ed.), A versenyjog legújabb fejleményei európai uniós kitekintéssel. (Budapest: Dialóg Campus, 2017), pp. 75–95.

Darázs, Lénárd. A kartellek semmissége Complex, Budapest, 2009. [The automatic invalidity of restrictive agreements].

Darázs, Lénárd. Vertikális kartellek. (Budapest: Complex, 2007). [Vertical restraints].

Eörsi, Gyula. *Összehasonlító polgári jog (Jogtípusok, jogcsoportok és a jogfejlődés útjai),* (Budapest: Akadémiai Kiadó, 1975).

Fuglinszky, Ádám. A versenyjogi jogsértések esetén alkalmazható polgári jogi jogkövetkezmények. In: Kisfaludi, András (ed.), Versenyjogi jogsértések – magánjogi jogkövetkezmények. ELTE Eötvös Kiadó (Budapest: 2012).

Gombos, Katalin. A versenyjog legújabb fejleményei – európai uniós kitekintéssel. In: Gombos, Katalin (ed.), A versenyjog legújabb fejleményei európai uniós kitekintéssel. (Budapest: Dialóg Campus, 2017), pp. 9–18.

Grad-Gyenge, Anikó. *The Law of Intellectual Property,* In: Business Law in Hungary, ed. István Sándor, (Budapest: Patrocinium, 2016).

Havasi, Péter. 'A személyek polgári jogi védelmére vonatkozó szabályozás kritikai elemzése, javaslat az új szabályozásra', *Polgári Jogi Kodifikáció* 1 (2002).

Nagy, Csongor István. Competition Law in Hungary, (Hague: Wolters Kluwer, 2016).

Nagy, Csongor István. Kartelljogi kézikönyv. A közösségi és a magyar kartelljog kézikönyve. HVG Orac 2006. [Handbook of Restrictive Agreements. Handbook of Restrictive Agreements in Community and Hungarian Competition Law].

Jerney, Leona. A kartelljogi jogsértések magánjogi jogkövetkezményei. In: Gombos, Katalin (ed.), A versenyjog legújabb fejleményei európai uniós kitekintéssel. (Budapest: Dialóg Campus, 2017), pp. 49–56.

Jobbágyi, Gábor. *Magyar polgári jog I., Általános rész, Emberi személy, Családjog, Szellemi alkotások joga,* (Budapest: Szent István Társulat, 2013).

Juhász, László. *A magyar magáncsőd kézikönyve* (A Handbook of Personal Bankruptcy in Hungary). (Budapest: HVG Orac, 2017).

Károlyi, Géza. 'Az egyszemélyes társaságokról', *Jogtudományi Közlöny* 9 (1999).

Kecskés, László. 'A civilisztika és a civilisztikai gondolkodás rétegei', *Jura* 1 (2015).

Kisfaludi, András. *Company Law* (Budapest: Complex Kiadó, 2007).

Kovács, Kázmér & Kovács, Szabolcs. *Indemnification and the Insurance Contract,* In: Business Law in Hungary, ed. Sándor, István, (Budapest: Patrocinium, 2016).

Kovács, László. 'A szellemi alkotások múltja és jövője', *Magyar Jog* 2 (2016).

Lábady, Tamás. *A magánjog általános tana,* (Budapest: Szent István Társulat, 2013).

Muzsalyi, Róbert. *Csődeljárások a számok tükrében* (Reorganisation Procedures by the Numbers). Gazdaság és Jog, 2015/9.

Nochta, Tibor. 'A magánjog kereskedelmi jogias szemléletéért', *Jura* 2 (2004).

Nochta, Tibor. *Társasági jog,* (Budapest – Pécs: Dialóg Campus Kiadó, 2007).

Novotni, Zoltán. *Polgári jog, A gazdasági társaságok és a gazdálkodás egyéb jogalanyainak joga,* (Miskolc: Miskolci Egyetemi Kiadó, 1992).

Osztovits, András (ed.). *A Polgári Törvénykönyvről szóló 2013. évi V. törvény és a kapcsolódó jogszabályok nagykommentárja*, (Budapest: Opten Informatikai Kft., 2014).

Papp, Tekla & Jakab, Tamás. 'The Present Situation of the Insurance System and Insurance Contracts in Hungary', *Wiadomosci Ubezpieczepiawe* 4 (2014).

Papp, Tekla (ed.). *Atipikus szerződések*, (Budapest: Opten Informatikai Kft., 2015).

Papp, Tekla (ed.). *Company Law*, (Szeged: Lectum Kiadó, 2011).

Papp, Tekla. 'Corporate governance – felelős társaságirányítás', *Acta Juridica et Politica* (Tomus LXXIII, Fasciculus 1-64, Szeged: 2008).

Papp, Tekla. *Atipikus jelenségek szerződési jogunkban, Atypical Phenomena in Our Contract Law*, (Szeged: Lectum Kiadó, 2009).

Papp, Tekla. *Corporations and Partnerships Hungary, International Encyclopaedia of Laws*, Suppl. 81 (Alphen aan den Rijn: Wolters Kluwer, 2015).

Papp, Tekla. *Law of Business Enterprises*, In: Business Law in Hungary, ed. István Sándor (Budapest: Patrocinium, 2016).

Papp, Tekla. *Opuscula civilia, Magánjogi látlelet, Report on Hungarian Private Law, Befundbericht über das ungarische Privatrecht*, (Szeged: Lectum Kiadó, 2013).

Pázmándi, Kinga (ed.). *Magyar fogyasztóvédelmi és reklámjog*, (Budapest: HVG Orac, 2010).

Whish, Richard & Bailey David. Competition Law, (Oxford: Oxford University Press, 2015).

Sándor, István. *A bizalmi vagyonkezelés és a trust, Jogtörténeti és összehasonlító jogi elemzés* (Budapest: HVG Orac, 2014).

Simon, Emese Réka. Versengő alapjogok. In: Gombos, Katalin (ed.), A versenyjog legújabb fejleményei európai uniós kitekintéssel. (Budapest: Dialóg Campus, 2017), pp. 57–63.

Szalma, József. 'A polgári és a kereskedelmi jog kapcsolata az új Ptk. fényében', *Jogtudományi Közlöny* 10 (2014).

Szikora, Veronika (ed.). *Magyar fogyasztóvédelmi jog – európai kitekintéssel*, (Debrecen: FOME, 2010).

Tóth, Tihamér. A versenytörvény újdonságai az összefonódások ellenőrzése és a kártérítési perek tekintetében. Jogtudományi Közlöny 2017/5. pp. 243–255.

Tóth, Tihamér. Az Európai Unió versenyjoga, (Budapest: Wolters Kluwer, 2014). [Competition law of the European Union].

Tóth, Tihamér. Competition Cases from the European Union – Hungary, In Kokkoris, Ioannis (ed.), Competition Cases from the European Union, (London: Sweet & Maxwell, 2010), pp. 629–672.

Vadas, György & Weltner, Andor. *Gazdasági jog*, (Budapest: Magyar Magánalkalmazottak Szabad Szakszervezete kiadása, 1949).

Vékás, Lajos (ed.). *A Polgári Törvénykönyv magyarázatokkal*, (Budapest: Complex, 2013).

Világhy, Miklós & Eörsi, Gyula. *Magyar polgári jog*, (Budapest: Tankönyvkiadó, 1965).

Vörös, Imre. Az európai versenyjogok kézikönyve. Logod Bt. (Budapest: 1996). [The handbook of European competition laws].

Wellmann, György & Petrik, Ferenc (ed.). *Az új Ptk. magyarázata* VI/VI., (Budapest: HVG Orac, 2013).

Index

The numbers here refer to paragraph numbers.

Index

Index

Made in the USA
Monee, IL
18 October 2026

66041391R10151